# Jonathan Edwards

# Jonathan Edwards

*An Introduction to His Thought*

Oliver D. Crisp and Kyle C. Strobel

William B. Eerdmans Publishing Company
Grand Rapids, Michigan

Wm. B. Eerdmans Publishing Co.
2140 Oak Industrial Drive N.E., Grand Rapids, Michigan 49505
www.eerdmans.com

ISBN 978-0-8028-7269-2

**Library of Congress Cataloging-in-Publication Data**

Names: Crisp, Oliver, author. | Strobel, Kyle, 1978– author.
Title: Jonathan Edwards : an introduction to his thought /
    Oliver D. Crisp and Kyle C. Strobel.
Description: Grand Rapids, Michigan : William B. Eerdmans Publishing Company, 2018.
    | Includes bibliographical references and index.
Identifiers: LCCN 2017042036 | ISBN 9780802872692 (paperback)
Subjects: LCSH: Edwards, Jonathan, 1703–1758. | BISAC: RELIGION /
    Christian Theology / History. | RELIGION / Christian Theology / General. |
    BIOGRAPHY & AUTOBIOGRAPHY / Religious.
Classification: LCC BX7260.E3 C665 2018 | DDC 230/.58092—dc23
    LC record available at https://lccn.loc.gov/2017042036

*To George Marsden,*
  *"a remarkable instance of true and eminent Christian piety*
  *in heart and practice" (Jonathan Edwards)*

# Contents

# Acknowledgments

Many different individuals have helped us in the writing of this volume. Kenneth Minkema and Adriaan Neele at the Jonathan Edwards Center at Yale University offered information and assistance on all things Edwardsean. We are most grateful to them for their help over the years. Mark Hamilton read and commented on various sections of the manuscript as it developed. George Marsden has enabled us (and many other readers of his work) to have a better picture of Edwards in the round. We dedicate this book to him as a token of our grateful thanks for his seminal work. Thanks are also due to our respective institutions, Fuller Theological Seminary and Biola University, for their support along the way.

We would also like to thank people individually. First, Oliver's thanks: David Kling, Ava Chamberlain, and Douglas Sweeney were of considerable help in the writing of the first chapter. Doug also offered suggestions for the Further Reading section at the end of the book. Gerald McDermott and Michael McClymond helped me to see connections I had overlooked and pressed me on various important matters of detail, prompting me to evaluate aspects of Edwards's thought with more care. Along the way I have also enjoyed the help of Stephen Crocco, Stephen Holmes, Stephen R. C. Nichols, Amy Plantinga Pauw, and William Wainwright. They have read and commented on material and responded to queries I have put to them over the years. I have also benefited from the critical eye of Brian Lee, who has read through and commented on a number of the chapters, as well as my research assistant, Tim Scheuers. As ever, my family has borne with me in all sorts of practical ways, helping a most impractical person.

And now Kyle's thanks: As I worked on my chapters, several people generously provided critical feedback. Thanks in particular to the

ACKNOWLEDGMENTS

Theology Reading Group at Biola. It is incredible to have such a fine group of theologians reflecting upon my work, and I am humbled and encouraged by your friendship. In the midst of writing this book I also had the opportunity to give a plenary talk at the Jonathan Edwards Congress in Melbourne on Edwards's theological anthropology. The folks at the conference, my friend Rhys Bezzant in particular, served as helpful conversation partners on various themes covered in my chapters. James Merrick, Kent Eilers, and Matt Jenson all provided helpful feedback on the conclusion, and their insights, as usual, made it much better. My friend Jamin, who is always available to wrestle through ideas, and Robbie Goforth and Ty Kieser read through chapters and provided helpful feedback. I am thankful for all of you. For my wife, Kelli, my daughter, Brighton, and my son, Oliver, you are so precious to me. Thank you for your joy, encouragement, and laughter in the midst of my work.

# Abbreviations

The standard critical letterpress edition of Edwards's works is that published by Yale University Press (1957–2008) in twenty-six volumes. A list of these works is given in the section at the end of this book entitled Further Reading. All references to Edwards's works are to the Yale edition and are given as WJE, followed by page reference (e.g., WJE 1:50). A fully searchable, open-access edition of Edwards's works can be found online at the Yale Center for Jonathan Edwards (http://edwards.yale.edu/). This database includes a wealth of sermon outlines and fragments not published in the print edition of Edwards's works; the online version of the works is therefore much larger than the print version. Reference is also made to this online version of the Yale edition of Edwards's works in what follows, cited as WJE Online, followed by the reference.

# Introduction

The nineteenth-century American educationalist and statesman George Bancroft once wrote, "he that would know the workings of the New England Mind in the middle of the last [i.e., eighteenth] century, and the throbbings of its heart, must give his days and nights to the study of Jonathan Edwards."[1] Taking up these words at the bicentenary commemoration of Edwards's birth in Andover, Massachusetts in 1903, Frederick Woodbridge pronounced, "Time has at last set the limit to the truth of such remarks. To understand the philosophy and theology of today in New England or the country at large, the student must undoubtedly seek his foundations elsewhere than in the thought of Jonathan Edwards."[2]

If the revolutions of time since the beginning of the twentieth century have not shown Woodbridge's comments to be baseless, they have nevertheless demonstrated that his pessimism was premature. The study of the Northampton Sage, as Edwards is sometimes called, has flourished since the end of the Second World War, and today there is a rich and variegated literature on almost all aspects of his thought. Some of this is historical in nature. But increasingly, there has been interest in him from theologians, philosophers, literary critics, and scholars of cultural and religious studies. Although not all of this literature is concerned with rehabilitating Edwards's ideas, there has been a significant amount of recent work in this direction too. He is no longer merely an interesting and

1. George Bancroft, "Jonathan Edwards," in *The New American Cyclopedia*, ed. George Ripley and Charles A. Dana (New York: D. Appleton and Co., 1867), 7:20.
2. Frederick J. E. Woodbridge, "Jonathan Edwards," *The Philosophical Review* 13, no. 4 (1904): 393.

important, though, perhaps, somewhat eccentric figure from the pages of the past. His thought is now placed alongside that of other comparable early modern theologians and philosophers of the first rank. It is considered to be of intrinsic interest as well as being a resource for contemporary constructive philosophy and theology.

This book offers an overview of Jonathan Edwards's thought. Its emphasis is upon making clear to the reader the importance and originality of his ideas without trying to domesticate them or apologize for aspects of his work that may seem strange or unfamiliar to the modern reader. In particular, attention is given to the shape and coherence of the different aspects of his thought, with reference to the theological and philosophical significance of the ideas he espoused. Since it is important to ensure such exposition is done with sensitivity to intellectual and cultural contexts, as well as to the history and development of ideas, we also try to give a sense of the rich variety of his output with some account of their place in history. Nevertheless, the primary focus of this book is upon Edwards as a theologian of a philosophical disposition.

It is tempting to write a considerably larger book, which might capture more of the depth and profundity of the work of a great mind such as Edwards. There is much in his varied publications that is intellectually arresting and worthy of serious scholarly interest—perhaps too much to be adequately covered in a book like this one. But there is also a place for the shorter introduction that might assist those coming to Edwards for the first time, or those wanting a more manageable overview of key themes in his work. This is just such a volume.[3]

By focusing on core aspects of Edwards's thinking, the reader is introduced to some of the most important areas of his thought. Some of the conclusions in the chapters that follow are controversial in contemporary Edwardsean studies. But if one were to take any interesting theological or philosophical doctrine and consider the literature on it, all sorts of contentious views would be found expressed there. Such is the

---

3. For larger works on Edwards's theology as a whole, see Oliver D. Crisp, *Jonathan Edwards on God and Creation* (New York: Oxford University Press, 2012); Sang Hyun Lee, *The Philosophical Theology of Jonathan Edwards*, expanded edition (Princeton: Princeton University Press, 2000); and Kyle C. Strobel, *Jonathan Edwards's Theology: A Reinterpretation* (London: Bloomsbury, 2013). Readers might also consult Michael McClymond and Gerald McDermott, *The Theology of Jonathan Edwards* (New York: Oxford University Press, 2011), as well as the annotated guide to further reading on Edwards at the end of this book.

nature of the scholarly enterprise, and such is the effect of almost any significant conundrum upon the thinking of the intellectually curious. The work of Jonathan Edwards has a way of becoming like a splinter in the mind, working its way into the reader's thoughts long after having put it down. Like other great thinkers, Edwards can be both fascinating, arresting, and remarkably insightful as well as frustrating, peculiar, and, at times, maddeningly myopic. But, as almost all who have borne with Edwards will testify, to read and engage him is to encounter a singular individual, one whose thought challenges and unsettles what was previously believed to be secure and conventional. These characteristics surely mark the presence of a great mind, and they provide a very good reason to pick up Edwards in order to interrogate his views for oneself. If this book facilitates that pursuit, then it will have served its purpose.

## The State of the Art

Another reason for writing a short introduction to Edwards's thought at this juncture has to do with the current state of Edwards scholarship. When Bancroft penned his admiring words in the middle of the nineteenth century, Edwards's works were widely read and appreciated, and his thought had borne fruit in the various branches of the New England Theology, a movement that flourished for a century after Edwards's demise. But by the turn of the twentieth century, Woodbridge's caustic remarks were more in vogue. Edwards had become an embarrassment; his philosophy was no longer fashionable, and his theology was no longer acceptable to an era of liberal progressivism. Edwards remained in relative obscurity until after the Second World War, when the Harvard historian Perry Miller sparked renewed interest in Edwards's thought.[4] This revival eventually led to the publication of the Yale edition of Edwards's works, the production of which continued into the early twenty-first century. In addition to Miller's study of Edwards and his milieu, Ola Winslow wrote a Pulitzer Prize–winning biography of Edwards.[5] Both scholars regarded him as a figure of tragedy—a first-rate intellect trapped in the medievalism of Puritan thought-forms—who nevertheless had moments of great brilliance in his forays into early natural science and philosophy.

4. Perry Miller, *Jonathan Edwards* (New York: William Sloane, 1949).
5. Ola Winslow, *Jonathan Edwards, 1703–1758* (New York: Collier Books, 1940).

The legacy of Miller was mixed. On the one hand, his efforts were important in securing for Edwards a new hearing among twentieth-century theologians and church historians. On the other hand, his picture of the "Tragic Edwards" was misleading in important respects. In the period immediately after the Second World War, interest in Edwards gradually gained ground, stimulated by the resurgence of work being done by historians of early colonial America. During this period, studies of Edwards's thought were also produced by philosophers like Douglas Elwood, theologians like Conrad Cherry, and students of aesthetics like Roland Delattre.[6] As the Yale Works of Edwards began to roll off the presses in 1957, their editorial introductions also marked significant re-engagement with Edwards's ideas. The pace of production picked up in the early 1980s with works by Norman Fiering on the sources of Edwards's thought and Robert Jenson on the shape of his theology, as well as a popular hagiography by Iain Murray.[7] As the century drew to a close, the volumes of the Yale Works provided new impetus to study the Northampton Sage. Interest in Edwards increased even more significantly with the advent of the online edition of the Works at Yale, which not only made the breadth of Edwards's works available to a much wider audience in a fully searchable digital format but also set a new standard for online scholarly archives (see http://edwards.yale.edu/).

The twenty-first century opened, like the twentieth, with controversy over Edwards's legacy. However, scholarly dispute now centers on the correct interpretation of Edwards's thought, rather than the question of whether his thought is worthy of interpretation at all. The twentieth-century battle over Edwards's place among the theologians has been won: he is now regarded as a theologian worth studying alongside Athanasius, Anselm, Aquinas, Luther, Calvin, Schleiermacher, or Barth.[8]

6. See Douglas Elwood, *The Philosophical Theology of Jonathan Edwards* (New York: Columbia University Press, 1960); Conrad Cherry, *The Theology of Jonathan Edwards: A Reappraisal* (Bloomington: Indiana University Press, 1966); and Roland A. Delattre, *Beauty and Sensibility in the Thought of Jonathan Edwards* (New Haven: Yale University Press, 1968).

7. See Norman Fiering, *Jonathan Edwards's Moral Thought in Its British Context* (Chapel Hill: University of North Carolina Press, 1981); Robert W. Jenson, *America's Theologian: A Recommendation of Jonathan Edwards* (New York: Oxford University Press, 1988); and Iain H. Murray, *Jonathan Edwards: A New Biography* (Edinburgh: Banner of Truth, 1988).

8. As evidence of this, see the essays collected together in Kyle C. Strobel, ed., *The*

Nevertheless, two competing streams of Edwards interpretation have emerged since the early 2000s. The first of these is associated with the work of the Princeton theologian Sang Hyun Lee. His study, entitled *The Philosophical Theology of Jonathan Edwards*, was a landmark work when it was first published in 1988, and it remains in print in an expanded edition from Princeton University Press.[9] Lee argues that Edwards's philosophical theology is a bold attempt at reconfiguring classical theological themes in an early modern key. Previous studies have not fully grasped how modern Edwards's theological ideas were. According to Lee, Edwards's thought depended in a fundamental way upon what has become known as a dispositional ontology. This is the idea that the world is a nexus of dispositions and habits that God actualizes at each moment, bringing them from potentiality to actuality. By means of this interpretive key, Lee attempts to unlock the whole of Edwards's thought, presenting readers with a fascinating vision that has far-reaching implications. Lee's interpretive scheme has been taken up and adapted by the likes of Amy Plantinga Pauw, Michael McClymond, Gerald McDermott, Anri Morimoto, and, in some respects, also by Stephen Daniel. This loose affiliation of scholars with a similar (though by no means identical) view of Edwards's dispositional ontology has produced a number of influential outputs.[10]

Since 2003, however, a rather different view of Edwards's project has emerged. This alternative perspective regards Edwards as much more traditional in his theology. This line of interpretation holds that, although Edwards is clearly a highly original thinker, his thought does not represent as pronounced a departure from classical theological norms as some scholars have suggested. Rather, he was attempting to reconfigure classical theology in light of early Enlightenment thought. This recalibration does indeed lead to some unusual conclusions in Edwards's thought, such

---

*Ecumenical Edwards: Jonathan Edwards and the Theologians* (2015; repr., Oxford and New York: Routledge, 2016).

9. Lee, *The Philosophical Theology of Jonathan Edwards*, expanded edition (1988; Princeton: Princeton University Press, 2000).

10. These include (in order of publication) Stephen H. Daniel, *The Philosophy of Jonathan Edwards* (Bloomington and Indianapolis: Indiana University Press, 1994); Anri Morimoto, *Jonathan Edwards and the Catholic Vision of Salvation* (University Park: University of Pennsylvania Press, 1995); Amy Plantinga Pauw, *The Supreme Harmony of All: The Trinitarian Theology of Jonathan Edwards* (Grand Rapids: Eerdmans, 2002); and Gerald R. McDermott and Michael J. McClymond, *The Theology of Jonathan Edwards* (New York: Oxford University Press, 2012).

as his views on idealism, occasionalism, and panentheism, but—importantly—defenders of this interpretation maintain that he did not seek to depart from the classical essentialist ontology of his forebears, adopting a dispositional ontology in its place.

The present work is written by two advocates of this second line of Edwards interpretation (who have two slightly differing views of Edwards as well!). In recent times this interpretation has become known as the British school, as opposed to the American school, of Edwards studies. The idea behind this nomenclature is that those associated with the second line of interpretation are either British theologians and philosophers or have received their doctoral degrees from British institutions, whereas the scholars aligned with Lee's interpretation of Edwards have all been schooled in America. The present authors are not convinced of the merits of these designations, not least because the points at issue have nothing to do with geography and everything to do with the shape of Edwards's ontology (that is, whether it was dispositional or essentialist). What is more, there are not two clearly defined schools of thought in Edwards studies, and not every Edwards scholar falls into one of these two groups.[11] Be that as it may, readers should be alerted to the fact that this introduction takes a particular view on the interpretation of Edwards's thought, consistent with the notion that he was a theologian formed by post-Reformation Reformed theology, who sought to utilize early modern philosophy to recast his classical theological heritage in new idioms while retaining much of the substance of the theological worldview that had formed him. We do not think that Edwards sought to construct his ontology along dispositional lines, as will become apparent as the chapters unfold.[12]

### Overview of the Chapters

This brings us to a consideration of the topics covered by the book. The first chapter considers the context in which Edwards wrote. It differs from

11. This is true of the renewed scholarly interest in Edwards's religious ethics, where discussion has been focused elsewhere, namely, on Edwards's place in the tradition of virtue ethics.

12. It should be noted that, as with any scholarly literature, both authors of the present work have learned much from Edwards scholars with whom they disagree. Moreover, any such disagreement should not detract from the esteem in which we hold these scholars whose work has provided great stimulus to the study of Edwards's thought.

a biographical sketch, although it does reference the events that shaped his life. Specifically, this chapter is more concerned with identifying the people, places, institutions, and so forth that shaped Edwards as a thinker and influenced the work he produced.[13] We argue that *where* Edwards wrote—that is, his geographical context—as well as the *time* at which he wrote had arguably as much influence on the sort of things he concerned himself with in his writings as the effect made upon him by important personalities and ideas at formative stages of his career.

Edwards was a remarkable intellectual by the standards of any age. But his relative geographical and political isolation from the early Enlightenment in Europe and Great Britain, as well as the lack of real intellectual peers in colonial New England, meant that his thought took on an entirely different shape than it would have had he been born in one of the great metropolitan centers of European learning at the time, such as London, Edinburgh, or Paris. Growing up on the periphery of what was then considered to be the civilized world had a deep and important effect upon Edwards. It made him a life-long intellectual magpie—gathering into his theological nest all manner of ideas and notions as he encountered them. Only if this intellectual context is properly understood can the reader of Edwards grasp why he fixates on certain issues and thinkers at the expense of others. And only when one has understood Edwards's background can one see why the fundamental ideas that underpin his theology are, by and large, the product of a certain intellectual eclecticism forced upon Edwards by his social and geographical situation at the margins of eighteenth-century intellectual culture.

Chapter two focuses on Edwards's doctrine of the Trinity, which, as much recent scholarship has argued, is at the heart of his intellectual project. Our point of departure is Edwards's most developed, though unfinished, work on the topic, entitled "Discourse on the Trinity." In this work, Edwards offers a remarkable and original account of the divine life, in which he distinguishes the divine persons in ways that go beyond the notion of subsistent relations bequeathed to Protestantism by medieval theology, while at the same time maintaining a strong doctrine of divine unity. In essence, Edwards reasons that the understanding and will of God

---

13. There are a number of recent biographies of Edwards as well as biographical sketches in various symposia of the last decade through which readers of Edwards can get acquainted with the chronology of Edwards's life. Interested readers should consult the section on Further Reading at the end of this volume.

are *person-constituting.* That is, the understanding of God *is* the second person of the Trinity, and the divine will *is* the third person of the Trinity. Thus, according to Edwards, there is only *one* understanding and *one* will in God. Moreover, the understanding and will of God interpenetrate one another in the divine life as the Son and the Spirit. This means that the relation between unity (or oneness) and diversity (or threeness) in God is mutually reinforcing, rather than two different theological poles pulling in opposite directions. God is one, having one understanding and one will. Nevertheless, it is only in virtue of this understanding and will that there are distinct divine persons. This picture of the divine life is fleshed out with reference to Edwards's other works—in particular, his sermons, in which he has much to say about the relations of the divine persons respecting their work in creation and salvation, as well as about the person of Christ.

Chapter three concerns Edwards's philosophical theology and its bearing upon his doctrine of God. Edwards denied the existence of material objects, claiming instead that the world is comprised of minds and their ideas. This view constitutes his idealism. Edwards also pictured God as a perfect being in keeping with the tradition of classical Christian theism that he inherited from the Reformed orthodox theology and that formed him as a student at Yale College. This chapter provides an outline of Edwards's idealism and shows how it is intimately related to his views about the divine nature.

Chapter four deals with Edwards's understanding of divine dispositions, panentheism, continuous creation, and occasionalism, as well as his views on determinism. Splitting the treatment of his metaphysical thought into two parts (in chapters three and four, respectively) enables the reader to see clearly the ways in which his thought endorses important aspects of classical orthodox Christian theology, while at the same time pushing at the boundaries of what is commonly regarded as theologically acceptable views about God and his relationship to creation. Although Edwards does affirm perfect being theology, he also entertains some unusual ideas about creation as the fitting, or perhaps necessary product of God's essential creativity. Also unusual are his views on the non-persistence of the created order through time and God's immediate causation of all that obtains in the world. When these ideas are set alongside Edwards's determinism, which applies to both God and creation, the picture that emerges—though broadly internally consistent—is much more creative and exotic than has sometimes been appreciated, and is not without problems.

Chapter five segues from metaphysics to constructive theology, which is the focus of the remaining chapters of the book. Specifically, this chapter treats the subject of the atonement. Although Edwards did not write a treatise on the reconciling work of Christ, he developed his views on the topic across several sermon series and in remarks made in a number of different notebooks. This chapter brings together much of that material to give an account of Edwards's view of the atonement, which he considered to be a work of divine wisdom in which God the Son takes upon himself the role of mediator in the *pactum salutis*, or covenant of salvation.

Chapter six follows on from the chapter on atonement to focus on Edwards's understanding of salvation. Edwards holds that Christ's reconciling work on the cross brings about human salvation. But the application of this salvation to particular human beings is the work of the Holy Spirit. In recent scholarship, much discussion has centered on the question of whether Edwards's doctrine of justification represents a truly Protestant view, or whether Edwards was a kind of crypto-Catholic. This debate turns on his language about the infusion of the Spirit as grace and its relation to imputation, and it is associated in particular with the scholarship of Anri Morimoto. Rather than weighing in on that debate, this chapter reframes the discussion in terms of the language of participation in the life of God that is at the heart of Edwards's understanding of the Christian life. Viewed in this light, justification and regeneration (the act whereby fallen human beings are morally and spiritually revived by the secret, inner working of the Holy Spirit) are considered as part of a bigger picture, namely, the gracious action of God in redeeming human beings so that they may participate in God's life by glorifying and enjoying him forever.

Chapter seven deals with Edwards's understanding of human beings (theological anthropology) and his moral thought. According to Edwards, the good life is concerned with true virtue. Some Christian thinkers have conceived of moral theology primarily in terms of living according to God's commandments. Edwards does have things to say about this topic, but his moral theology—which is of a piece with his broader concerns about participation in the life of God—focuses instead upon the apprehension of *true* virtue. The reception of true virtue requires the gracious action of God within the human heart. God regenerates the human person, so that by means of a "new sense of things" given through divine grace she or he is able to delight in God's presence and desire once more to find pleasure in things of a religious nature. The Holy Spirit activates virtue in the human heart, which properly orders human nature so that human beings can effectively participate in the life of God—the end to which they are called.

The eighth and final chapter attempts to retrieve Edwards's project by asking whether and to what extent Edwards's work can be of service to systematic theology today. As a way of approaching this topic, we again consider the relation between God and creation, as well as Edwards's views on free will. We argue that there are significant problems with Edwards's doctrine as it stands and that some adaptation of his views—by stepping back from his occasionalism and (perhaps) some aspects of his doctrine of continuous creation—may be necessary in order to make his work serviceable for contemporary theology.

As previously indicated, the book also contains a guide to further reading on the literature by and about Jonathan Edwards, which serves as an aid to the further study of his life, work, and intellectual legacy.

# CHAPTER ONE

# Intellectual Context

In a recent essay on the shape of the Reformed tradition, the distinguished historian of doctrine, Brian Gerrish, writes that "Schleiermacher was the greatest theologian of the Reformed church between Calvin and Barth." Of all the other theologians between these two giants of the Reformed tradition, he maintains that "only Jonathan Edwards comes close."[1] Elsewhere, he goes as far as to say that Edwards is the greatest theologian in the English-speaking world.[2] Even if he is not *the* greatest English-speaking theologian, he is surely one of the greatest. Among the firmament of English-speaking theologians Edwards's star shines brightly indeed, though there are other Anglophone divines whose work is similarly luminous—the Puritan John Owen being one notable example. Yet Edwards is a theologian unlike many others. Not only was he at home in both the Reformed and (more broadly) Western traditions of theology; he was also a thinker engaging with cutting-edge early modern philosophy. This is not what distinguishes him as the most important English-speaking theologian, however. What makes him such a singular figure in the history of theology is his startling originality. He was a person who really did think for himself, tracing out ideas and arguments in his many notebooks in the isolation of his study for hours at a time. He literally worked through philosophical and theological problems by writing. In his work he was unafraid to affirm ancient theological truths using the tools

---

1. See Brian Gerrish, "Constructing Tradition: Calvin, Schleiermacher, and Hodge," in *Thinking with the Church: Essays in Historical Theology* (Grand Rapids: Eerdmans, 2010), 160.

2. Gerrish, "Revelation and the Religion of Reason," in *Thinking with the Church*, 13.

of the emerging Enlightenment philosophy to demonstrate that, far from undermining traditional orthodoxy, the new ideas actually undergirded and reinforced the sort of Reformed faith with which he aligned himself.

Gerrish's estimate of the relative importance of Schleiermacher, Barth, and Calvin is common enough among historians of Reformed doctrine. But the inclusion of Edwards as a thinker next only to Schleiermacher in theological importance between the polestars of the French Reformer and the Swiss dogmatician is rather more unusual. Nevertheless, here too, Gerrish's judgment appears sound. Schleiermacher's genius was to reconceptualize the basis for doing Christian theology in the wake of devastating attacks upon the rationality of theism. For him, religious experience was front-and-center in the Christian life, doctrine being the codification of that experience, which must be subjected to critical scrutiny in light of further such experiences. His was a sort of Romantic account of Christian doctrine. Edwards lived a generation before his German successor (Schleiermacher was born a decade after Edwards's death), at the beginning of the seismic changes that signaled the end of the period of Protestant Orthodoxy in the post-Reformation period and the beginning of the Enlightenment. Like Schleiermacher, Edwards was a theologian of the heart. That is, he was concerned not merely with the articulation of Christian doctrine but also with the way in which it affected the life of the Christian. Religious experience was a fundamental theological datum for both thinkers. Unlike Schleiermacher, Edwards did not attempt to recalibrate his understanding of the relationship between doctrine and experience in order to make the former comprehensible in light of the latter. He had a high view of the inspiration and authority of Scripture. But he conjoined this with a serious and enduring interest in spiritual experience. In some respects both Edwards and Schleiermacher were concerned with similar theological projects: how to reconcile the religion of the Book with the religion of the heart. But the solutions they proposed were very different, though the theology of both was, in many ways, a response to different phases in the developments of the same cultural and ideological change that was sweeping across Western culture.

## Socio-political Context

We might press Gerrish's estimation of the Northampton Sage in a slightly different direction. Not only was Edwards arguably one of the most important English-speaking theologians to date. He was also the greatest British colonial theologian, and arguably one of the greatest of all British theologians. This may strike some readers as an audacious statement, not because of the honor it confers upon Edwards but because of the nationality it assigns him. For Edwards is usually hailed as one of the greatest of *American* theologians. This is accurate in one, purely geographical respect. Edwards lived in New England and died in (what is today) the state of New Jersey, never leaving the Eastern Seaboard of the American continent. But in another, deeper sense Edwards was just as clearly *not* an American theologian—at least, not as that term would be applied to an American thinker after the Revolutionary War that brought about the declaration of an independent nation of federated states in 1776. For he lived and died nearly two decades before the United States of America came into existence.

Edwards was born into colonial New England, a society that had been settled by English refugees who sought a better life free from the religious persecution they had endured in the Old World. But it was not an American society, in the sense we use the term today. After the acts of Union by which the Scottish Parliament was amalgamated with the English at Westminster whereupon Great Britain became a legal and political entity, New England became part of the British Empire. It comprised several of the thirteen colonies of British citizens that owed their allegiance to the British Crown and were governed by aristocrats appointed by the British government. Although the pilgrim fathers had sought to build a very different society in the New World from the one they had left in the Old, this changed after the demise of the short-lived Commonwealth of Oliver Cromwell's Protectorate, and the restoration of the monarchy in England after 1660. As Kenneth Minkema observes,

> The Puritan political experiment effectively ended in 1684, with the revocation of the Massachusetts Bay Charter; the entity to replace it was the Dominion of New England, and, though Puritan religious culture endured, this was the beginning of a process by which the colonists came more and more to conform to the sociopolitical ways and means of the mother country.[3]

3. Kenneth Minkema, "Edwards's Life and Career: Society and Self," in *Understanding Jonathan Edwards: An Introduction to America's Theologian*, ed. Gerald R. McDermott (New York: Oxford University Press, 2009), 17.

Jonathan was formed, flourished, and ended his days in this political climate. And it is clear from one or two references in his works that he saw himself as an Englishman and British subject, rather than as an American. For instance, in *Some Thoughts Concerning the Revival* (1743), Edwards offers the following remarks:

> And though it may be thought that I go out of my proper sphere to intermeddle in the affairs of the colleges, yet I will take the liberty of *an Englishman* (that speaks his mind freely concerning public affairs) and the liberty of a minister of Christ (who doubtless may speak his mind as freely about things that concern the kingdom of his Lord and Master) to give my opinion in some things with respect to those societies; the original and main design of which is to train up persons, and fit them for the work of the ministry.[4]

So to describe him as an American theologian without qualification is to court misunderstanding and anachronism. This is recognized even by established American Edwardsean scholars. Kenneth Minkema, who is one of the most distinguished historians working on Jonathan Edwards today, concedes that "we ugly Americans are quick to claim Edwards as one of us, as America's most significant religious figure, but our European colleagues, and especially those from the United Kingdom are right to point out that he was a British subject, and saw himself as such."[5]

It is important to grasp something of this cultural context in order to appreciate Edwards's development as a thinker. As his biographer George Marsden writes,

> Eighteenth century Britons viewed their world as monarchial and controlled by hierarchies of personal relationships. On both these counts, their assumptions were almost opposite to

---

4. WJE 4:510. Emphasis added.

5. Minkema, "Edwards's Life and Career: Society and Self," in *Understanding Jonathan Edwards: An Introduction to America's Theologian*, 16. There is not a little irony in what Minkema says here, given the subtitle of the book to which his piece is a contribution. Similarly, George Marsden points out that "Edwards was not an 'American' in the modern sense, but an English colonial loyal to the British crown." See his essay "Biography," in *The Cambridge Companion to Jonathan Edwards*, ed. Stephen J. Stein (Cambridge: Cambridge University Press, 2007), 19.

those of most Westerners today, who tend to think of society
as in principle egalitarian and in fact controlled by impersonal
forces. Eighteenth-century British-American society depended
on patriarchy.[6]

Edwards's world was indeed very different from our own, something
closer to the society reflected in the novels of Jane Austen or Samuel
Richardson than any social or political context with which we are familiar. (Indeed, Richardson's novels *Pamela* and *Clarissa* were read and
enjoyed in the Edwards household.) Contemporary Western societies are
much more secular in outlook than the world in which Edwards lived.
As Marsden is at pains to point out in his monumental biography, it is
very difficult to engage sympathetically with Edwards without also entering imaginatively into that world. For Edwards and his contemporaries
in New England, religion was not a trivial or merely private matter—or
worse, a malaise from which human beings needed liberation. In the
eighteenth century theological views still divided the European powers
and were dominant themes in public discourse, a matter that influenced
foreign and domestic policies. And in colonial society this was even more
the case, despite the gradual religious atrophy that had occurred since
the time of the Founding Fathers, which saw fewer members of society
confessing faith or becoming church members.[7]

Daily life was significantly different from that in modern complex
liberal democracies, such as the democracy that succeeded the British
colonial society of New England. Not only was it essentially hierarchical
in nature, with each person aware of his or her place in the established
order; society was regulated by the demands of a largely rural, agrarian
culture. Eighteenth-century New England was only beginning to wake up
to the monumental changes that would transform the way most people

6. George Marsden, *Jonathan Edwards: A Life* (New Haven: Yale University Press,
2003), 3.

7. By the time Edwards was an adult the religious monopoly enjoyed by the Congregationalist churches that had for some time been effectively the state-church of the region
had been eroded. Anglicans, Baptists, and other "nonconformists" were tolerated. During
the same period fewer people made public confession of faith or took the steps necessary to
become full church members. But church attendance was still the expectation and norm.
Colonial society in the early eighteenth century was still profoundly shaped by religious
concerns. For more on this see Gerald R. McDermott, *One, Holy, Happy Society: The Public
Theology of Jonathan Edwards* (University Park: Pennsylvania State University Press, 1992).

lived in the century that followed. Such a largely pastoral existence was reflected in the social stratification of society as well. There was little personal freedom or social mobility, and most communities were networks of family and marital relationships that would, by modern standards, be little more than hamlets or small rural towns. There were very few urban centers in colonial New England, and even major ports like Boston or New York—bustling, international communities of the period—were a far cry from their modern urban counterparts.

The political arrangements of the period were frequently subject to disruption. The chance that a local township would meet with serious violence was much greater than many such rural communities today. There were frequent skirmishes with the local Native American population, including the infamous Deerfield massacre, which happened the year after Edwards's birth and touched his own wider family. There were also wars between the English settlers (as they saw themselves) and other colonial powers of the period, epitomized in conflicts such as the French and Indian War of the late 1750s. The worry that lands would be taken, that "civilized" Englishmen would be ravaged by "savages," and that Protestant New England would be turned over to a Roman Catholic power were all real concerns at a time when the security of the Protestant settlement in Great Britain was far from assured. The Jacobite rebellion of "Bonnie" Prince Charlie in 1715–16 is perhaps the most celebrated example of such upheaval back in the mother country during Edwards's lifetime. These events impacted daily life in tangible ways for the Edwards family. For a brief period Jonathan's father was a military chaplain in the latter phase of Queen Anne's war in 1711 (and wrote a fascinating letter to Jonathan's mother about how the children should be educated in his absence). Jonathan himself had to billet British troops in his house in Stockbridge in the last phase of his life, when, while he served as a missionary to the Native Americans, the frontier towns were being fortified against foreign aggression.

Thus, it would be a great mistake to think that the society in which Edwards grew up and worked was a gentle, rural idyll. Although for much of his adult life Edwards could ride out to spend a morning in secret prayer or devote the majority of his time to cloistered study, he managed to live in this way *despite* the interruption of political instability and violence, and the fears and worries that such upheaval brought. Given the times in which he lived, he had to endure significant periods when such daily routine was set aside in preference for the more pressing political and social issues of the day.

## Family Connections

This social, political, and religious situation fashioned the sort of person Edwards became in important respects. We can see this by considering the way in which his family shaped him. He was raised as the only son of a strict and rather severe Congregationalist minister, Timothy Edwards, and his wife, Esther, the daughter of a family of well-to-do and influential New England clergy. Her father, Jonathan's grandfather, the Reverend Solomon Stoddard, was one of the most powerful ministers in provincial New England outside Boston. Stoddard was known in his own lifetime as the "Pope of the Connecticut River Valley," such was the shadow he cast over the region. He was also the person Edwards later served under as an assistant in Northampton during the first phase of his parish ministry there, before becoming the sole minister of that congregation.

Timothy Edwards was of Welsh ancestry. His family had come to New England after the death of his great-grandfather, and his father, Richard, had been a prosperous cooper. From what is reported of her erratic behavior, a number of Edwards scholars have drawn the conclusion that Timothy's mother was mentally ill, a weakness that appears to have run in her side of the family. She was also (allegedly) a serial adulterer, even bearing another man's child. Her behavior was supposed to have been so irregular and alarming—including physical threats to her husband and a spell of desertion—that he eventually divorced her, which was a rare occurrence at that time that carried a not inconsiderable social stigma. It took him two attempts to have the divorce passed through the courts. Richard went on to remarry and have another six children. However, this story about Edwards's paternal grandmother has recently been challenged: it may be that Elizabeth Tuttle, Timothy Edwards's "notorious" mother was not quite the pariah she is sometimes thought to have been.[8] Nevertheless, she did bring disrepute upon the family, and divorce in colonial New England was no trivial thing. Undoubtedly the family scandals left their mark on Timothy, who was the product of a broken home. In light of this it is perhaps not surprising that in later life he paid close attention to forming the character of his children, especially his only

---

8. See Ava Chamberlain's fascinating revisionist monograph, *The Notorious Elizabeth Tuttle: Madness and Murder in the Family of Jonathan Edwards* (New York: New York University Press, 2012). Chamberlain works directly with many of the primary sources in order to give a very different account of Tuttle's character.

son Jonathan. His meticulous oversight of their development suggests a certain paternal overcompensation, as if to ensure that his offspring were given the right sort of formation so as to be above moral reproach.[9]

His father's perfectionism gave Edwards a taste for the impractically high standards that he demanded of himself and, to some extent, of those around him in later life. Timothy Edwards was not only his father and the minister of the church in which Edwards was raised. He was also Jonathan's schoolmaster and the one who prepared him to enter the fledgling Collegiate School (later Yale College) at the tender age of twelve.[10] This paternal gold standard was not only evident in Jonathan's intellectual formation. It was also present in his spiritual ambition. Timothy Edwards was very much an heir of Puritan theology, who strove to improve the doctrine he preached week by week in the pulpit, in the hope that God would bless his labors with an ingathering of converted souls. Jonathan's first experience of revivals was had under his father's ministry in East Windsor, Connecticut. It may also be that the seeds of some of the less commendable aspects of Jonathan's character were sown through his relationship with his father. Jonathan's pride and aloofness in company are traits that also seem to have belonged to Timothy Edwards and appear to have contributed to the rather difficult dealings his father sometimes had with his congregation. This fact is not unimportant when one considers the strained exchanges in the latter stages of Jonathan's relations with the church at Northampton that contributed to his dismissal.[11]

9. In addition to the allegations regularly reported concerning Elizabeth Tuttle, there were reports about her family. Timothy's aunt (Jonathan's great-aunt) murdered her own child while his uncle (Jonathan's great-uncle) killed his sister with an axe. Concerning these grisly events, Marsden writes, "Jonathan Edwards has sometimes been criticized for having too dim a view of human nature, but it may be helpful to be reminded that his grandmother was an incorrigible profligate, his great-aunt committed infanticide, and his great-uncle was an ax-murderer." Marsden, *Jonathan Edwards*, 22.

10. Timothy Edwards supplemented his ministerial stipend by schooling local children. His sizable library included a significant number of textbooks for this purpose. See WJE 26 for a detailed annotated inventory of Timothy's library, compiled by Kenneth Minkema.

11. Interestingly (perhaps *uncannily*), Jonathan's son, Jonathan Edwards Jr., was also expelled from his ministerial position and latterly became a college president like his father. The intellectual vices of the family seem to have been passed down from one generation to the next along with considerable intellectual gifts. For an account of the life of Jonathan Edwards Jr., see Robert L. Ferm, *Jonathan Edwards the Younger, 1745–1801: A Colonial Pastor* (Grand Rapids: Eerdmans, 1976).

However, it would be grossly unfair to place all the blame for Jonathan's character faults at the paternal door. Being the only male child among eleven siblings had important implications for Edwards's development. What is more, women in the Edwards family were well educated and given considerable freedom to express themselves, even choosing their own husbands (which was not a common practice at the time). Jonathan not only had sisters aplenty. Those sisters were brought up to think and argue as well as any of his peers as a boy; and they appear to have doted on Jonathan. Marsden comments, "Jonathan grew up surrounded by women. As the only boy, he was the center of attention. From early years his parents groomed him for college and the ministry, and his older sisters often oversaw his lessons." It is no wonder, then, that in later life he "especially admired female piety, which he first saw in his mother and sisters."[12]

In fact, although Edwards stayed within the accepted social norms for behavior between men and women, and does not seem to have seriously questioned the subservient role almost all women had in colonial society of the period, his attention to the piety of women and his respect for female spirituality are noteworthy. His upbringing in an almost entirely female household no doubt accounts for some of this. But his relationship to his wife, Sarah Pierpont Edwards, is another important factor. Edwards was clearly deeply in love with his wife, and not a little in awe of her profound spirituality, which she seems to have exhibited from an early age. When he was a young man and first came into contact with her, he penned a short piece about a young woman that he knew, who appeared always to be in conversation with some invisible person, and whose mind was focused on heavenly things and the life to come.[13]

This spiritual temperament appealed to Edwards on several levels. Not only was he someone for whom serious spiritual concern was a given. He was also someone who saw in the (apparently) anonymous young lady something of the sweetness and ethereal beauty that he had begun to associate with the highest and best things in life, all of which were spiritual in nature. Undoubtedly, Sarah had charms other than her

12. George M. Marsden, *A Short Life of Jonathan Edwards* (Grand Rapids: Eerdmans, 2008), 15.

13. The full text of this occasional piece by Edwards (called his "Apostrophe to Sarah Pierpont," despite the fact that its subject is never named by the author) can be found in John E. Smith, Harry S. Stout, and Kenneth P. Minkema, eds., *A Jonathan Edwards Reader* (New Haven: Yale University Press, 1995), 281.

pious disposition. Jonathan's apostrophe to the unnamed lady is typical of a certain kind of devotional literature that can be found in Puritan as well as Catholic piety and that extols the spiritual virtues of those thought to be particularly saintly. But in Jonathan's case, his early infatuation with the young, pious Sarah became a lifelong hobby. In *Some Thoughts Concerning the Revivals,* one of his early pieces written around the time of the regional ingathering at Northampton that presaged the Great Awakening, Edwards describes the religious ecstasy enjoyed by a person who seems to be a thinly veiled sketch of Sarah Edwards. And when Jonathan was away preaching at a neighboring parish on one occasion, the minister who filled his pulpit found that Mrs. Edwards was overcome with spiritual concern almost to the point of intoxication, swooning and bursting into song, in a state of apparent bliss for several days after the Sabbath meeting.

It is perhaps not too much to say that Jonathan thought of his wife as a paradigm of true spirituality. Her devotion to matters of the heart certainly seems to have deeply marked his view of the revivals. And it is interesting that a man so committed to the aristocratic structures of colonial New England society was not ashamed to credit female piety in the way he does in his writings, although it should also be said that Jonathan's reporting of Sarah's spirituality disguised her sex. If he admired female piety he was sufficiently aware of the social climate in which he lived to ensure that he did not jeopardize his publications on the revivals by overstepping conventions that tended to view female religion with much less enthusiasm.[14]

Although Sarah and Jonathan did have a long and happy marriage by all accounts, like all couples they had their misunderstandings and disputes. Sometimes the Edwards marriage has been held up as an ideal of perfect human union. (The itinerating evangelist George Whitefield and Edwards's disciple and subsequent leader of the New Divinity, Samuel Hopkins, were well-known early admirers of the marriage of Jonathan

14. Jonathan also used the testimony of other women in his revival works. These included Abigail Hutchinson, a frail young woman dying of an esophageal obstruction, and Phebe Bartlet, who was only four years old when converted, but whose evident religious zeal and persistence in her new-found faith deeply impressed Jonathan. This is remarkable on two counts. Phebe was very young and both she and Abigail were female, two reasons that would usually have excluded them from serious consideration as candidates for credible religious experience, given the social conventions of the time. See Edwards, *A Faithful Narrative,* in WJE 14.

and Sarah Edwards.) But Jonathan was, after all, his father's son. By contrast, Sarah was something of a charismatic personality, and a woman of not inconsiderable intelligence, wit, and ability. One recorded but unpublished dispute between them concerned some matter of prudence, for which Sarah feared her husband would horsewhip her out of town, which is hardly the response one might expect of an otherworldly saint.[15]

Beyond the circle of his immediate family, Jonathan's relations also played important roles at key points in his career, sometimes, sadly, to his personal and professional detriment. Take, for instance, the Williams clan, relatives on his mother's side who had suffered loss at the Deerfield massacre. Toward the end of the 1740s, as his ministry at Northampton came to an unhappy and premature end, his cousin, Solomon Williams, wrote a treatise in order to discredit Jonathan's change of views on the qualifications necessary for participation in communion, which was the matter that had precipitated the crisis at Northampton. Ironically, Jonathan's Northampton parishioners sponsored Solomon Williams's work. Other members of the Williams clan who had settled in Stockbridge, the small frontier hamlet to which Jonathan removed after leaving Northampton to be a missionary to the Mahicans, made his time there much more difficult than it otherwise might have been. They repeatedly and maliciously interfered with his work and placed strain upon his relations with the native peoples and colonial British neighbors in the village.

Clearly, Jonathan Edwards was formed in important respects by the actions of his family, and their relations with him had important implications at crucial junctures in his ministerial career.

## Intellectual Formation

With this in mind, we may now turn more directly to the matter of Jonathan Edwards's intellectual formation. In the mid-twentieth century, Edwards scholarship was reinvigorated by the work of the Harvard intellectual historian Perry Miller. He conceived of Edwards as a visionary thinker ahead of his time, a person whose genius was thwarted by be-

15. This reference is given in Kenneth P. Minkema's illuminating essay "Personal Writings," in *Cambridge Companion*, 48. Minkema also detects an underlying note of spiritual envy in Edwards's "Apostrophe to Sarah Pierpont"—a longing for spiritual experiences that may have eluded him but were all too apparent in the life of his future spouse. See Minkema, "Personal Writings," 47.

ing expressed in the outmoded thought of Puritan theology, which was the only medium available to him at the time. In Miller's estimation it was Edwards's philosophical and scientific forays that indicate his real substance as a thinker, not his sermons or theological treatises.[16] This conception of Edwards as an intellectual has been largely discredited by subsequent work on the Northampton Sage's formation. For one thing, Miller's picture of Jonathan Edwards is rather one-dimensional. It places him as a protean disciple of the English philosopher John Locke and the natural scientist Sir Isaac Newton, as if these were the only two important thinkers to shape Jonathan's mature work. But in fact, he was a lifelong intellectual magpie who promiscuously gathered into his nest ideas and arguments from many different sources. Another problem with Miller's account is that it makes of Edwards a tragic figure whose early intellectual promise was cut short by being shackled to a moribund theology. However, it is indisputable that from a very early age Jonathan regarded his life work as centered upon theology and as chiefly concerned with the greater glory of God.

His time at Yale provides one important example of this (although even there he could not escape the influence of his relatives). Edwards was an impressionable teenager when he matriculated for his studies at the Wethersfield branch of the Collegiate School, as it was then known. At that time there were two locations vying to be the place at which the college was settled. (Eventually, the decision was made to erect the first buildings at New Haven, and Edwards and his compatriots moved there for their studies.) Jonathan was granted his Bachelor of Arts degree by the time he was sixteen and was a Master of Arts before he was twenty, joining the social elite at a time when only one in a thousand people in Colonial America had a higher education.[17]

The young Collegiate School had its fair share of scandals to deal with while Edwards was a student there. Timothy Cutler, the rector of the college, became a *cause célèbre* when he converted to Anglicanism the year after Edwards graduated with his baccalaureate degree. Samuel Johnson, another Anglican defector, was a senior tutor whose doubtful orthodoxy led a group of students, including Edwards, to decamp from

16. See Perry Miller, *Jonathan Edwards* (New York: Sloane & Associates, 1949).

17. This information and much else about Edwards's intellectual, social, and theological formation can be found in Douglas A. Sweeney's remarkable and insightful book *Jonathan Edwards and the Ministry of the Word: A Model of Faith and Thought* (Downers Grove: InterVarsity, 2009), especially 22–39.

the official site of the college at New Haven back to the previous site at Wethersfield, until his removal from office toward the end of Jonathan's undergraduate studies. During his sojourn at Wethersfield Jonathan's education was overseen by his cousin, Elisha Williams. It is noteworthy that Jonathan's MA *quaestio* (that is, his formal oration, which was a condition of passing his graduate degree) on justification by faith, given the year after Cutler's defection, was a ringing endorsement of the theological *status quo* and an intimation of his lifelong engagement with the problem posed by "Arminianism."[18]

While a graduate student at Yale College, Edwards had access to the controversial collection of books provided by the philanthropist Jeremiah Dummer, which included many fashionable authors. The bequest included volumes that set forth ideas far from Calvinistic orthodoxy and contributed to the "apostasy" of Rector Timothy Cutler and Tutor Samuel Johnson. On the basis of Samuel Hopkins's claim that Edwards devoured John Locke's *Essay Concerning Human Understanding* while still an undergraduate, Perry Miller presumed that Edwards had been an intellectual prodigy in the making. However, recent work has shown that Edwards almost certainly did not have access to Locke prior to finding his *Essay Concerning Human Understanding* in the Dummer collection. What is more, although Locke did leave a lasting influence upon Jonathan's thought, he was not the only philosopher to affect Edwards. In addition to Newton, Edwards was drawn to the ideas of the French Cartesian, Nicholas Malebranche, and his English disciple John Norris. He was also deeply influenced as a young man by the Cambridge Platonists, particularly the work of John Smith, traces of whose idealism can be found in Edwards's early scientific and philosophical works, such as *"The Mind."*

However, in addition to these philosophical influences Edwards was shaped by the curriculum at Yale, which was modeled on that of Harvard. Edwards would have closely studied a number of Reformed scholastic theologians as central components of his course of studies. This included working through William Ames's *Marrow of Theology*, a standard body of divinity in Puritan England, as well as Johannes Wollebius's *Abridgement*

---

18. A number of Edwards scholars have pointed out that in eighteenth-century New England "Arminian" was a term used rather indiscriminately to describe a range of non-Calvinist freethinking, not all of which would have been embraced by those of the Arminian theological persuasion. When Edwards castigates a thinker or view as Arminian it is not always clear whether he means historic Arminianism or this broader, cultural "Arminianism." For discussion of this, see Paul Ramsey's editorial introduction to WJE 1.

*of Christian Divinity* and works of logic by the Dutch Reformed thinkers Franciscus Burgersdicius and his disciple Adriaan Heereboord. In fact, William Morris has drawn attention to the fact that these elements of Edwards's education were at least as important as the much-touted intellectual discovery of Locke, Newton, and the Cambridge Platonists—perhaps more important in laying the groundwork for Edwards's formation as a Christian thinker.

Like Harvard, the daily routine for scholars at Yale consisted in oral displays of rhetorical, logical, and argumentative prowess in debate and recitation. This was similar to the medieval university curricula on which New England collegiate education was modeled. According to Morris, "these oral exercises and the habits they inculcated were far more important in the formation of the mind of Edwards than has been realized. They contributed to that essentially Scholastic bent of much of his thinking and writing."[19] On the basis of this pedagogy, "Edwards early learned to contend in argument for victory, and he never forgot that lesson."[20] Nor, in light of the curriculum he was taught, did he forget that divinity had a number of branches that included biblical, systematic, dogmatic, and practical theology. His works are shot through with these different facets of his theological training.

Edwards amassed his own library as a minister, which eventually amounted to more than 800 items.[21] It included many theological and controversial works, some philosophy and natural science, as well as other volumes including fiction. But recent work has shown that he was also involved with an association of local ministers in a book-lending cooperative, which significantly augmented the works to which he had access. These included a number of digests or learned journals, such as the *Republick of Letters* and the *Ladies Journal*, which were widely circulated among his associates. They contained abstracts of fashionable works of literature, philosophy, and history that were much more than mere pastiche. Through these works Edwards was able to access the latest ideas circulating in Europe, and he may even have used them to locate works he then sought for himself, such as those of David Hume, whom Edwards appears to have read toward the end of his life.

19. William Sparkes Morris, *The Young Jonathan Edwards: A Reconstruction* (New York: Carlson Publishing, 1991), 536.

20. Morris, *Young Jonathan Edwards*, 526.

21. Minkema, "Personal Writings," 54.

He squirreled away the ideas he gleaned from the books and magazines he read in numerous notebooks and ledgers that he kept with typical fastidiousness throughout his adult life. These repositories for his ideas served several purposes. He used them in the training of ministerial candidates who came to lodge in the Edwards household, testing their theological knowledge through what he called his familiar method of questioning a candidate and getting him to reflect and respond for himself, using the resources Edwards placed at his disposal, including his "Miscellanies" notebooks. This was a kind of Socratic method of learning that made use of his notebooks as resources for theological reflection. But his voluminous notebooks also served as cribs for his mature works. Edwards used them as sources for his treatises, especially when composing the so-called Stockbridge treatises of the last few years of his life while a missionary to the Native Americans. Samuel Hopkins says that Edwards always thought with pen in hand. He was a thinker who wrote as he read and as he reflected in his hours of study each day. This was so much the case that Edwards's hands were permanently stained with ink from his daily intellectual endeavors.

Although he was a voracious and eclectic reader, drawing upon as wide a range of materials as he could in order to fashion his own works, it would be a mistake to think of Edwards as a scholar in the modern, secular sense of the word. No doubt he was a fine metaphysician and surprisingly well read for someone living so far from the centers of high society. But, contrary to the Miller thesis about the character of Edwards's outputs, his work was all bent to a single purpose, namely, the glory of God. To this end, he read and studied the Bible more than any other work. At first glance, it is rather surprising that modern secondary scholarship on Edwards has not made more of this fact. After all, Edwards was a minister almost all of his professional life, spending hours a day in prayer, in Bible study, in the writing of minute notebooks on Scripture and typology, and in the construction of sermons and midweek lectures for his congregation. One of his major projected works, which remained unfinished at the time of his death, was a *Harmony of the Old and New Testaments*, for which he had been gathering notebook materials over a protracted period.

But this relative modern neglect of Edwards the biblical scholar is rather more understandable when we consider that his interest in Scripture was in many ways that of the pre-critical scholar. This is not to say that Edwards's biblical concerns were flat-footed, although they were decidedly more theologically conservative than many contemporary secular academicians would find palatable. If anything his biblical concerns were extremely elaborate. It was precisely this rather baroque approach to Scripture that made his work in this area rather less accessible to later generations. For Edwards, the Bible was a vast set of types and antitypes, a labyrinthine complex of signs, whose polyvalence points to different theological truths that only a lifelong immersion in Scripture will reveal. The Bible was, for Edwards, a palimpsest, upon which were inscribed and reinscribed various images that connote an array of theological truths to the discerning reader. So complex was his understanding of the typology of Scripture that it is difficult for anyone not steeped in the sort of biblically literate society in which Edwards grew up to penetrate.[22]

Although Edwards's work was largely centered upon rightly understanding and interpreting Scripture, this does not mean his intellectual interests were *narrowly* biblical, though he spent more time in biblical study than any other. For Edwards, all truth was God's truth since God was the Creator of all things. So it made perfect sense to him to read, say, early Enlightenment epistemology or natural philosophy alongside the Bible because he saw the truth in each area of knowledge as part of one seamless and divinely generated whole. This explains why he bent all his work to the glory of God. It also explains why he found no difficulty in segueing between his different intellectual interests. Unlike many of his contemporaries who saw in the new learning something to be feared, Edwards regarded the philosophical and scientific advances of his own age as something to be celebrated and embraced, from which theologians could learn about the created order and about better ways of thinking God's thoughts after him.

In his widely read hagiography of Edwards, Iain Murray has claimed, "The plain fact is that Edwards' excursions into philosophy were only occasional and peripheral to his main thought; it was theology, or 'divinity,' which belonged to the warp and woof of his life. Edwards' place in his-

---

22. There is still a dearth of material on this topic, although a significant step forward has been made with Douglas A. Sweeney's monograph, *Edwards the Exegete: Biblical Interpretation and Anglo-Protestant Culture on the Edge of the Enlightenment* (New York: Oxford University Press, 2015). Earlier noteworthy studies in this area include Robert E. Brown's *Jonathan Edwards and the Bible* (Bloomington: Indiana University Press, 2002), as well as the work of Stephen J. Stein. A recent discussion of Edwards's use of the two biblical testaments can be found in Stephen R. C. Nichols, *Jonathan Edwards's Bible: The Relationship of the Old and New Testaments* (Eugene, OR: Wipf & Stock, 2012).

tory is not alongside Locke, Berkeley or Kant. His life and impact were essentially religious."[23] But any careful student of Edwards will quickly recognize this as a false dichotomy. Edwards's excursions into philosophy, like the excursions of many of his contemporaries—including Locke and Newton—were not peripheral to his thought. They were the essential metaphysical underpinning of his theological reflections. Edwards sought to understand the doctrine of Scripture. But he also sought to comprehend how this made sense given the latest discoveries in the sciences and philosophy precisely because he thought that the whole truth of the matter could be grasped only by immersion in all the different academic disciplines. For if God has created the world and all it contains, and if God is an absolute sovereign, then the whole of creation will carry his signature. Revelation is to be found not only in the words of Holy Writ, although such words provide a vital key by means of which we may understand creation's underlying unity and purpose.

So Murray is mistaken in dividing Edwards's work in this way, though theology undoubtedly was the central focus of his lifework. In fact, it would be a mistake to divide the work of many early Enlightenment thinkers in this fashion. For many intellectuals working in the late seventeenth and early eighteenth century, the world was still to be understood as the handiwork of a Creator, not the upshot of happenstance and random but nevertheless adaptive mutation. Many of these scholars and scientists spent a great deal of time in the study of Scripture, trying to make sense of it in light of the (then) new discoveries of science and philosophy. This was true of John Locke, whose *Reasonableness of Christianity* is just one example of his desire to understand the Bible. It was also true of the great light of the age, Sir Isaac Newton, who, as is well known, spent the last years of his life poring over biblical images, trying to fathom the numerology of Scripture. The list could go on. The metaphysician Nicholas Malebranche was a French Oratorian priest; Gottfried Wilhelm Leibniz was a deeply pious Christian who wrote a systematic theology; and so on. Although there are notorious "freethinkers" in the early Enlightenment period in which Edwards worked (such as Baruch Spinoza or David Hume), and even some whose study of Scripture led them to unorthodox conclusions about its content (such as John Tindal, whose work Edwards singled out for particular criticism), many of the

---

23. Iain H. Murray, *Jonathan Edwards: A New Biography* (Edinburgh: Banner of Truth, 1987), xx.

most important thinkers of the age were deeply engaged with theological matters. The hard-and-fast distinctions between sacred and secular concerns were not yet part of the republic of letters in the way they are today.[24] Sometimes such anachronistic distinctions have marred secondary literature on early modern thought (Edwards included). This work attempts to provide an account of Edwards's thought that better tracks the sensibilities that motivated him.

## Character and Personal Habits

Edwards's social standing as the scion of prominent ministerial families certainly gave him a head start in life. Being of ministerial stock was tantamount to being aristocracy in colonial New England. It provided him with access to education, to books, and to a collegiate formation, which was something restricted to the socially privileged Europeans. But it also placed upon him expectations. Perhaps because of his upbringing and the gender imbalance in his immediate family, he was reserved in company even as an adult. He could appear proud, "stiff and unsociable" as one early biographer puts it,[25] and this was certainly a besetting sin with which he struggled throughout his career, and which most probably contributed to his dismissal from his ministerial position at Northampton. He was a little too quick to criticize others, and on occasion to delight in their misfortunes; and he was a little too thin-skinned when it came to receiving criticism in turn.[26] His erstwhile teacher, the Anglican rebel Timothy Cutler, remembered Edwards as being "critical, sad and peculiar," a "sober person" and "pretty recluse, austere and rigid," as well as "a

24. Gerald McDermott, among others, has shown that Edwards was deeply engaged in refuting deism, one of the principal freethinking products of the early Enlightenment. Whereas deists thought God had fashioned the world like a vast clockwork machine that he simply wound up and left to run independent of his interference, orthodox theologians like Edwards believed God was deeply involved in the creation and upholding of what he had made, a matter to which we shall return later in the book. For more on this matter, see McDermott, *Jonathan Edwards Confronts the Gods* (New York: Oxford University Press, 2000).

25. Samuel Hopkins, *The Life and Character of the Late Learned Mr Jonathan Edwards, President of the College of New Jersey, Together with Extracts from His Private Writings and Diary, And Also Seventeen Select Sermons On Various Important Subjects* (Northampton, MA: Andrew Wright, 1804), 44.

26. See Minkema, "Personal Writings," 44–45.

man of much sobriety and gravity" and "odd in his principles, haughty stiff and morose."[27]

To be fair, Edwards was aware of some of these shortcomings and did try to combat them. Reflecting upon his own character toward the end of his life, he wrote in his *Personal Narrative*: "I am greatly afflicted with a proud and self-righteous spirit; much more sensibly, than I used to be formerly. I see that serpent rising and putting forth its head, continually, everywhere, all around me."[28] As a young man Edwards briefly kept a diary, like other pious youths of the period, in which he confided the mercurial nature of his spiritual pilgrimage as well as the sort of morbid musings that teenage journaling often produces. But these pages also reflect an unflinching honesty in the forensic diagnosis of his character flaws. For instance, on May 4, 1723, as a teenager of nineteen, he wrote:

> Although I have in some measure subdued a disposition to chide and fret, yet I find a certain inclination, which is not agreeable to Christian sweetness of temper and conversation: either by too much dogmaticalness, too much of the egotism; a disposition to be telling of my own dislike and scorn; and freedom from those that are innocent, yea, common infirmities of men; and many other such like things.[29]

And at the beginning of September of that year just over a month before he turned twenty, he could admit "there is much folly, when I am quite sure I am in the right, and others are positive in contradicting me, to enter into a vehement or long debate upon it."[30]

He may well have found it temperamentally difficult to suffer fools gladly. But then, Edwards had no real intellectual peer in his social circles. There were other thinkers of importance in colonial America, such as Benjamin Franklin, whom he does not appear to have met, although they both had a mutual friend in the English evangelist George Whitefield. But there was no one who was able to match him in his raw intellectual ability, his grasp of logical precision, finer points of argument, and theological and metaphysical minutiae. He stands alone among colonial figures of

---

27. Cited in Minkema, "Personal Writings," 56.
28. WJE 16:803.
29. WJE 16:769.
30. WJE 16:781.

his period as the one truly great mind whose peers were the European thinkers of the age. It was impossible for him not to be aware of this in his interactions with those around him. And this, in turn, meant it was sometimes difficult for him to tolerate those of inferior talents, which meant almost everyone with whom he came into contact on a daily basis.[31] Marsden sums up Edwards well when he says that "his prowess as a logician made him exceedingly sure of his opinions, sometimes given to pride, overconfidence, tactlessness, and an inability to credit opposing views."[32]

This rather semi-detached demeanor was reinforced by his scholarly and personal habits. From an early age, Edwards had installed into himself Puritan habits of mind, whereby "redeeming" or "improving the time" one had was regarded as a *sine qua non*. He kept a series of resolutions as a young man, to which he strictly adhered and which he reviewed on a weekly basis. His fifth resolution reads, "Resolved, never to lose one moment of time; but improve it the most profitable way I possibly can," a clear reference to biblical passages such as that in Ephesians 5:16. He was schooled in the ancient biblical tongues as a child so as to be able to matriculate to Yale, where Latin was still regarded as the language of culture and was the tongue in which most textbooks were written. And as a minister he developed formidable habits of study, which he passed on to his closest disciples such as Joseph Bellamy and Samuel Hopkins.

Hopkins, who was also one of his early biographers, records that Edwards commonly spent thirteen hours a day in study.[33] He rose early, usually around 5 a.m., and went to bed, as most people did before electric lights, when the day ended in the early evening. His daily routine was punctuated by regular occasions for prayer: first thing in the morning, at meals, in the evening, riding out into the fields, and holed up in his study. He did not make pastoral visits as a matter of course, preferring instead to "improve" his time through prayer and study, which he thought of as the chief means by which he might serve the purposes of God. Parishioners were able to visit and consult Edwards, and there is evidence that this did occur. But he did not venture to visit them; the onus was upon

---

31. An example of his early intellectual self-confidence: with the encouragement of his father, Jonathan had sent a careful description of the working of a spider to a colonial member of the Royal Society, with hopes of its publication. (It was not published.) The letter is reproduced, along with other early attempts at scientific writing, in WJE 6:147–69.

32. Marsden, *Jonathan Edwards*, 5.

33. Hopkins, *The Life and Character of the Late Learned Mr Jonathan Edwards*, 43.

the church member to come to see him. Not that the Edwards house was a quiet sanctuary dedicated to the bookish ways and scholarly habits of its master, which could not be disturbed. After all, Edwards had a large family to oversee. What is more, for some periods of his ministerial career the house was full not just of children, but also of visitors, such as the ministerial candidates that lodged with Edwards or (in Stockbridge) the soldiers billeted in the town during the French and Indian war in the late 1750s. The ailing missionary David Brainerd stayed and died in the house, tended by one of Edwards's children, Jerusha. Her loving care for Brainerd as his life ebbed away due to consumption (i.e., tuberculosis) actually led to her own demise. She died shortly afterwards and is buried in the Northampton cemetery.

Although as a minister Edwards owned some property that was farmed and had an increasing and eventually large family, the household management was something almost entirely turned over to his wife. Hopkins tells us that "he was less acquainted with most of his temporal affairs than many of his neighbors; and seldom knew when and by whom his forage for winter was gathered in, or how many milk kine he had; and whence his table was furnished, etc."[34] Edwards was able to spend his hours in intensive study because his household revolved around him. And, of course, the Edwards household was assisted in the daily chores by slave labor. It is a sad fact for which there is no moral justification that Edwards even wrote in support of slavery, unlike his closest disciples whose work against slavery marked the emerging New Divinity, as it was called.[35]

Yet this picture of an otherworldly Edwards, the ivory-tower minister and scholar, should be tempered by recent discoveries about his accounting book, which contains careful lists of transactions and borrowings, as well as the markings of his cows so that they would not be lost! Like his father, who was fastidious about keeping his accounts in order, Edwards seems to have had a mania for ensuring he knew what he owed, to whom, and when. Although by the end of his ministry in Northampton he was one of the best-paid ministers in his surrounding area, the fact that his stipend was paid in arrears and often in kind (i.e.,

34. Hopkins, *The Life and Character of the Late Learned Mr Jonathan Edwards*, 53–54.

35. Edwards's slaveholding was unremarkable for someone of his social standing in colonial New England of the period. As is well known, other important historical figures of the time such as Thomas Jefferson and George Washington had large numbers of slaves in their households.

in produce not money), coupled with the large family and trappings that went with ministerial social standing (e.g., china tableware, fashionable dresses for his wife, and silver buckles for his knee-breeches), Edwards was often struggling to make ends meet. So, although the daily running of his household was largely taken out of his hands in order that he might concentrate on his studies, it appears that he kept a rather close eye on the financial and other transactions that occurred in his home, which tempers the otherworldly picture of Edwards the closeted, heavenly minded scholar.[36] That said, his contribution to the management of these practical aspects of his household was very much in keeping with his scholarly habits: the accountant and book-keeper rather than the foreman or manager of his smallholding.

Edwards was not only scrupulous about how he spent his time. He was careful about his other personal habits too, especially his diet. He ensured that he only ate what was necessary for him to continue his work, never to capacity; and he regularly fasted and prayed in secret. This is also reflected in his early resolutions, where number 20 states, "Resolved, to maintain the strictest temperance in eating and drinking," and number 40 takes up a similar theme: "Resolved, to inquire every night, before I go to bed, whether I have acted in the best way I possibly could, with respect to eating and drinking. *Jan. 7, 1723.*" Sometimes he would forego a meal in order to continue his studies, such was the seriousness with which he pursued his intellectual interests.[37] In his admiring biography of his mentor, Samuel Hopkins tells us that these bodily strictures were demanded in part by his constitution:

> He was very careful and abstemious in eating and drinking, as doubtless was necessary [for] so great a student, and a person of so delicate and tender a bodily make as he was. . . . When he had, by careful observation, found what kind and what quantity of diet best suited his constitution, and rendered him most fit to pursue his work, he was very strict and exact in complying with it; and in this respect *lived by rule*, and herein constantly

---

36. For more on this, see Minkema, "Personal Writings."

37. In a diary entry for January 22, 1734, Edwards remarks, "I judge that it is best, when I am in a good frame for divine contemplation, or engaged in reading the Scriptures, or any study of divine subjects, that ordinarily I will not be interrupted by going to dinner, but will forego my dinner, rather than be broke off." WJE 16:789.

practiced great self-denial, which he also did in his constant early rising, in order to redeem the time for his study.[38]

This is reinforced by Edwards's own words to the Trustees of the College of New Jersey (now Princeton), which called him to succeed his son-in-law, Aaron Burr, as president in what would be the last year of his life. Edwards's reply in October of 1757 includes comments about his physical unfitness for the job, due to what appears to be chronic problems associated with indigestion and the general bodily weakness from which he suffered. He remarks that

> I have a constitution in many respects peculiar unhappy, attended with flaccid solids, vapid, sizy and scarce fluids, and a low tide of spirits; often occasioning a kind of childish weakness and contemptibleness of speech, presence, and demeanor; with a disagreeable dullness and stiffness, much unfitting me for conversation, but more especially for the government of a college.[39]

Yet he took regular exercise, often chopping wood or riding several miles into the woods for prayer. The concatenation of these different habits of mind and body may well have contributed to his physical frailty, which was the subject of comment at the time. There were several periods of his life during which he endured very serious illness, which seems to have weakened him permanently and may well have precipitated his premature decline at Princeton, when the inoculation for smallpox that had been given to him led to complications in his swallowing and his eventual death. Edwards described one of the most serious of these bouts while he was still at college as a teenager as a pleurisy, which, if accurate, would suggest that he suffered from a serious chest infection, perhaps even pneumonia. It was to be the first of a series of recurring health crises, which may well have been in large measure due to this initial, serious damage done to his health.[40] This would certainly explain the

38. Samuel Hopkins, *The Life and Character of the Late Learned Mr Jonathan Edwards*, 43. Emphasis in the original.

39. Edwards, Letter to the Trustees of the College of New Jersey, October 27, 1757, Letter no. 230, in WJE 16:726.

40. In his *Personal Narrative*, Edwards says this: "Indeed, I was at some times very uneasy, especially towards the latter part of the time of my being at college. Till it pleased God, in my last year at college, at a time when I was in the midst of many uneasy thoughts

periodic interruptions to his extremely demanding routine, sometimes lasting several months. It would also explain why his constitution was so frail and why the recurrence of his physical ailment was precipitated by prolonged periods of physically and mentally exhausting work. Like a number of other evangelical leaders of the eighteenth century (most famously, George Whitefield), Edwards literally worked himself into the ground.

Jonathan was tall for a man of his times, at around six feet. But he was wan and drawn through his ascetic habits of life. In this respect, the healthy and robust-looking portrait of Edwards painted by Joseph Badger and reproduced on a steady stream of book covers may be more than a little fanciful, since it depicts a middle-aged minister in the full bloom of health. Contemporary descriptions of his disposition, his eating habits, and his general constitution give the lie to this artistic license. Garbed in his ministerial black with his periwig atop his high, receding brow, and gaunt from a life of austerities and illness, the severe, serious minister of Northampton must have cut a very singular figure.

Yet although Edwards was most certainly a patrician, something of an autocrat, and a thinker whose abilities tempted him to intellectual pride, he was also a loving father and devoted friend and mentor. His children clearly loved him, and his closest friends held him in the highest esteem. Although he may have been difficult to get to know, those who were intimate with Edwards counted their relationship as something to be treasured. One example of many that could be given will make the point. Jonathan's daughter, Esther Edwards Burr, wife to Aaron Burr who became the president of the College of New Jersey (i.e., Princeton), whom Edwards succeeded, kept a detailed diary over a three-year period that has been preserved and published in full transcription. It is a fascinating window onto a lost world, cast in the form of letters to a friend. In one entry, dated September 19, 1756, a Sabbath, she speaks of seeking counsel from her father (she was then married to Burr), in these terms:

> Last eve I had some free discourse with My Father on the great things that concern my best interest—I opened my difficulties to him very freely and as he freely advised and directed. The conversation has removed some distressing doubts that dis-

---

about the state of my soul, to seize me with a pleurisy; in which he brought me nigh to the grave, and shook me over the pit of hell." WJE 16:791.

couraged me much in my Christian warfare—He gave me some excellent directions to be observed in secret that tend to keep the soul near to God, as well as others to be observed in a more publick way—What a mercy that I have such a Father! Such a Guide![41]

On the basis of such effusive filial testimony, it would be difficult to sustain the view that Edwards's character left him aloof and friendless. But it would also be true to say that in some cases he gained and then lost friends, the most spectacular example of which is his falling in and out of love with his congregation at Northampton. This also tells us something about the man as well as about the times in which he lived and the people among whom he ministered.

## Places and Spaces

Social historians of the last thirty or more years have shown us that the location in which a particular thinker grew up or flourished has often proven to be an important influence upon subsequent intellectual outputs. David Hume's success would be difficult to conceive of without the high society of Edinburgh and its place as a hub of early Enlightenment thinking. And, to take a very different example, John Bunyan's *Pilgrim's Progress* reflects the topography as well as the ideas to which Bunyan was exposed—his description of mountains (of which he had no personal experience) being a famous case in point. The same could be said for a multitude of other intellectuals of the early modern period, whose thought was dependent in important ways upon the culture and geography with which they were familiar. Edwards is no different in this respect. In fact, the places in which he grew up, and where he pastored, were of profound importance for his spirituality and theology. By modern standards, he did not travel very far in the course of his life. He lived his entire life in Massachusetts, Connecticut, New York, and (briefly at the end) New Jersey. He never left what we would think of as the Northeastern Seaboard of America. Compared to his contemporaries John and Charles Wesley,

41. Esther Edwards Burr, *The Journal of Esther Edwards Burr, 1754–1757*, ed. Carol F. Karlsen and Laurie Crumpacker (New Haven: Yale University Press, 1984), 224. The antique spelling is preserved from the diary.

or his friend the evangelist George Whitefield, or even Bishop George Berkeley, he was not a well-traveled man. He never went to any of the major urban centers of learning. Boston, the most significant city in New England, was a small provincial town by contemporary standards. Most of Edwards's life was spent in rural villages or on the frontier.

This had an impact on Edwards in several respects. We have already had cause to note the connection between Edwards's practical habits of study and the fact that the places in which he lived were removed from major places of learning. But it is also true to say that the physical environment he inhabited had an important influence upon his work. Edwards delighted in the natural world, in its apparent design, intricacies, proportion, beauty, and excellence. He spent many hours in prayer wandering in the woodlands of his hometown in Northampton. He mused over the natural world in things like his short work on the spider. But, perhaps most important of all, this intoxication with the natural order led him to develop an extremely sophisticated, even hypertrophied typological account of the whole of creation. For Edwards, the whole created order was an image or shadow of divine things. It spoke with great eloquence of its Creator for anyone who had the eyes (and sufficient grounding in Puritan ways of thinking about Scripture) to see. Even everyday things like the sun shining became for Edwards the occasion for reflection upon the divine order of things. The sun was an analog to the Trinity: the celestial body itself being like the Father, its rays like the Son, its warmth like the Spirit.

Standing on the summit of Mount Holyoke, one can see the vista of the Connecticut River valley below, including the town of Northampton. In one sweep it is possible to take in most of the places in which Edwards spent his life, the river down which he traveled in moving house, the hills beyond which the frontier and Stockbridge lay, and the direction in which he went to go to Yale, to New York, and eventually to Princeton. Even today, it is a green, wooded valley that it is easy to imagine Edwards inhabiting. Perhaps it is no wonder that such a place produced a thinker so concerned with the beauty and order of all God's creation, as well as the tiny part that human beings play in the grand scheme of God's purposes. For it is a place that leaves one feeling larger, better, more complete, just as it seems to have left the Sage of Northampton.

## Conclusion

Edwards's most distinguished modern biographer points out that "if we are to appreciate Jonathan Edwards as a real person and not just as an intellectual or spiritual prodigy who appears out of nowhere in the American wilderness, we must try to get a sense of his contexts."[42] This introductory chapter has been written with these comments in mind. Knowledge of the context that formed a great figure of the past, and in which that figure worked and flourished, is fundamental to rightly understanding his or her contribution and work. For when we see something of the context in which a person worked, it helps us to understand better what it is that makes a thinker both familiar and yet strange. Edwards stood at the intersection of several different worlds. He worked in a culture where Puritanism was dying and the modern world was beginning to make significant inroads in terms of science, economics, politics, and religion. Sometimes Edwards has been accused of being a medieval; at other times he has been heralded as so ahead of his time that we are only just beginning to catch up with him. Paradoxically, there is something true about both judgments. The explanation for this apparent antinomy lies in the contextual crucible that formed him. He was a minister in a Puritan ecclesiastical polity, a student of traditional Reformed theology, a reader of early modern philosophy, and an adept of the emerging natural science. In the tumultuous period in which he lived one world was passing away and another much more recognizably modern environment was beginning to emerge. His life's work reflects this concatenation of different religious, social, and political factors. It is, in many respects, Janus-faced: looking backwards to the post-Reformation Reformed theological hegemony that obtained from the founding of New England, and forward to a much more uncertain, complex world in which the natural sciences held sway. If we do not attend to these contexts that shaped him, we will fail to understand something fundamental about the nature of Edwards's project and what it was that drove him to make the contribution he did. For, like any great thinker, Edwards was a man of his times, a product of his immediate intellectual, cultural, and religious environment. What makes him a truly remarkable individual is the fact that his work transcended these particularities. It is not reducible

42. Marsden, "Biography," in *Cambridge Companion*, 19.

to the historical context that shaped him or comprehensible as the sum of the parts that fashioned him. But to acknowledge this is not to belittle the importance of his context in the shaping of his thought. It is to recognize its place as a crucial constituent in the formation of Edwards as a thinker of the first rank.

# CHAPTER TWO

# God of Beauty and Glory

Having considered Edwards's intellectual context, we turn to his theology. We begin with his doctrine of God. God's life *in se* (in himself) is the foundation and end of all of Edwards's theologizing. The inner plenitude of the divine life grounds and guides the theologian's quest to seek understanding. To adequately address Edwards's doctrine of God, we start with an overview of his doctrine of Trinity and utilize this material to advance a discussion of God's emanation and remanation. We conclude with a discussion of Edwards's aesthetics. This overarching vision of God will be important for our discussion of Edwards's philosophical theology, as well as the remaining theological material on the atonement, soteriology, and ethics, which we turn to in later chapters of the book.

## Trinity

In broadest terms, the tradition offers two ways to talk about God—from the temporal missions back to the eternal processions, or from the eternal processions to the missions.[1] Edwards doesn't hesitate, in a way foreign to our own context, to provide a robust description of the eternal divine life, claiming, "Those doctrines which relate to the essence, attributes, and subsistencies of God, concern all; as it is of infinite importance to common people, as well as to ministers, to know what kind of being God

---

1. Fred Sanders's chapter "Incarnation and Pentecost," in his book *The Triune God*, is particularly insightful here. Fred Sanders, *The Triune God*, New Studies in Dogmatics (Grand Rapids: Zondervan, 2016), 95–121.

is."[2] Whereas twentieth-century theologians tended to lean so heavily on the triune missions that any vestige of God's life *in se* seemed to dissipate, Edwards "sets his mind on things above" (Col. 3:2) and doesn't hesitate to "put together reason and Scripture." This impulse leads Edwards to say, somewhat provocatively, "There has been much cry of late against saying one word, particularly about the Trinity, but what the Scripture has said . . . I am not afraid to say twenty things about the Trinity which the Scripture never said."[3] Edwards's boldness does not necessarily unearth an overly realized faith in reason; instead, his boldness is a response to God's condescension in Son and Spirit and the riches Edwards finds in God's self-revelation in Scripture. God's inner life, far from being cut off from human inquiry, has been revealed in the giving of the Son and Spirit and has been unveiled through Scripture to human reason. In the light of God's self-revelation the Christian can penetrate into the divine depths to gaze upon the infinite beauty that defines the eternal effulgence of the divine being.

To describe the infinite fullness of the divine life and how that life overflows into the created order, three interrelated emphases define Edwards's doctrine of God: *personhood*, through the employment of a psychological analogy,[4] *perception*, as the Father gazes upon his perfect image and understanding (the Son), and *affection*, the flowing forth of the Holy Spirit as the will and love of God.[5] God is the divine mind, whose

2. WJE 22:92.

3. WJE 13:256–57.

4. Whereas this view assumes something like a psychological analogy in his development of the Trinity, it may be a mistake to categorize it as such. One of the reasons for this is that it is unclear to me (Strobel) that Edwards is employing an analogy at all. Edwards utilizes the category of personhood to delineate the threefold reality of the divine essence (something like mind, understanding, and will). But Edwards does not seem to be utilizing an analogy. This is just what it means to be personal: God or human. Edwards claims, "Though the divine nature be vastly different from that of created spirits, yet our souls are made in the image of God: we have understanding and will, idea and love, as God hath, and the difference is only in the perfection of degree and manner." WJE 21:113. While Edwards collapses God and humanity within the broad category of "personal creatures," he reinforces his Creator/creature distinction through his use of infinity. See, for instance, WJE 13:135.

5. Reconstructing Edwards's doctrine of God comes with some minor difficulties. Most of Edwards's reflections on the Trinity are scattered through notes, sermons, and published works, and while he did devote a specific discourse to the Trinity, it was never completed or readied for publication. A close reading of Edwards's "Discourse on the Trinity" reveals that he is taking his previous reflections and advancing them into a rough

intellection and affection are the generation and motion of the divine life. This makes personhood central to Edwards's account, and his doctrine of God is formed deeply by this focus. This emphasis on personhood also unveils the development of Edwards's argument in his "Discourse on the Trinity" (hereafter "Discourse"). Edwards begins his account with the singular personhood of God, which was a place of common ground with the anti-trinitarians of his day, and then advances a psychological analogy to argue that God has understanding and will, and that, as an infinite personal being, God is infinitely happy. To talk about God is to talk about a being in utter fullness, flowing forth in the pure actuality of love and delight. Notice how Edwards begins his work on the Trinity:

> When we speak of God's happiness, the account that we are wont to give of it is that God is infinitely happy in the enjoyment of himself, in perfectly beholding and infinitely loving, and re-joicing in, his own essence and perfections. And accordingly it must be supposed that God perpetually and eternally has a most perfect idea of himself, as it were an exact image and representation of himself ever before him and in actual view. And from hence arises a most pure and perfect energy in the Godhead, which is the divine love, complacence and joy.[6]

Edwards's God is a God of infinite happiness (known as the "divine blessedness").[7] This God has his own image ever before him, and a "pure and perfect energy" of love, complacence, and joy pours forth in an infinite

---

argument but mature analysis. For more on this, see Kyle Strobel, *Jonathan Edwards's Theology: A Reinterpretation* (New York: T&T Clark, 2012). In that work, I argue that Edwards changed his view of how the divine persons relate to the divine essence as he was writing the "Discourse." It was this issue, I argue, that caused Edwards to write it in the first place. For a slightly different reading of the "Discourse," see Oliver D. Crisp, *Jonathan Edwards among the Theologians* (Grand Rapids: Eerdmans, 2015), ch. 3.

6. WJE 21:113.

7. Edwards gave a sermon on the divine blessedness to articulate his doctrine of God (1 Timothy 6:15; November 23, 1738). His doctrine was: God is a Being possessed of the most absolutely perfect happiness. Whereas I prefer to label Edwards's doctrine of the Trinity "religious affection in pure act," it could be more theologically helpful to label it simply "the divine blessedness." This idea is clearly foundational for Edwards's doctrine of God. The way he develops it is through personhood and the beatific vision, but the goal is an articulation of God as the Being who is infinitely happy in himself. This is clear from the first line of the "Discourse."

fountain of delight. The foundation of this view is the psychological analogy, but its architecture is the beatific vision—a vision of God generating perfect happiness. Whereas most theologians focus the beatific vision on the experience that *believers* have in glory, Edwards locates this experience in God's own life of blessedness. By using the beatific vision as the structure of his doctrine, the categories of personhood, perception, and affection are given priority. To categorize this view of the Trinity, we can say that God's life is religious affection in pure act.[8] In this sense, God is the archetype of the purely *religious* life. This description assumes personhood, but the details focus on the kind of personal existence this Being has. God's life is the infinite actuality of divine blessedness—beatitude known and experienced in the eternal fullness of the divine being.

### The Divine Processions

Seeking to articulate his primary theological foundation, as well as the ontological grounding for the missions of Son and Spirit, Edwards proceeds according to the order of being by addressing the divine processions. To do so, Edwards utilizes his understanding of personhood as the construct to describe God's fullness. In short, a person is a being with understanding and will. God the Father is infinitely attending to his understanding (procession of the Son), and love flows forth between the Father and Son in the procession of the Spirit. The processions serve to fund a broader reality, namely, the Father and Son in the beatific actuality of the Spirit. How the processions fund this broader reality depends on Edwards's doctrine of perichoresis, which will be addressed below. The development thus far unveils Edwards's inclinations in four key ways, each reaching beyond theology proper to assert pressure across Edwards's theological system. First, Edwards is starting with a singular divine mind, sharing common ground with the anti-trinitarians of his day (for the purpose of his anti-trinitarian polemic).[9] Second, Edwards uses the psy-

8. Oliver Crisp has argued, persuasively in my mind, that Edwards's doctrine of God should be understood in light of the *actus purus* tradition. See Oliver Crisp, *Jonathan Edwards on God and Creation* (Oxford: Oxford University Press, 2012); and Crisp, "Jonathan Edwards and the Divine Nature," *Journal of Reformed Theology* 3, no. 2 (2009): 175–201.

9. The most important, for Edwards, would have been Samuel Clarke. Clarke states, "The reason why the Son in the New Testament is sometimes stiled [*sic*] God, is not so much upon account of his metaphysical substance, how divine soever; as of his relative

chological analogy to argue that this singular divine person of the Father has both understanding and will, and that the divine understanding is a *generation* of the divine essence, and the will is a *movement* of the divine essence between them. Third, Edwards assumes divine simplicity: "that there is no distinction to be made in God between power or habit and act"; and that "there are no distinctions to be admitted of faculty, habit and act, between will, inclination and love: but that it is all one simple act."[10] God is infinite fullness; he sees and knows his perfect idea and loves it without ceasing. Last, Edwards's description of God's life *in se* unites knowledge and love (i.e., understanding and will) together, grounding them in the divine essence, such that God's self-knowing is always affectionate self-knowing.

### *The Divine Idea*

The first major hurdle in Edwards's analysis is to give an account of the divine idea. The divine idea is a perfect generation of the divine essence, Edwards avers. "The sum of the divine understanding and wisdom consists in his having a perfect idea of himself," and, furthermore, "I do suppose the Deity to be truly and properly repeated by God's thus having an idea of himself; and that this idea of God is a substantial idea and has the very essence of God, is truly God, to all intents and purposes, and that by this means the Godhead is really generated and repeated."[11] God is, in some sense, his own object, and therefore "there is nothing in the pattern but what is in the representation—substance, life, power, nor anything else—and that in a most absolute perfection of similitude; otherwise it is not a perfect idea. But that which is the express perfect image of God, and in every respect like him, is God to all intents and purposes, because there is nothing wanting."[12] God's idea of himself is a generation of the

---

attributes and divine authority over us." Samuel Clarke, *The Scripture-Doctrine of the Trinity: In Three Parts* (London: Printed for James Knapton, 1712), 296. Clarke uses relative attributes to subordinate the Son in an attempt to develop a monarchian account of the Trinity. See Clarke, *Scripture-Doctrine of the Trinity*, 280–82, 296–97, 359, and Thomas C. Pfizenmaier, *The Trinitarian Theology of Dr. Samuel Clarke (1675–1729): Context, Sources, and Controversy* (Leiden: Brill, 1997), 118.

10. WJE 21:113.
11. WJE 21:114.
12. WJE 21:114.

divine essence because it is a perfect contemplative act. Edwards qualifies what this perfect idea entails:

> But this will more clearly appear if we consider the nature of spiritual ideas, or ideas of things purely spiritual. Those that we call ideas of reflection—such as our ideas of thought, love, fear, etc.—if we diligently attend to them, we shall find they are repetitions of those very things either more fully or faintly; or else they are only ideas of some external circumstances that attend them, with a supposition of something like what we have in our own minds that is attended with like circumstances.

He continues, drawing a possible analogy between human contemplation and the procession of God's understanding.

> And if it were possible for a man by reflection perfectly to contemplate all that is in his own mind in an hour as it is and at the same time that it is there, in its first and direct existence; if a man had a perfect reflex or contemplative idea of every thought at the same moment or moments that that thought was, and of every exercise at and during the same time that that exercise was, and so through a whole hour: a man would really be two. He would be indeed double; he would be twice at once: the idea he has of himself would be himself again.[13]

In this act, the divine essence is generated. But this is not an act in time, it is the eternal generation of God's own idea.

Importantly, we must not read into what Edwards is saying and go beyond his intentions. Edwards is trying to make one simple point: The Father has a perfect and eternal generation of himself ever before him, and, as such, "that idea which God hath of himself is absolutely himself."[14] Edwards's first move is to develop an account of the divine idea, and he has not yet attempted to give an account for the divine idea as the second *person* of the Trinity. The way he does this will be shown below, but Edwards's next move is to turn to Scripture. Edwards's exposition of Scripture reveals

---

13. WJE 21:115–16. In God's perfect self-contemplation, the divine essence is generated as the divine idea.
14. WJE 21:116.

that the divine idea has become incarnate as Jesus, and that this is how the Bible talks about Jesus's identity. For instance, the Son is the image of the invisible God (2 Cor. 4:4; Col. 1:15), is in the form of God (Phil. 2:6), and is the "brightness of his glory" and the "express image of his person" (Heb. 1:3).[15] "What can [be] more properly called the image of a thing than the idea?," Edwards questions. "If you have seen me you have seen the Father," Jesus asserts (John 12:45; 14:7–9), which leads Edwards to argue that Jesus is the divine idea. Furthermore, Scripture claims that Jesus is the Logos (John 1), and we are told that Jesus is the wisdom of God (compare Prov. 8:22–31; Matt. 23:34; Luke 11:49; 1 Cor. 1:24), both notions pointing to the infinite and eternal depths of Jesus's person. It was Christ's presence that was with Moses, Edwards argues, and he believes it was Christ who was called the "face of God" (from Exod. 33:14).[16] While Edwards's description of the divine life is often presented as if it was disengaged from revelation, it is an account driven by his exegetical commitments. Far from being an arbitrary development of the psychological analogy, with no real biblical weight behind it, Edwards is seeking to advance the abundance of scriptural imagery into an account that takes seriously the infinite depths of the divine being. At this point in his development, what seems clear to him is that God has an eternal idea, and that idea, somehow, is the same one who becomes incarnate as the man Jesus.

### The Divine Will

From this biblical material, Edwards turns his attention to the Spirit. Now, he states, "there proceeds a most pure act, and an infinitely holy and sweet energy arises between the Father and Son: for their love and joy is mutual, in mutually loving and delighting in each other."[17] Edwards continues, "This is the eternal and most perfect and essential act of the divine nature, wherein the Godhead acts to an infinite degree and in the most perfect manner possible. The Deity becomes all act; the divine essence itself flows out and is as it were breathed forth in love and joy."[18] The pure actuality of

---

15. WJE 21:117.

16. WJE 21:118–19.

17. WJE 21:121.

18. WJE 21:121. Edwards's use of "becomes" here can seem troubling. It seems reasonable to conclude that this language is simply an aspect of talking about God's life in progressive movements, and should not be taken as actual change in God's eternal life.

God's life is the procession of the Spirit as the divine will, love, holiness, and beauty. Once again, Edwards turns to exegesis. Edwards uses Proverbs 8 to narrate the divine reality; here wisdom proclaims, "I was daily his delight, rejoicing always before [him]."[19] God and his wisdom rejoice in each other. This is the Father and the Son flowing forth in delight, which is the Holy Spirit—the "infinitely holy and sweet energy" between the Father and Son. Similarly, Scripture defines God as love (e.g., 1 John 4:8). The way this unfolds for Edwards is that the Holy Spirit is the divine love. On this view, this is why Jesus prays, "I have made Your name known to them, and will make it known, so that *the love with which You loved Me* may be in them, and I in them" (John 17:26 NASB; emphasis added). How is the Father's love of the Son given over to God's people? Edwards believes this is clear; the Father's love of the Son is received upon the infusion of the Holy Spirit in regeneration. Edwards takes these references (and others) as evidence for his view that the Spirit is God's eternal movement of love that was poured out at Pentecost and received in regeneration.

While we might not be entirely satisfied by all of Edwards's exegetical maneuvering, he works closely with the biblical material to argue that the Spirit's proper nature is holiness, love, grace, and peace, canvassing Scripture to argue for overarching types now revealed as the Spirit. Regardless of our own exegetical tradition, it should be clear that Edwards refuses to allow the scriptural witness to be ignored, and believes Scripture itself governs his typology and trinitarian theology. Two examples are evident of this. First, Edwards turns to the Spirit's name as the Holy Spirit, claiming this name "naturally expresses the divine nature as subsisting in pure act and perfect energy, and as flowing out and breathing forth in infinitely sweet and vigorous affection." This is "confirmed both by his being called the *Spirit*, and by his being denominated *Holy*."[20] Second, he questions why Paul wishes grace and peace from God the Father and the Lord Jesus Christ, but never from the Spirit. Edwards suggests that this can be explained only by the simple reality that the Holy Spirit is, in fact, the grace and peace of the Father and the Son given over to his people. Edwards concludes this section with a nod to the depth of the biblical witness, and he levels a subtle critique for those (perhaps us?) who refuse to pay closer attention to its language: "I think the Scripture reveals a great deal more about it than is ordinarily taken notice of."[21]

19. WJE 21:121.
20. WJE 21:122. Emphasis added.
21. WJE 21:131.

## Natures and Distinctions in the Godhead

By following the contours of Edwards's argumentation in the "Discourse," we have seen how the divine idea and the divine will are generated based on a psychological analogy and God's beatific self-knowledge. Before explaining how the divine idea and will *are persons*, it is important to highlight how the inner life of God governs God's economic life, such that the identity and nature of the Son and Spirit are brought over with them into the economy. Therefore, it is particularly important to attend to the inner life of God, as it is revealed, to recognize the eternal, ontological grounding of God's redemptive activity.[22] In particular, it is important to understand the order and nature of the processions to identify the meaning of the divine mission. Edwards claims,

> though the Holy Ghost proceeds both from the Father and the Son, yet he proceeds from the Father mediately by the Son, viz. by the Father's beholding himself in the Son. But he proceeds from the Son immediately by himself by beholding the Father in himself. The beauty and excellency and loveliness of the divine nature, though from the Father first and originally, yet is by the Son and nextly from him. The joy and delight of the divine nature is in the Father by the Son, but nextly and immediately in the Son.[23]

Whereas the Spirit flows forth from the Father originally, he[24] does so by the mediation of the Son.[25] The Son's act in the procession of the Spirit is secondary, but immediate (not mediated): "For though it be from

22. God establishes an "economy" for functioning among the Father, Son, and Spirit that is not identical to the processions but is based upon them. Edwards calls this agreement the "mutual free agreement," and it is this agreed-upon economy that leads to what looks like subordination in God's life. This is not a "natural" subordination, however, but a willed one. See WJE 20:431. This willed subordination in God's life is still an eternal act, because it "precedes" the eternal covenant of redemption, but it is a willed subordination and not "natural." WJE 20:432.

23. WJE 21:143.

24. We are following Edwards's use of "he" for the Spirit here and for the rest of this volume.

25. Edwards was troubled by the rise of anti-trinitarian subordination within the Godhead, and so he seeks to protect the Son's dignity and equality through his understanding of the processions (not unlike the original emphasis on the *filioque*).

the Son by his beholding the Father," Edwards explains, "yet he beholds himself in himself." The Son's gazing upon the Father "is nothing else but his existing: for 'tis nothing else for an idea of a thing to behold that thing that it beholds, but only for an idea to exist. The idea's beholding is the idea's existing."[26] The Son's existence is his beholding of the Father, embracing that the Father is in him and that he is of the Father. But this mutual vision between the Father and the Son is not complete without the movement of the Spirit. God's life is not a disinterested knowledge—a passive gazing upon the ceaseless truth of himself—but is an affectionate overflow of infinite love. God the Father gazes upon the Son, and the pure actuality of divine love flows to him, and from the Son back to the Father, embracing them both in the uniting love of the Spirit.

In the divine life, the Father is the "first in order" and the "fountain of Godhead" that sustains the "dignity of Deity."[27] "All is from him, all is in him originally."[28] Whereas the Father has a "particular honor" in being the fountain from which all else flows, the Son has a "particular honor" by having all else come "nextly" by him. The Son is not simply an instrumental cause, but all comes by him immediately (including, as we have seen, the Holy Spirit).[29] Edwards's articulation of the fountain of the deity reveals that the ordering of the divine processions serves as particular relations, honors that differentiate the persons of God. Therefore, while the divine persons have an equal honor, it is still possible to predicate a relative honor among them: "Thus God the Father be the first person from whom the others proceed, and herein has a peculiar personal honor. And the Holy Ghost is the last that proceeds from both the other two, yet the Holy Ghost has this peculiar dignity: that he is as it were the end of the other two, the good that they enjoy, the end of all procession."[30] Although the Holy Spirit is in some sense "the end of all procession,"

---

26. WJE 21:143.

27. This is the order that makes it "fitting" for the agreed-upon economy among the persons to take on a subordination. But Edwards is clear that "there is no such thing as a natural superiority. . . . [There is] no proper dependence. Independence is an essential property of the divine nature, [and so there is] no natural subjection. Thus the Son of God is not by nature in any subjection to the Father. By nature [he is] under no obligation." WJE 25:147.

28. WJE 21:143.

29. Seng-Kong Tan makes this point well in his discussion. See Tan, *Fullness Received and Returned: Trinity and Participation in Jonathan Edwards* (Minneapolis: Fortress, 2014), 15.

30. WJE 21:146.

the nature of the movement of the Holy Spirit is to flow forth from both Father and Son. Therefore, the Spirit of love

> flows out in the first place [necessarily] and infinitely towards his only begotten Son, being poured forth without measure, as to an object which is infinite, and so fully adequate to God's love in its fountain. Infinite love is infinitely exercised towards him. The fountain does not only send forth large streams towards this object as it does to every other, but the very fountain itself wholly and altogether goes out towards him. And the Son of God is not only the infinite object of love, but he is also an infinite subject of it. He is not only the infinite object of the Father's love, but he also infinitely loves the Father. The infinite essential love of God is, as it were, an infinite and eternal mutual holy energy between the Father and the Son, a pure, holy act whereby the Deity becomes nothing but an infinite and unchangeable act of love, which proceed from both the Father and the Son.[31]

### Subsistence and Personhood

Edwards's account struggles (and he recognized this) to turn the corner from one divine mind with understanding and will to three divine persons partaking of one singular divine essence.[32] This is a common problem for accounts seeking to maintain a psychological analogy for a description of *triune* personhood. In focusing on the divine mind with understanding and will, one is left with aspects of the divine life (i.e., understanding and will) that are adequate faculties, but not adequate persons. To remedy this issue, Edwards turns to the mutual interpenetrating union of the subsistences, asserting that

> the whole divine essence is supposed truly and properly to subsist in each of these three—viz. God, and his understanding and love—and that there is such a wonderful union between them that they are after an ineffable and inconceivable manner one

31. WJE 8:373.
32. WJE 21:132–33.

in another; so that one hath another, and they have communion in one another, and are as it were predicable of one another.[33]

He continues to unpack this union and communion by adding, "the Father understands because the Son, who is the divine understanding, is in him. The Father loves because the Holy Ghost is in him. So the Son loves because the Holy Spirit is in him and proceeds from him. So the Holy Ghost, or the divine essence subsisting in divine love, understands because the Son, the divine idea, is in him."[34]

On this account, the processions are necessary but not sufficient conditions for personhood. Without the mutual interpenetration (often deemed "perichoresis"), what Edwards offers is an account of the "repeating" and "movement" of the divine essence, but not a full description of the divine persons. Rather than turning to a social analogy for the Trinity, where God is described as three persons (i.e., individuals) communing in love, Edwards reads the very notion of personhood through perichoresis, such that the three are three persons only insofar as they are one (i.e., persons as they interpenetrate each other). By mooring God's personal triunity in his union and oneness, Edwards's account refuses to slide toward either error, allowing for robust plurality from within a psychological analogy not known for those kinds of resources.[35] No matter how hard one tries to pull God's oneness apart from the individuality of the persons in the economy, this only pulls tighter the knot of God's intrinsic unity.

As Scripture narrates the divine missions in redemption, Edwards recognizes the wisdom, idea, and understanding of God's eternal life in the person of Jesus. Similarly, in the sending of the Spirit Edwards sees the love, peace, and holiness of God himself, sent forth to create so that

---

33. WJE 21:133.

34. WJE 21:133. Edwards admits that there is room to push back on his account, but he is able to simply ask, How does your account of God fare against mine? The orthodox, he notes, have always asserted one divine essence, along with one understanding and one will (see WJE 21:134–35). If God has an understanding and a will, and, if Edwards's biblical material is convincing, this understanding was made incarnate in Jesus Christ and this will is given over for believers to commune with God.

35. This can be seen, perhaps most obviously, by interpreters who believe that Edwards must have employed two different analogies, a social analogy and a psychological analogy, because they seem to assume that Edwards's social language is not possible from within a psychological analogy. But this is the genius of Edwards's account.

they may partake in God's beatific self-knowing. This focus on God's inner life, therefore, is not abstract speculation but the shape of God's self-revelation in the economy as revealed in Scripture. This means that the inner triune identities of the Son and Spirit are internal to their persons, and therefore communicable properties they carry over into their economic work. Far from communicating superfluous and esoteric knowledge to his creatures, God the Father gives himself to his people by sending his understanding and his love into the world. Salvation, therefore, entails communion with the Father in the Son by the Spirit (Eph. 2:18) and, as such, is a partaking of God's self-knowing in love and affection.[36] The Father and Son exist within the Spirit, so to speak, as the union of love between them—a bond that exists as the affection and pure action of the divine mind. In the economy this love overflows to the elect, and by receiving the Spirit believers receive God's own holiness, love, and beauty, an infusion, Edwards tells us, that reorients the human person by pulling one up within the divine life.[37]

## Emanation and Remanation

To address the self-giving of God to his creatures and the glory that returns back to him through their knowledge and love, Edwards employs the terms "emanation" and "remanation." Mirroring the divine fullness, where the processions of understanding and will define God *in se*, in the economy God's will and understanding emanate forth to the creature through a willed self-giving of God's understanding and love as the Son and Spirit. For God's understanding and love to be remanated for the glory of God, the creature must know God as God knows himself. This is religious affection. To remanate God's life back to him is to know God affectionately from within God's self-knowing. In Edwards's words,

---

36. "This is the divine partaking or nature that we are made partakers of (II Pet. 1:4)," Edwards claims, "for our partaking or communion with God consists in the communion or partaking of the Holy Ghost." WJE 21:122.

37. "When men are regenerated and sanctified, God pours forth of his Spirit upon them, and they have fellowship or, which is the same thing, are made partakers with the Father and Son of their good, i.e. of their love, joy and beauty." "Discourse on the Trinity," WJE 21:124. The claim that God "pulls creatures up" into the divine life is my own language to describe this reality. This does not undermine the creature/Creator distinction, but should be read in terms of communion or fellowship.

> In the creature's knowing, esteeming, loving, rejoicing in, and praising God, the glory of God is both exhibited and acknowledged; his fullness is received and returned. Here is both an *emanation* and *remanation*. The refulgence shines upon and into the creature, and is reflected back to the luminary. The beams of glory come from God, and are something of God, and are refunded back again to their original. So that the whole is *of* God, and *in* God, and *to* God; and God is the beginning, middle and end in this affair.[38]

God sends forth his Son as his perfect image; the image of the invisible God. The Spirit is the illuminating presence of God that makes the Son known, and therefore seen (and "if you've seen me," Jesus proclaims, "you have seen the Father"; John 14:9). Edwards's employment of the term "emanation" unites the immanent and economic life of God together, highlighting that the economic is an extension and image of the immanent. The God known in the divine economy is God as he really is. The order of the immanent life, therefore, is important. Edwards focuses his attention on God's eternal existence as a way to speak meaningfully about the sending of the Son and the Spirit. Their work in redemption is not foreign to them, but is intrinsically connected to their eternal identities and natures.

In God's eternal life, the Spirit flows out from the Father to the Son without measure (and vice versa). The Son, who takes on human nature to redeem, is the one through whom the Spirit flows forth to the creature. Pentecost follows the ascension because the resurrected and ascended Christ is the one who sends the Spirit. This is *his* Spirit, and it is by the Spirit that Christ unites people to himself. The Spirit, as Christ's Spirit, allows believers to see and know the Son by faith, and if they have seen him, they have seen the Father. The beatific vision is the goal of the creature, as theologians have always articulated: "Now we see through a glass darkly," Paul proclaims, "but then face to face" (1 Cor. 13:12). But the sight of God, for Edwards, is first and foremost determined by God's own beatific life. In God's life there is an emanation of the Son—the divine idea eternally generated—and there is remanation of the Spirit pouring forth from the Son to the Father.[39] Likewise, in the economy, there is a willed

---

38. WJE 8:531. Emphasis in the original.

39. Seng-Kong Tan's chapter "Communication of Being *Ad Intra*: The Trinity as

emanation: the divine revelation of the Son as the divine idea; and there is remanation: the creature seeing by faith and responding in affection through the indwelling work of the Holy Spirit.

The indwelling Spirit allows for a mediated immediate perception of God.[40] The perception is immediate because it is not based on our own rationalizing. We do not merely think our way to God. But, importantly, the sight of God is mediated because we come to see the Father in Christ, who mediates this vision by the Spirit.[41] As noted above, the mediate/immediate distinction is used in Edwards's doctrine of God to delineate how the Spirit proceeds forth from the Father. The Spirit proceeds mediately (in a mediated manner) through the Son from the Father, whereas from the Son in an immediate (not mediated) manner. In heaven, furthermore, there will be a kind of mediation of the vision of God in the Son, because, Edwards argues, "no creature can thus have an immediate sight of God, but only Jesus Christ. . . . And Jesus Christ, who alone sees immediately, [is] the grand medium of the knowledge of all others."[42] As the saints are members of the Son, so they see the Father immediately in Christ's mediation:

> The saints shall enjoy God as partaking with Christ of his enjoyment of God, for they are united to him and are glorified and made happy in the enjoyment of God as his members. . . . They being in Christ shall partake of the love of God the Father to Christ, and as the Son knows the Father *so they shall partake with him in his sight of God*, as being as it were parts of him as he is in the bosom of the Father.[43]

---

Origin, Medium, and End of the Divine Emanation and Remanation" is helpful in this regard. See Tan, *Fullness Received and Returned*, 5–24.

40. It would be too narrow to limit the Spirit's work to illumination alone. Rather, in the Spirit the elect commune with God. "Now the sum of God's temper or disposition is love, for he is infinite love"; and this "is the divine disposition or nature that we are made partakers of (2 Peter 1:4); for our partaking or communion with God consists in the communion or partaking of the Holy Ghost." WJE 21:122. Bernard J. F. Lonergan talks similarly about a "mediation of immediacy," in Lonergan, *Method in Theology* (Toronto: University of Toronto Press, 1971), 77.

41. WJE 18:427–34, WJE 17:64–65. For more on this, see Strobel, *Jonathan Edwards's Theology*, 139–40.

42. WJE 18:428.

43. JEC, Unpublished Sermon, Romans 2:10, #373 [L. 44v] (hereafter Romans 2:10 with leaf number). Emphasis added.

In the Son, the believer partakes in his own sight and enjoyment of the Father. In the life of faith—a life of sight through a dark glass—believers still have an immediate sight of God, but now that needs further qualification. As believers receive the Spirit, they see the Father in a mediated manner through the Son, but in Christ it is an immediate knowledge of God (because of Christ's nature as the divine idea). Christ is the subject and revelation by which God is known and seen.[44] The sight believers have, even through the dark glass of faith, is still an unmediated sight of God as it is known in Christ by the Spirit, because Christ is not ultimately an intermediary but true God of true God. But Edwards is careful. Right after saying that the saints' view of God here and now is, in a sense, immediate, he affirms another sense where it is mediated: "But yet in another sense they are [the saints' discoveries of God] mediate; that is, as they are by means of the gospel through a glass."[45] Edwards's concerns are clear. By God's self-revelation in Son and Spirit, the saints truly receive God's glory. "As all the revelation that God has made of his glory by Christ the Father is never seen but by Christ. Therefore he is said in Colossians 1:15, 'to be the image of the invisible God,' which intimates to us that God the Father in himself is invisible and never can be seen immediately."[46] This sight is of God, as it is a vision of the invisible God in Christ by the Spirit through the means of the gospel (i.e., the means of grace). We do not merely think our way to God; God reveals himself, giving us eyes to see *in* his Son and Spirit and *through* the means of grace.[47] So Edwards will say explicitly,

> The discoveries that the saints have of God's excellency and grace here, they are immediate in a sense; that is, they don't

44. Edwards explains his usage saying, "When it is said that this light is given immediately by God, and not obtained by natural means, hereby is intended, that 'tis given by God without making use of any means that operate by their own power, or a natural force. God makes use of means; but 'tis not as mediate causes to produce this effect." WJE 17:416.

45. WJE 17:65.

46. Edwards, "Jesus Christ Is the Shining Forth of the Father's Glory," in *The Glory and Honor of God: Volume 2 of the Previously Unpublished Sermons of Jonathan Edwards*, ed. Michael D. McMullen (Nashville: Broadman & Holman, 2004), 230.

47. The distinction here I am drawing between "in" and "through" is somewhat arbitrary, but helpful, I hope, nonetheless. Edwards is carefully navigating what it means to know God directly, even while we seem to be dealing with God indirectly (through a sermon, for instance). But by grace (i.e., having the Holy Spirit dwelling in one's heart), there is an immediacy to God's working and communicating to the person.

depend on ratiocination. But yet in another sense they are mediate; that is, as they are by means of the gospel through a glass. But in heaven God will immediately excite apprehensions of himself without the use of any such means.[48]

In eternity we will not need the means of grace because we will have a vision of God in the mediated immediacy of the Son by the Spirit. Importantly, here and now these means of grace do not erect a mediator between God and his people other than Christ, but mediately offer God to us in Christ. The offer of wisdom and grace, or the economic movement of the divine idea (Son) and grace itself (Holy Spirit) is the self-giving of God. Edwards explains, "'Tis rational to suppose that this blessing should be immediately from God; for there is no gift or benefit that is in itself so nearly related to the divine nature, there is nothing the creature receives that is so much of God, of his nature, so much a participation of the Deity: 'tis a kind of emanation of God's beauty, and is related to God as the light is to the sun."[49]

The Spirit, as divine grace, provides communion with God through a participation in God's own life: "Grace is a thing supernatural and divine not only in the way it is from God, but in that 'tis a participation in God . . . for where grace dwells, there God dwells."[50] By sending forth himself and his life into the world, God is calling creatures into the movement of vision and love that define his fullness. There is emanation and there is remanation, as creatures receive and flow forth themselves—receiving knowledge of God in the Son and responding in love and affection—and this is had through communion with God, in Christ, by the Spirit. God's life and presence given over to his creation is God's movement of redemption and reconciliation. God's life is infinite happiness and delight, and so God wills an emanation of that life so creatures can partake in it:[51]

48. WJE 17:65.

49. WJE 17:422.

50. 1 John 4:12, Transcription #498.

51. In comparing, for instance, the eternal generation of the Son and the creation of the world, Edwards states "that it [eternal generation] is not an arbitrary production but a necessary emanation. Creation is an arbitrary production. They are the effects of the mere will and good pleasure of God." Edwards, "Jesus Christ Is the Shining Forth of the Father's Glory," 228. Edwards uses the term "emanation" to refer either to the eternal generation of the Son or Spirit or to God's life *ad extra*. For Edwards, the differentiation is found in the nature of God's being, his emanating the Son and the Spirit as the reality of his existence,

> As there is an infinite fullness of all possible good in God, a fullness of every perfection, of all excellency and beauty, and of infinite happiness. And as this fullness is capable of communication or emanation *ad extra*; so it seems a thing amiable and valuable in itself that it should be communicated or flow forth, that this infinite fountain of good should send forth abundant streams, that this infinite fountain of light should, diffusing its excellent fullness, pour forth light all around. And this is in itself excellent, so a disposition to this in the Divine Being must be looked upon as a perfection or an excellent disposition; such an emanation of good is, in some sense, a multiplication of it; so far as the communication or external stream may be looked upon as anything besides the fountain, so far it may be looked on as an increase of good.[52]

God created so that his glory could emanate beyond his own life to another and so that creatures could partake of his life in him and with him.

> Thus it appears reasonable to suppose that it was what God had respect to as an ultimate end of his creating the world, to communicate of his own infinite fullness of good; or rather it was his last end, that there might be a glorious and abundant emanation of his infinite fullness of good *ad extra*, or without himself, and the disposition to communicate himself or diffuse his own *fullness*, which we must conceive of as being originally in God as a perfection of his nature, was what moved him to create the world.[53]

This is not a God who is desperately seeking fulfillment, nor is it a God who emanates himself uncontrollably. Edwards's God is infinite perfection that wills to overflow so that others can partake in the fullness of

---

and will, the emanating externally to himself. Edwards, "Jesus Christ Is the Shining Forth of the Father's Glory," 229.

52. WJE 8:432–33. Edwards's use of "amiable," "valuable," "in some sense," and "it may be looked on," are in place to protect him from being read too strictly. See Stephen R. Holmes, "Does Edwards Use a Dispositional Ontology?," in *Jonathan Edwards: Philosophical Theologian*, ed. Paul Helm and Oliver Crisp (Aldershot, UK: Ashgate, 2003), 114n50.

53. WJE 8:433–34.

this perfection. This perfection, following the contours of God's own life, is an overflow of knowledge to be both perceived and loved according to its greatness, goodness, and beauty. It is fitting, Edwards notes, "that as there is an infinite fullness of joy and happiness, so these should have an emanation, and become a fountain flowing out in abundant streams, as beams from the sun."[54] Just as the Father and the Son are bound together in the Spirit of love, so too are God's elect united to God in Christ by the Spirit of love. God looks upon his people as his own, and therefore he ties the communication of himself (emanation) to his own end, such that their response (affection as remanation) is seen to be a part of God's own life. God is, in a sense, incomplete without it.

> *God looks on* the communication of himself, and the emanation of the infinite glory and good that are in himself to belong to the fullness and completeness of himself, *as though* he were not in his most complete and glorious state without it. Thus the church of Christ (toward whom and in whom are the emanations of his glory and communications of his fullness) is called the fullness of Christ: *as though* he were not in his complete state without her; as Adam was in a defective state without Eve. . . . Indeed after the creatures are intended to be created, God may be conceived of as being moved by benevolence to these creatures, in the strictest sense, in his dealings with, and works about them.[55]

Edwards is careful here, using "as though" as an important qualifier. He wants to use the strongest possible language while still recognizing God's aseity. God emanates his self-knowledge to his elect so that they can see and know the love of God that surpasses knowledge. Edwards points to a God that is communicative within himself, and who overflows to communicate his own life to his people. Within God's eternal existence there is an emanation and remanation (between the Father and Son). The Spirit, Edwards claims, is, in some sense, the end of the Trinity; the Spirit is "the good that they [Father and Son] enjoy, the end of all procession."[56] As such, the pouring forth of the Spirit within the life of God

---

54. WJE 8:433.
55. WJE 8:439–40. Emphasis added.
56. WJE 21:146.

defines that life. This is mirrored in the economy. The God who is pure act, the infinite movement of emanation and remanation, reveals himself to his people (emanation) to bring a return to himself in glory through his people (remanation). This broad movement is mirrored in miniature, as a movement of religious affection (i.e., emanation and remanation in a person's relating to God in Christ) and revival (i.e., emanation and remanation in community). In this, as well, the Spirit is the end: the *telos* of the divine life overflowing and flowing back in glory.

## Beauty and Excellency

As an account of the divine blessedness, where God is known as infinite knowledge and love in the overflowing effulgence of eternal delight, the category of beauty becomes fundamental for Edwards's doctrine of God. "God is God, and distinguished from all other beings," Edwards boldly declares, "chiefly by his divine beauty, which is infinitely diverse from all other beauty."[57] Edwards's conception of beauty entails a description of God's own life, a life that is, in some sense, *sui generis*. This is why divine beauty is infinitely diverse from other notions of beauty. And yet, beauty is a category of intelligent being, and therefore of persons, and is one of the categories Edwards utilizes to link humanity to the life of God. The difference between God's beauty and all others concerns the degree of virtue and greatness of being, concepts linked in Edwards's thought, and the reality that beauty is found internal to himself (whereas all other creatures primarily know beauty in relations external to themselves).[58]

While the preceding emphasis on perception and affection has assumed beauty, it has been left implicit. Making Edwards's aesthetics explicit is not ushering in new material to his doctrine of God but is shifting registers to reveal the breadth of his doctrine and its reach across the theological spectrum. Recalling the threefold focus on personhood, perception, and affection in Edwards's doctrine of God, God

57. WJE 2:298.
58. See Roland A. Delattre, *Beauty and Sensibility in the Thought of Jonathan Edwards: An Essay in Aesthetics and Theological Ethics*, The Jonathan Edwards Classic Studies Series (Eugene, OR: Wipf & Stock, 1968), 30–35. For a critique of Delattre's model, see Kin Yip Louie, *The Beauty of the Triune God: The Theological Aesthetics of Jonathan Edwards*, Princeton Theological Monograph Series 201 (Eugene, OR: Wipf & Stock, 2013), 82–83.

is beautiful because he is personal and because he partakes in the "consent, agreement and union of being to being" within his own life.[59] Edwards's description of beauty is discovered first and foremost in God's affectionate knowledge in his eternal beatific gazing. In this sense, he is the ultimate example and definition of primary beauty. Primary beauty, what Edwards will also call spiritual beauty, is persons uniting in love.[60] Spiritual beings are the primary instance of beauty, whereas physical beauty points beyond itself to the primary.[61] Edwards takes it for granted that "this is an universal definition of excellency: The consent of being to being, or being's consent to entity. The more the consent is, and the more extensive, the greater is the excellency."[62] Consent, as will become clear, is a work of the will within persons to unite personally to another. Edwards's God is the God of beauty within his own life, because he is the pure actuality of persons perceiving in the consent of love. On this understanding, for God to be beautiful, God has to be triune. As Edwards states explicitly,

> One alone, without any reference to any more, cannot be excellent; for in such case there can be no manner of relation no way, and therefore, no such thing as consent. Indeed, what we call "one" may be excellent, because of a consent of parts, or some consent of those in that being that are distinguished into a plurality some way or other. But in a being that is absolutely without any plurality there cannot be excellency, for there can be no such thing as consent or agreement.[63]

59. WJE 8:561.

60. This is why the word "consent" is used, which is used in a way that directly relates to the will. In his notes on excellency, Edwards states, "When we spake of excellence in bodies we were obliged to borrow the word 'consent' from spiritual things. But excellence in and among spirits is, in its prime and proper sense, being's consent to being. There is no proper consent but that of minds, even of their will; which, when it is of minds toward minds, it is love, and when of mind towards other things it is choice. Wherefore all the primary and original beauty or excellence that is among minds is love, and into this may all be resolved that is found among them." WJE 6:362.

61. WJE 8:561–63.

62. WJE 6:336. Paul Ramsey explains Edwards's view by claiming, "God's peculiar excellency is his 'beauty within himself, consisting in being's consent with his own being, or love of himself in his own Holy Spirit; whereas the excellence of others is in loving others, in loving God, and in the communications of his Spirit.'" WJE 8:701.

63. WJE 6:337.

This is why the Spirit is the beauty of God. Beauty, properly perceived, is consent, proportion, and affection, and the type and degree of beauty are determined by the nature of the being's consenting. The Spirit is the consent and affection of the divine life and the infinite proportion of love between Father and Son. Therefore, the Spirit can be called divine beauty because he is the infinite consent of love in God's life. Edwards outlines this life of love accordingly, claiming:

> There must have been an object from all eternity which God infinitely loves. But we have showed that all love arises from the perception, either of consent to being in general, or consent to that being that perceives. Infinite loveliness, to God, therefore, must consist either in infinite consent to entity in general, or infinite consent to God. But we have shown that consent to entity and consent to God are the same, because God is the general and only proper entity of all things. So that 'tis necessary that that object which God infinitely loves must be infinitely and perfectly consenting and agreeable to him; but that which infinitely and perfectly agrees is the very same essence, for if it be different it don't infinitely consent. Again, we have shown that one alone cannot be excellent, inasmuch as, in such case, there can be no consent. Therefore, if God is excellent, there must be a plurality in God; otherwise, there can be no consent in him.[64]

God's pure actuality is the Spirit's consenting spiration, serving as the union between Father and Son. The infinite greatness of the divine being, the perfection of God's contemplative intellection, and his infinite consent of love as the procession of the Spirit establish God's life of beauty. By locating beauty in the procession of the Spirit, Edwards binds beauty together with goodness, holiness, and love (all aspects of the Spirit's nature). As the foundation and fountain of these realities, the Spirit's work in the economy carries these over to creatures. By having *this* Spirit, one is now in a relation of beauty with God that requires affection and contemplation to be true knowledge of God. As holiness itself, infused into the regenerate, the Spirit creates freedom to consent in affection in ever greater and greater ways to the life of God.

---

64. WJE 13:283–84.

## *The Excellency of Christ*

As the God of beauty, God makes his beauty manifest through Jesus. The Christ that captivated Edwards's attention, therefore, is the *excellent* Christ. The notion of excellence derives from a close meditation on Hebrews 1:3, which claims that Christ "is the radiance of the Father's glory, and the exact representation of his nature." Christ himself, of course, affirmed that no one has ever seen the Father, but then supplied an extremely important qualification: No one has seen the Father except the One who is from God, Jesus himself (John 6:46). Likewise, Jesus claims that anyone who has seen him has seen the Father (John 14:9), and that eternal life is knowing both the Father and Jesus Christ whom he has sent (John 17:3).

Christ is the revelation of God to his people, people who have eyes but cannot see and ears but cannot hear. Just as Jesus healed the blind and the deaf, so too does the Spirit open ears and illuminate eyes to the spiritual depths of God's revelation of himself in the Son. Believers truly see God the Father in the Son as they are caught up in the movement of the Spirit to bind them to the life of God. The illumination of God is not the passive sight of a distant being but is a participation in God's own self-knowing through the missions of Son and Spirit. God's life is archetypal blessedness—the beatific fullness of glory that is available to the creature in eternity. God's economy is an emanation of *this* life; that he might allow the beauty of his life to overflow to creation. In Edwards's words,

> How good is God, that he has created man for this very end, to make him happy in the enjoyment of himself, the Almighty, who was happy from the days of eternity in himself, in the beholding of his own infinite beauty: the Father in the beholding and love of his Son, his perfect and most excellent image, the brightness of his own glory; and the Son in the love and enjoyment of the Father. . . . 'Twas not that he might be made more happy himself, but that [he] might make something else happy; that he might make them blessed in the beholding of his excellency, and might this way glorify himself.[65]

The blessedness of God and God's desire to communicate his own delight to his creature drive Edwards's account. This picture of salvation is

65. WJE 14:153.

centered in the Son, whom the Father beholds in love. In Christ, the glory of God has broken into the creaturely realm in a way previously unknown:

> As the glory of Christ appears in the qualifications of his human nature, it appears to us in excellencies that are of our own kind, and are exercised in our own way and manner, and so, in some respects, are peculiarly fitted to invite our acquaintance, and draw our affection. The glory of Christ as it appears in his divinity, though it be far brighter, yet doth it also more dazzle our eyes, and exceeds the strength or comprehension of our sight: but as it shines in the human excellencies of Christ, it is brought more to a level with our conceptions, and suitableness to our nature and manner, yet retaining a semblance of the same divine beauty, and a savor of the same divine sweetness. But as both divine and human excellencies meet together in Christ, they set off and recommend each other to us.[66]

Christ manifests virtues that "are of our own kind." Creaturely virtues, like humility, are not properly predicated of God's life *in se*, but are made manifest in Christ. By revealing himself in this way, through the person of Christ in his humanity, God can be received according to our comprehension.

Christ, "the image of the invisible God" (Col. 1:15), is sent by the Father to reveal his glory, but his glory is revealed in a mode that his creatures could bear: "The manifestation of the glory of God in the person of Christ is, as it were, accommodated to our apprehensions. The brightness is suited to our eyes."[67] God's glory is appropriately veiled for humanity when the Son takes on flesh.[68] Christ's excellency is an important doctrine for Edwards, both in his thought generally and for him personally. When he looked back over his spiritual life, he states, "my mind was greatly engaged, to spend my time in reading and meditating on Christ; and the beauty and excellency of his person."[69] In contrast, when Edwards reflects upon his earlier affections that failed to be truly converting, he claims,

---

66. WJE 19:590.

67. Edwards, "Jesus Christ Is the Shining Forth of the Father's Glory," 233.

68. "But Christ being a person who is come to us in our nature has, as it were, softened the light of God's glory and accommodated to our view." Edwards, "Jesus Christ Is the Shining Forth of the Father's Glory," 233.

69. WJE 16:793.

"Those former delights, never reached the heart; and did not arise from any sight of the divine excellency of the things of God."[70] Note what is implied. For delight to be truly of God, it has to arise from a sight of the divine *excellency*. Edwards states, "I have sometimes had a sense of the excellent fullness of Christ, and his meetness and suitableness as a savior. . . . The person of Christ appeared ineffably excellent, with an excellency great enough to swallow up all thought and conception."[71]

In perhaps his most focused exposition of the excellency of Christ (his sermon "The Excellency of Christ" on Revelation 5:5–6), Edwards narrates the tension revealed in the imagery of Christ as both lion and lamb. In using these opposing images to refer to Christ, Scripture reveals that in Christ there are "diverse excellencies." The excellencies of a creature are the perfections of its nature, known in relation to perfections within its genus (e.g., lions or lambs) as well as creation as a whole.[72] For instance, a lion excels in its strength, majesty of appearance, and its voice, whereas a lamb excels in meekness and patience, and its being good for food and clothing.[73] Edwards employs the language of excellencies to talk meaningfully about the person of Jesus having both a divine and a human nature, and to highlight what both those natures bring to the single personhood of Christ.[74] It is here, for instance, where infinite justice and infinite grace meet in one being: "Though his justice be so strict with respect to all sin, and every breach of the law, yet he has grace sufficient for every sinner, and even the chief of sinners."[75] Likewise, in Christ meet "the deepest

70. WJE 16:795. Note how the ordering of one's knowledge of God is supposed to work: "they [the saints] first rejoice in God as glorious and excellent in himself . . . they first have their hearts filled with sweetness, from the view of Christ's excellency, and the excellency of his grace . . . and then they have a secondary joy, in that so excellent a Saviour, and such excellent grace is theirs." WJE 2:250.

71. WJE 16:801.

72. In his "Blank Bible," Edwards writes, "But the excellency of wisdom is that wisdom giveth life to them that have it." WJE 24:593. *Excellency* is a term of relation, like all of Edwards's aesthetic terminology. Therefore, it can be mapped onto moral as well as natural categories (to use Edwards's language). In other words, Christ's humility is a moral excellency, whereas the limitedness of Christ's humanity is a natural excellency. We see both of these revealed in his discussion of excellency.

73. WJE 19:565.

74. Edwards notes how the circumstances of Jesus's birth and life highlight the diversity of these excellencies. For instance, Christ was born a king in a stable; his birth seemed relatively ordinary and yet wise men came to worship him; he was upholding the universe and yet he submitted to his human parents. WJE 19:574.

75. WJE 19:567.

reverence towards God, and equality with God."[76] It is only in the person of Christ, the mediating God-man, that these attributes come together:

> In the person of Christ do meet together, infinite glory, and the lowest humility. Infinite glory, and the virtue of humility, meet in no other person but Christ. They meet in no created person; for no created person has infinite glory: and they meet in no other divine person but Christ. For though the divine nature be infinitely abhorrent to pride, yet humility is not properly predicable of God the Father, and the Holy Ghost, that exist only in the divine nature; because it is a proper excellency only of a created nature. . . . But in Jesus Christ, who is both God and man, these two diverse excellencies, are sweetly united.[77]

It should be noted that the human excellencies do not add to Christ's divine excellency, which is infinite. Christ, as a person of God, has an infinite fullness of excellency. Rather, the excellencies the Son has as a human being are "communications and reflections" of his divine excellency.[78] When expositing the excellency of Christ, therefore, Edwards is talking about how the divine is revealed through created forms, most specifically the human nature of Christ. In the life of Christ, who has two natures within a single person, we see excellencies that are unique to him. These excellencies are "sweetly united" because they do not contrast but refract the divine light through creaturely mediums. In doing so, God is revealing himself in a register that human persons can see and comprehend, even though they point beyond themselves to the infinite depths of God's life. "Never was his divine glory and majesty covered with so thick and dark a veil" than during his suffering and death, Edwards admits, but, in apparent contrast, "never was his divine glory so manifested, by any act of his, as in that act, of yielding himself up to these sufferings."[79] This is how the divine glory and beauty are revealed in an apparent paradox, because Christ is a divine person who has condescended to take upon himself a nature much lower and more base than his own, so that creatures may see and know the truth of God in the flesh.

---

76. WJE 19:569.
77. WJE 19:568.
78. WJE 19:590.
79. WJE 19:576.

Edwards's depiction of the excellency of Christ takes what is true of the divine nature, "infinite glory" for instance, and relates this to an excellency of Jesus in his humanity that seems contrary (humility is one of his examples). These are both true of Jesus, because Jesus is sensible of who he is as a divine person, but because he is also sensible of who he is in his human nature he is aware of the incredible distance between himself and God the Father.[80] As a human being Jesus recognizes his lowliness beneath God, and this is considered to be the "lowest" humility, because Jesus is a divine person who has humbled himself. Humility, while a virtue in general, is a virtue that depends upon one's position for its greatness. A king and a peasant both submitting to one another and serving each other do not have the same humility. Their position and level of greatness alter the depth of their humility. A king's submission, because of his stature, will always have a greater depth of humility.[81] In Christ's excellency the infinite beauty of God is refracted through Christ's humanity, but it is this excellence that is visible spiritually only through the illuminating presence of the Spirit.

## Secondary Beauty

Whereas Christ refracts the divine beauty through the prism of his humanity, creation itself reflects divine beauty as it mirrors the same relational principles through physical-relational features of creation. So whereas primary beauty is the highest form of beauty and is "the union or propensity of *minds* to mental or spiritual existence,"[82] Edwards also gives an account of "secondary beauty." God's life provides the archetype of true beauty; revealing the content (i.e., the divine understanding) and the mode (i.e., consent) of the beautiful. Yet, Edwards explains, "there is another, inferior, secondary beauty, which is some image of this, and which is not peculiar to spiritual beings, but is found even in inanimate things: which consists in a mutual consent and agreement of different things in form, manner, quantity, and visible end or design; called by the various names of regularity, order, uniformity, symmetry, proportion, harmony, etc."[83]

---

80. See WJE 19:568, 581.
81. WJE 19:568.
82. WJE 8:561. Emphasis in the original.
83. WJE 8:561–62.

Physical realities can be considered beautiful in this secondary sense. This notion of beauty is not untethered from primary beauty but serves as a sign of it, as a physical representation of the harmony of God's ideas in creation. Physical reality points beyond itself to true spiritual beauty, and it does so through symmetry, proportion, and harmony as "the mutual agreement" of the objects, sounds, or events that are beautiful.[84] The harmony of color, shape, and sound are the echoes of an eternal harmony of love that establishes the tune of all creation. Seeing the beauty of the world does not, somehow, take our eyes off of God. Rather, by basking in the beauty of the world in relation to God, we are coming to enjoy reality as he does—as a reflection of his own infinite beauty and harmony of ideas that gives meaning to all things.

As a fundamental feature of his doctrine of God, Edwards's theological aesthetics act like a thread woven throughout his entire thought. We will see this thread in God's economic work, strung through Edwards's soteriology, down to his moral theology. In his moral theology, most specifically, we will once again address the notion of beauty in relation to believers becoming beautiful. The focal point in redemption will be Christ, who is uniquely beautiful in all of God's creation as he pulls together the divine and human beauty and serves as the archetype for creaturely beauty through union with God. Because Edwards follows the traditional understanding of the beatific vision as the goal of creaturely existence, beauty serves him as a helpful way to address God's beatific life and creaturely participation within that life (initially through the dark glass of faith).[85] The longing of the creature is fulfilled ultimately in God, who is beauty itself, and therefore every aspect of the Christian life—worship, mission, and theology—should be beautiful and beautifying.

---

84. WJE 8:562. Edwards links this aspect of his thought to Francis Hutcheson. See WJE 8:562–63.

85. In the Reformed "High Orthodox" period, which Edwards fits into, there was a recovery of the scholastic distinction between archetypal and ectypal theology. Christ, as the God-man, was given a *sui generis* category of union in ectypal theology in contrast to believers who were either categorized as "pilgrim" (revelation) or "beatific" (vision). Richard Muller helpfully outlines this impulse; see Richard A. Muller, *Prolegomena to Theology: Post-Reformation Reformed Dogmatics*, vol. 1 (Grand Rapids: Baker Academic, 2003), 230.

# CHAPTER THREE

# God and Idealism

In the previous chapter we focused on a central motif of Edwards's thought, namely, the Triune God. We saw that Edwards developed a novel account of the Trinity, making a significant contribution to discussion of that fundamental Christian dogma. In this chapter we turn to consider some of the most important philosophical-theological aspects of his doctrine of God. Edwards the dogmatician or systematic theologian (as we would now think of it) is not something different from Edwards the philosophical theologian. His theological and philosophical works are two aspects of one intellectual project. Nevertheless, Edwards primarily saw himself as a Christian thinker—a pastor and theologian—and not as a philosopher, even though his work includes important treatments of philosophical themes. Importantly, it was his theological sensibilities that drove him to pursue particular philosophical notions, even when they took his thinking in unusual directions. As we shall see, this is particularly true with respect to the bearing his philosophical thought had upon his doctrine of God.

## Idealism

Although Edwards never wrote a treatise on the doctrine of God, he had a lot to say about the subject of the divine nature. The sources of Edwards's thinking on this matter are complex. They include the Protestant orthodox and Puritan theology of the post-Reformation period in which he had been schooled; British philosophers and scientists such as John Locke, Isaac Newton, and the Cambridge Platonists; as well as continental metaphysics, particularly the influence of the French philosopher Nicholas Malebranche.

In any historical period certain ideas are in the air, so to speak, and can be found cropping up in the works of different thinkers, often recombined in slightly different ways. Sometimes particular thinkers at a given time end up espousing very similar sorts of views, although they have been schooled in different places, and perhaps they have not even been aware of the work of others relevant to their own intellectual pursuits.[1] Often, this is called the Zeitgeist of a particular age. A celebrated eighteenth-century example of this phenomenon is the startling philosophical convergences to be found in the works of Edwards and Bishop George Berkeley. Berkeley was an Irish Anglican clergyman who had been educated at Trinity College, Dublin. As a consequence of coming into contact with the ideas of John Locke, and having developed an aversion to the sort of materialist philosophy espoused by Thomas Hobbes,[2] Berkeley embraced a rather radical metaphysical vision based on a particular account of how human beings come to understand the world. This account derived from the Lockean insight that our apprehension of the world around us comes by means of a myriad of sense impressions and ideas that we then associate with other ideas, recombining them in different ways in order to make sense of the universe in which we live. Thus, an impression of, say, a large, stationary green and brown object in my visual field might give rise to the idea of a tree. This impression is further associated with other ideas, such as its location in the college quadrangle. But these ideas can be recombined: trees clustered together in a copse, or woodland, or the picture of a tree used as a symbol for life and fertility, and so on. After reflecting upon this doctrine, Berkeley

1. A classic example of this, which occurred a generation before Edwards was active, was the controversy between Sir Isaac Newton and Gottfried Leibniz over which of them invented mathematical calculus. It seems likely that each one developed his notation independent of the other, albeit around the same time in the last decades of the seventeenth century.

2. It was widely understood that Hobbes's metaphysics committed him to, among other things, the claim that the only meaning one could give to the term "substance" was something that was material. Needless to say, the theological implications of this were not lost on his seventeenth- and eighteenth-century readers. A clear indication of his materialism about substances can be seen in Hobbes, *Elementorum Philosophiae Sectio Prima De Corpore* 3.4 (London: Andrew Crook, 1655), 22. A modern English translation of this portion of his text can be found in Hobbes, *De Corpore, Part I*, trans. A. P. Martinich (New York: Abaris Books, 1981).

became convinced of two things. First, he believed that the world is an ideal world. There is no such thing as matter, strictly speaking. There are only minds and their ideas, whether the divine mind or created minds. All the stuff of the universe can be made sense of on this basis: "From the principles we have laid down, it follows, human knowledge may be reduced to two heads, that of ideas and that of spirits."[3] But, second, Berkeley thought that this doctrine was simply what all reasonable human beings understand as the deliverance of common sense.[4] The first of his convictions was directed against the sort of materialist philosophy then gaining ground, chiefly through the work of Hobbes. If the world is an ideal one, then it is not merely the case that some entities are immaterial and some material; there is no such thing as matter at all. All that exists is ideal, or mental.

Whatever the merits of Berkeley's position as a means of staving off materialism (and atheism), it is certainly true to say that there are striking similarities between Berkeley's idealism and that of Edwards. Like Berkeley, Edwards was worried by the materialism of Hobbes. The Hobbesians reasoned that all substances are material; God is a substance; so God is a material object. In order to avoid embracing this conclusion, Edwards, like Berkeley, took the opposite view: all existing things are ideal. It seems, however, that Edwards formed his view on this matter independent of Berkeley's work.

Following in the footsteps of his Reformed teachers, Edwards conceived of ontology—that branch of philosophy dealing with what exists, or being—in terms of essentialism. Roughly speaking, essentialism is the doctrine according to which things that exist consist of properties or predicates and the substances that exemplify them. In fact, the Aristotelian essentialist doctrine assumed by much of medieval and post-Reformation theology also maintains that substances have substantial forms that organize the matter of which the particular substance is composed—a bit like a blueprint that is used to inform or organize the materials used to construct a motorcar. The substantial form of a given substance somehow organizes, and gives coherence to, a particular sub-

3. George Berkeley, *Principles of Human Knowledge*, with an introduction by Roger Woolhouse (1710; repr., Harmondsworth: Penguin Classics, 1988), §86.

4. Famously, Berkeley affirms that "we ought to 'think with the learned, and speak with the vulgar.'" He goes on to say, "A little reflection on what is here said will make it manifest, that the common use of language would receive no manner of alteration or disturbance from the admission of our tenets." See Berkeley, *Principles*, §51.

stance. But the relation between form and substance on this Aristotelian version of essentialism is more intimate than that between a blueprint and the fully assembled product, since, on the Aristotelian way of thinking, every individual existing thing has a particular substantial form that organizes it.

An example will make this view clearer. According to Christian thinkers who adopted Aristotelian essentialism, humans are composed of a material substance (a human body) that is organized by the immaterial substance that informs corporeal substance, namely, the human soul. Like a number of other early modern thinkers, Edwards's essentialism departs from the doctrine of Aristotle and his epigone in excising the concept of substantial forms. According to Edwards, the world is composed of ideas and minds, that is, of predicates—properties or attributes of a given thing—and the immaterial substances that exemplify these attributes (for example, souls). Thus, a tall dark-haired man consists of the immaterial substance of which he is composed (his soul or mind) and the attributes that make up the apparently corporeal part of this entity, including his being tall, dark-haired, and so forth. The situation shifts when it comes to common objects that are not moral agents or persons, such as tables and chairs. Like Berkeley, Edwards seems to have believed that the attributes of many common, non-personal objects are bundled together and collocated at a particular place by the direct activity of God. The table continues to appear rectangular, solid, wooden, and brown-colored because God ensures these different properties are collocated together in one place.

If human beings are composed of two substances, bodies and souls, as Edwards believed, then, in this Edwardsean version of idealism, there are certain kinds of ideal entities—souls and minds—that are immaterial substances. But there are also other sorts of ideal entities (properties, predicates, attributes) that appear to be material substances like bodies, though they are, in fact, merely clusters of properties collocated in a particular place. Strictly speaking, then, there are no material substances on Edwards's view. The world appears to be material. But it is actually ideal; even things that appear to be material are in fact immaterial. Edwards is perfectly serious about his viewpoint. For instance, in his early fragmentary notebook, "Things to be Considered an[d] Written fully about," item twenty-six reads, "To bring in an observation somewhere in a proper place, that instead of Hobbes' notion that God is matter and that all substance is matter; that nothing that is matter can possibly be God, and that no matter is, in the most proper sense, matter."[5] As if to underline this point, later, in the same work, item forty-seven reads, "body is nothing but an infinite resistance in some part of space caused by the immediate exercise of divine power."[6] These are not isolated comments. They reflect Edwards's early rumination upon things metaphysical as he studied and taught at Yale as a tutor in the early 1720s. Thus, in his early work *The Mind*, he has this to say about the relationship between the body and soul:

> Seeing the brain exists only mentally, I therefore acknowledge that I speak improperly when I say, the soul is in the brain only as to its operations. For to speak yet more strictly and abstractly, 'tis nothing but the common connection of the operations of the soul with these and those modes of its own ideas, or those mental acts of the Deity, seeing the brain exists only in idea.[7]

Elsewhere, in his "Miscellanies," Edwards sounds very much like Berkeley: "Supposing a room in which none is, none sees in that room, no created intelligence; the things in the room have no being any other way than only as God is conscious [of them], for there is no color, nor any sound, nor any shape, etc."[8] This avowed idealism does not stop Edwards from speaking, like Berkeley, in the vulgar mode when necessary. He is perfectly capable of addressing his congregation with the most lurid illustrations of coming judgment using images that imply some corporeal punishments in hell. The best-known example of this may be his sermon "Sinners in the Hands of an Angry God," but there are many others like it in his extant body of sermons and sermon outlines. When speaking with the learned, however, it is clear that Edwards truly believes that all

---

5. WJE 6:235. Edwards explicitly cross-references the excerpt from *Of Atoms* just cited with entry twenty-six in *Things to be Considered*. Incidentally, it should be obvious from the foregoing that the statement "matter is not matter," strictly speaking, is simply trivially true given idealism.

6. WJE 6:241.

7. WJE 6:355. He goes on to say, "But we have got so far beyond those things for which language was chiefly contrived, that unless we use extreme caution we cannot speak, except we speak exceeding unintelligibly, without literally contradicting ourselves."

8. WJE 13:188. Edwards explicitly denies material substance in the short list, "Notes on Knowledge and Existence," where he states in response to Hobbesianism that "What we call body is nothing but a particular mode of perception; and what we call spirit is nothing but a composition and series of perceptions, or an universe of coexisting and successive perceptions connected by such wonderful methods and laws" (WJE 6:398).

such physical things are really ideas or collections of ideas, and not anything material. In short, he denies that there are any extended, unthinking substances.

## Immaterial Antirealism

I have said that Edwards's ontology is a version of idealism, much like that of Bishop Berkeley. Given Edwards's statements above, however, it would perhaps be better to describe his position as a version of immaterial antirealism. This view holds that every existing thing is immaterial (like ideas and minds). According to Edwards, however, all ideas, including the created minds that have them, continue to exist because they are held in the divine mind. Human beings and the ideas they exemplify continue to exist, provided God continues to think of them and the ideas they possess. Were God to cease thinking about humans and their ideas for a moment, they would cease to exist. The immaterialist component of this reasoning seems clear enough: what appears to be a physical object, like a table, is merely a collection of sensible percepts one has of the table. There is nothing more fundamental than this that somehow underlies the perceptions of the table. The hardness of the table, the sensation of a polished wooden surface one has upon touching it, and so forth, are all ideas.

This view is not without problems, and well-known philosophical objections to idealism do exist. We should note, however, that Edwards makes matters still more complex in that he speaks at various times and in a number of places about the physical world being a mere shadow of the spiritual world, of which it is a type. He says at one point,

> those beings which have knowledge and consciousness are the only proper and real and substantial beings, inasmuch as the being of other things is only by these. From hence we may see the gross mistake of those who think material things the most substantial beings, and spirits more like a shadow; whereas spirits only are properly substance.[9]

9. WJE 6:206. This is one way in which Edwards demonstrates his Neo-Platonist credentials, which he derives from the Cambridge Platonists, whose influence can be traced in his early philosophical works in particular. See especially WJE 6.

But if there really is nothing material at all, then this is a rather odd thing to say. It amounts to claiming that the ideal, but apparently physical, world that we inhabit is a mere shadow of the spiritual, ideal world. These two assertions, taken on their own merits, do not yield a contradiction. But it is a rather strange doctrine in that it entails one ideal, but apparently physical, world being the shadow of another ideal, spiritual world. Nevertheless, this is what his view implies: a sort of layering of ideal worlds, one of which (the unseen spiritual world) somehow underlies and is more real than the other (the apparently physical, perceptible world).

The antirealist aspect of Edwardsean immaterialism is, if anything, yet more contentious. One could argue that, provided we exist as divine ideas, or provided our minds are sustained by the divine mind—upon which our minds are radically dependent for their continuing existence—then realism is preserved. For then we really do exist; our ideas really do exist; and the world around us really exists independent of our minds, because all these things (the world, created minds, and their ideas) exist in the mind of God. In this way, God's continuing to think of the created world—you and me included—is, if you like, the objective guarantee that the world will persist through time. But if metaphysical realism entails some mind-independent reality that exists out there beyond human minds, then, strictly speaking, this Edwardsean picture of an immaterial world is antirealist, which is a rather surprising consequence of his immaterialism. For on the Edwardsean position outlined thus far, our minds and ideas are radically dependent on the divine mind. In fact, as far as Edwards was concerned, in the strictest sense nothing exists independent of the divine mind and its mental contents. All created things, including created minds, exist as ideas in God's mind or as ideas projected by God's mind (like the projection of a motion picture onto the screen of a movie theater). In this case, Edwards's immaterialist conception of the created order is also an antirealist view, and thus immaterial antirealism. His way of thinking entails that all created reality is mind-dependent—specifically divine mind–dependent, a set of ideas that subsist in the divine mind. Let us call this the Edwardsean immaterial antirealist consequence of his particular brand of idealism.[10]

10. It is true that Edwards nowhere develops a complete account of properties that explicitly states or otherwise strictly implies that all properties are mind-dependent. One might therefore think that there is some metaphysical wiggle-room here, sufficient to stave off the claim that Edwards's position is equivalent to a species of immaterial antirealism. Nevertheless, where Edwards does speak about universals, he speaks in ways that are con-

Admittedly, this is fairly strong metaphysical mead that it takes quite a bit of effort to swallow. Yet, in one respect, it sounds more radical than it actually is. Edwards's theistic idealism is of a piece with much of the Western tradition of Christian theology, in which some version of theistic idealism is presumed.[11] What is intriguing about Edwards's idealism, like that of Berkeley, is his belief that such a metaphysical picture of the world actually safeguards Christian thought against the threat of materialism and atheism that had begun to make inroads into early modern philosophy. In fact, Edwards was committed to other controversial metaphysical positions, which, taken together with his idealism, lead to even more extravagant conclusions about the creation and conservation of the world. But in order to make sense of what he has to say on that matter, we must turn, in the first instance, to consider his understanding of the divine nature.

## Perfect Being Theology

We have already noted in the previous chapters that Edwards's understanding of God was deeply influenced by post-Reformation Reformed orthodox theology. This is the theological tradition that developed in continental Europe in the period after the Reformation of the sixteenth century, and which declined around the time of (and in part, as a consequence of) the burgeoning Enlightenment toward the end of the seventeenth century. In particular, Edwards was indebted to the work of theologians such as Francis Turretin, Calvin's successor in Geneva, and the Dutch theologian Peter van Mastricht.[12] He was also conversant with a lot

---

sistent with immaterialism along the antirealist lines sketched out here. See, for example, the corollary to "The Mind," entry 43, in WJE 6:362. There are other reasons for thinking Edwards was committed to something like the metaphysical antirealism described above, for instance, his adherence to a doctrine of continuous creation and occasionalism. We shall address these matters later in this chapter and return to them in the next chapter as well.

11. Paradigms of such Christian theistic idealism can be found in St. Augustine's work (e.g., *Confessions*, Books XI–XII) and in St. Anselm of Canterbury. For a discussion of Anselm's theistic idealism, see Katherin A. Rogers, *The Neoplatonic Metaphysics and Epistemology of Anselm of Canterbury* (Lewiston: Edwin Mellen, 1997).

12. For a helpful introduction to this Reformed scholastic tradition, see Willem van Asselt, *An Introduction to Reformed Scholasticism* (Grand Rapids: Reformation Heritage Books, 2011). Scholastic theology is characterized by a careful analytical method that divides the subject matter of theology into topics that can be subdivided using precise

of Puritan theology (for example, that of John Owen, Richard Sibbes, and John Flavel), which was the strain of Reformed theology that flourished in Great Britain in the same period as continental Reformed orthodoxy.[13]

Following Anselm of Canterbury and the medieval school theologians from whom they derived their own scholastic method, the Reformed orthodox conceived of God as a perfect being.[14] Like their medieval counterparts, these Reformed theologians did not think about God in this way in order to put the God of the philosophers before the God of Scripture. Rather, perfect being theology was a way to draw together the variety of biblical data concerning the divine nature. The Reformed tended to conceive of the role of human reason as a helpmeet, or ancillary to theology. Reason was employed as a means to systematize the theological implications of biblical data, and organize their conceptual content in a rational, logical, and cogent manner. We might say that, for these divines, the God of the Bible is the perfect being of whom the philosophers speak—at least where they speak of him rightly. In putting the matter like this, it should be clear that the role of philosophy is subservient to theology in Reformed thought.

In several important respects, Western medieval theologians like Anselm and Thomas Aquinas were responsible for the development and dissemination of this picture of God as a perfect being, although it did not originate with them. If God is perfect, they maintained, then he must be immutable, that is, incapable of any substantive change whatsoever. Most perfect being theologians took this to imply that God must be atemporal, or eternal; he is outside of time, which he creates. He must also be omnipotent, omniscient, omnipresent, and a necessary being (he cannot *not* exist; in contemporary philosophical parlance, there are no possible worlds in which God does not exist). In a loose and non-philosophical

---

logical and metaphysical distinctions. Often this was presented in a Socratic method of question and answer.

13. A number of studies have drawn attention to Edwards's debt to the Reformed orthodox. See, for example, Norman Fiering, *Jonathan Edwards' Moral Thought in Its British Context*, Jonathan Edwards Classic Studies Series (1981; repr., Eugene, OR: Wipf & Stock, 2006); and William S. Morris, *The Young Jonathan Edwards: A Reconstruction*, The Jonathan Edwards Classic Studies Series (1955; repr., Eugene, OR: Wipf & Stock, 2005), ch. 3.

14. Anselm had spoken of God as the greatest conceivable being in his *Proslogion*, reflecting Hebrews 6:13–14. Other biblical passages reflect the notion of divine perfection, e.g., the idea that he is perfect "in all his ways" (2 Sam. 22:31; Ps. 18:30). From here it is a short step to the conclusion that God, as a perfect being, must have all his perfections to a maximal degree.

sense, the medieval school theologians were willing to speak of divine attributes as if God has a nature like his creatures. But strictly speaking, the
nature of the Deity is significantly different from any creaturely essence.
For one thing, whereas created beings can be understood in terms of the
distinction between wholes and parts, God cannot. Since this perfect
being conception of the divine nature is important for Edwards's doctrine
of God, it requires a brief explanation.

In recent times, Nicholas Wolterstorff has argued that medieval theologians worked with a particular ontology (doctrine of being) according to
which things are distinguished by being wholes or parts. He calls this *constituent ontology*.[15] Modern thinkers no longer think in these terms. They
understand the world according to a *relational ontology*, that is, how one
thing is related to another, or what internal relations it has that comprise
its own internal structure. The medieval thinkers Wolterstoff has in mind
maintained that created beings had natures or essences made up of certain
properties essential to that thing. Thus, a bird can lose a wing, let us say,
and still remain a bird, albeit a mutilated one. But a bird cannot lose the
property birdhood without ceasing to be a bird. Birdhood is an essential
property of birds. Necessarily, any bird exemplifies or possesses this property (whatever birdhood actually entails). Thus, it appears that there are
parts of entities like birds that are not essential to their continued existence,
and other parts of those objects that are essential, like birdhood. God is
unique in not having any non-essential attributes. All that we predicate of
God is his essentially. He must be immutable, omnipotent, omniscient,
etc. If he is not these essential attributes then he cannot be God. And if
God is perfect, he cannot lose any of his attributes on pain of ceasing to be
perfect. So God is eternally, essentially, and immutably all that he is; there
is nothing that God could cease to have, no attribute he could be without.
For students of modern relational ontology, such language sounds very
strange since it presumes that there are substances with essences and properties and that these are fundamental or metaphysically basic—they carve
up reality at its joints, so to speak. Relational ontologies begin in a rather
different place; namely, with the relations that one thing bears to another.
For some modern theologians, the relations we bear to one another are, in
fact, constitutive of the sort of beings we are.[16] This is not the purview of

---

15. See Nicholas Wolterstorff, "Divine Simplicity," in *Philosophical Perspectives 5:
Philosophy of Religion*, ed. James Tomberlin (Atascadero: Ridgeview, 1991), 531–52.

16. To take just one example in the contemporary theological literature, see John

the medieval thinkers. To understand their perspective, one must mentally set to one side the relational in order to focus on the constituent ontology.

## Divine Simplicity

It is a commonplace notion in medieval theology that a perfect being must be a non-composite being. A metaphysically non-composite being is what is called a simple substance. Plausibly, souls are metaphysically simple entities because they are immaterial substances, and such metaphysically simple substances cannot have parts as physical substances can. One cannot remove a part of a soul as one can remove a part of a body. Still, souls seem to have different properties, such as "being the soul of this particular body" or "being the soul with this particular mental state at this particular moment." Some of these properties might be lost by a given soul. A soul may, for example, cease to have an intimate causal relationship with the human body to which it is attached when the body dies. But it would remain the same soul—just a soul that now lacks a certain property. In this sense, a soul, though arguably a metaphysically simple substance, may yet gain or lose properties. Thus, a soul can gain or lose parts, in the sense of particular, contingent properties it possesses.

God is metaphysically simple in some ways like a soul. For instance, he cannot be carved up into parts on an analogy with a body, because he is an immaterial substance. But he is simple in a much stronger sense than a human soul because (so a number of medieval theologians thought) he can have no distinct parts *whatsoever*. Not only does this mean he cannot have any contingent properties, that is, properties that he might lose, like I might lose my arm in a nasty accident. Strictly speaking, on the medieval view, he cannot have distinct properties at all. Possession of distinct properties would mean God is not essentially simple. He would be composed of, or possess, parts, even if those parts are merely abstract objects such as properties. So, when referring to God's power or God's knowledge, what we must say is that such attributes are only predicates that we use to refer to something about God, but which do not refer to properties God has (that is, distinct, abstract objects that belong to God, and that he exemplifies).

Zizioulas, *Being as Communion: Studies in Personhood and the Church* (Crestwood: St. Vladimir's Seminary Press, 1997).

In the contemporary philosophical literature, the doctrine of divine simplicity has been subjected to searching criticism. For instance, Alvin Plantinga argues that if all God's properties are identical to one another and to God, then God must be a property. But clearly God is not a property. So something is wrong with the doctrine of divine simplicity as it has been traditionally understood.[17] But there are also scholars who argue that this is not a deliverance of the traditional doctrine. They maintain that there are various different views on divine simplicity, as there are different views on the Trinity, the incarnation, or any other Christian doctrine. But these differing versions of the doctrine share a common conception of divine simplicity as a piece of negative or apophatic theology. That is, they regard the doctrine as a sort of theological safeguard that prevents certain misunderstandings of the divine nature from developing. They do not think of it as a description of what the divine nature is like.

In a similar fashion, if someone were to discover a hitherto unknown color, it would be fruitless trying to describe it to those who had not yet seen it. Such persons would have no vocabulary or concepts adequate to the task of comprehending this new phenomenon. But the discoverer of this wonder could help those who had yet to see it to understand something of what it was like by saying what it was not. If she said, "it is not bright, like yellow, or dark, like navy blue, but it is more like a deep crimson in tone—though not exactly the same as crimson in color," we might have some inkling of what she had seen. But such an approach is really a way of saying what this new color is not, rather than what it is. It offers no description of that color. In like manner, divine simplicity is not a description of some fundamental aspect of the divine nature, but a piece of negative theology; it tells us that God is non-composite, though it does not explain how he is non-composite. It functions rather like the doctrine of the Trinity, according to which God is both one and three at the same time, though we do not have a complete description of how God is one and three at the same time. In this connection, the historian of post-Reformation Reformed theology Richard Muller remarks:

> If some of the late patristic and scholastic expositions of the doctrine class as philosophical and perhaps speculative, the basic concept is not: from Irenaeus to the era of Protestant or-

17. See Alvin Plantinga, *Does God Have a Nature?* (Milwaukee: Marquette University Press, 1990).

thodoxy, the fundamental assumption was merely that God as ultimate spirit is not a compounded or composite being. It is also the case that, from the time of the fathers onwards, divine simplicity was understood as a support of the doctrine of the Trinity and as necessarily defined in such a manner as to argue the "manifold" as well as the non-composite character of God.[18]

Dominican theologian Brian Davies expresses similar sentiments in connection with Thomas Aquinas, whose doctrine is the most influential of the medieval accounts of divine simplicity:

> Aquinas's doctrine of divine simplicity is not offered as a *description* of God, or as an attempt to suggest that God has an *attribute* or *property* of simplicity. It is not a description since (in keeping with Aquinas's promise to note ways in which God does *not* exist) it consists entirely of negations, of attempts to say what God *cannot* be. It also is not ascribing simplicity to God as an attribute or property since it explicitly denies that, in a serious sense, God has any attributes or properties. . . . It is not concerned to paint a portrait of God. Its aim is to put up "No Entry" signs in front of certain roads into which we might turn when trying to think about God.[19]

## Pure Act

The final component of this medieval picture of God concerns the relationship between God's nature (what he is, his essence or quiddity) and his actuality (roughly, his existence). The perfect being theologians argued that a simple, perfect, immaterial divine being must be a being that has no unrealized potentiality, a being for whom there is no distinction between being and actuality. The same is not true of creatures. To make this point clearer, consider the example of Smith. She is a human being.

18. Richard A. Muller, *Post-Reformation Reformed Dogmatics: The Rise and Development of Reformed Orthodoxy, ca. 1520 to ca. 1725,* vol. 3 (Grand Rapids: Baker Academic, 2003), 276.

19. Brian Davies, "Simplicity," in *The Cambridge Companion to Christian Philosophical Theology,* ed. Charles Taliaferro and Chad Meister (Cambridge: Cambridge University Press, 2010), 36.

She has a human nature. She exists (let us say). So in one sense, Smith is actual. Yet in another sense, there are many aspects of her nature that Smith will never actualize. Being a human, she has the capability to learn languages. But Smith has never learned a language other than English. So there are capacities that she never realizes, such as being able to speak fluent Russian or Spanish.

Now, medieval theologians like Thomas Aquinas thought that God is not like Smith in this respect. God has no unrealized potential. There is nothing about him that remains dormant or that could develop or grow with greater application. God's capabilities are completely realized in a way that no creaturely capabilities ever are. And this must be the case if God is immutable, omniscient, and omnipotent. He cannot change, for better or for worse, because he is already perfect. And he cannot come to know new things or forget things, because he knows everything completely and immediately (and, of course, unchangingly). He also has maximal power. There is nothing logically possible that he is unable to do. Interestingly, theologians such as Thomas Aquinas thought that this must mean that God's nature contains, as it were, an infinite number of possibilities. God knows by his natural knowledge all that is necessary and (logically) possible, which, on this medieval way of thinking, is simply a given if God is omniscient.[20] Thus, although God brings about this world, there are an infinite number of other possible worlds God could have created but did not bring about.[21] But all of these other worlds are present in the divine mind, since his nature is such that it contains all of these possibilities. This is part-and-parcel of what it means to say that God is a completely actualized being, or, as the medieval theologians put it, that God is *actus purus* (pure actuality). For if God did not comprehend all such possibilities, then there would be potentiality in God, specifically, the potential to know more, which is impossible if he is a perfect being.

20. In fact, for Thomas, God knows all possibilities pertaining to the created order by introspection; knowledge of created things derives from his self-knowledge.

21. However, as we shall see, this is not quite the same as Edwards's view. And it is important to note that not all the medieval theologians took this view either. When Aristotle's works became available in the west, largely due to the translations of Arab versions at the University of Toledo, they were received and understood according to the Arab commentators on Aristotle's works. Like Edwards, some of those commentators believed that this is the best and only world God could create. For discussion of this, see Mary Beth Ingham and Mechtild Dreyer, *The Philosophical Vision of John Duns Scotus* (Washington, DC: Catholic University of America Press, 2004), ch. 1.

But not only is God without potentiality on this way of thinking. He is also the only entity for whom there is no distinction between his being and his action. Whereas we can distinguish between "Smith exists" and "Smith is running," because Smith's existing does not necessarily entail or include her performing a particular action, such a distinction cannot obtain in the case of God. On the pure act view, God cannot do one action and then another. His nature is entirely realized without remainder. In fact, on this way of thinking, God is a single, eternal, pure act. He is entirely in act, as it were. And he is entirely one single act. This has to be the case if God is metaphysically simple; otherwise he would be composed of different actions. In fact, on the pure act view, the one, simple, eternal act that is God has numerous different temporal effects in time. God seems to be doing different things at different moments of history, at least from our point of view. But this is just an instance of anthropopathism, that is, of attributing to the divine nature human states. In reality, God is a timeless act. But this timeless act has many temporal effects, from creating and sustaining the world to intervening at particular moments of human history, as in the incarnation. If, in the final analysis, this seems to make God something beyond our ken, this is exactly what medieval theologians like Anselm and Aquinas intended. For them, God is indeed beyond our finite comprehension; the divine nature will forever remain mysterious to us because we are not capable of grasping what God is in a single moment of apprehension. We are just too limited to make such a leap of knowledge.

As I have already indicated, this medieval picture of God as a perfect, simple pure act is usually referred to as the pure act account of the divine nature. It was inherited by the post-Reformation orthodox theologians who looked back to the school theology of the medieval period to provide them with the careful, logical distinctions they needed to systematize the different topics of Reformation theology that now had to be taught to pastors and students. It was this picture of the divine nature that Edwards read about and imbibed while he was a student at Yale College. Although he did not expend a great deal of energy elaborating this conception of God, it is certainly evident in his published works. Indeed, the very fact that it crops up usually in a short, pithy remark with very little elaboration is evidence of the fact that Edwards assumed this picture of God without feeling the need to make much comment on it. It was the standard way of thinking about the divine nature in the continental post-Reformation and Puritan theology in which he had been schooled.[22]

As evidence for this, consider the example of the British Puritan divine and professor at Franeker University, William Ames, whose *Marrow of Theology* (*Medulla Theologia*) was a standard textbook of divinity at Yale in the early part of the eighteenth century. It was a familiar work to Edwards, one that he had read with care.[23] Ames endorses the pure act account of the divine nature and its corollary, divine simplicity, without cavil, affirming of the divine attributes that "these attributes are God's act—single, most pure, most simple." Furthermore, "the effecting, working, or acting of God, insofar as they are in God in action, are not other than God himself. For no compositeness or mutation of power and action can have a place in God's perfectly simple and immutable nature."[24]

## Edwardsean Perfect Being Theology

Edwards is happy to speak of God as a perfect being. Indeed, he maintains that there is "great absurdity" in thinking that there is no God or in conceiving of an "eternal, absolute, universal nothing," rather than an "eternal, infinite, most perfect being."[25] If human beings had the intellectual capacity to perceive the divine essence at a glance, then we would not need to argue for the existence of God, he says. Instead, our knowledge of God would be intuitive, or (to borrow a word from contemporary philosophical parlance) basic. In other words, we would simply know there is a God without inferring that belief from some other belief we already held. But, according to Edwards, we do not have such "strength

22. This has been contested in recent literature on Edwards. See, for example, Amy Plantinga Pauw, "'One Alone Cannot Be Excellent': Jonathan Edwards on Divine Simplicity," in *Jonathan Edwards: Philosophical Theologian*, ed. Paul Helm and Oliver D. Crisp (Aldershot: Ashgate, 2003), ch. 8. A response to this article can be found in Stephen Holmes's essay in the same volume, as well as in Kyle C. Strobel, *Jonathan Edwards's Theology: A Reinterpretation* (London: T&T Clark, 2012), and Crisp, *Jonathan Edwards on God and Creation* (New York: Oxford University Press, 2011).

23. John Eusden notes that Edwards came into possession of his copy in 1721 when he was eighteen. It is currently housed in the Beineke Library at Yale University. See Eusden's Introduction to his English translation of William Ames, *The Marrow of Theology* (1968; repr., Grand Rapids: Baker, 1997), 2.

24. Ames, *Marrow of Theology*, IV.20 and VI.2, 84, and 91, respectively.

25. WJE 1:182.

and extent of mind," so we need to utilize argumentation based upon the creation, as (he presumes) the apostle has in mind in Romans 1:20. Thus, fallen human beings have to reason to the existence of a perfect being. "We first ascend, and prove *a posteriori*, or from effects, that there must be an eternal cause," says Edwards. Then, "secondly, prove by argumentation, not intuition, that this being must be necessarily existent; and then thirdly, from the proved necessity of his existence, we may descend, and prove many of his perfections a priori."[26]

Elsewhere Edwards speaks of divine perfection in language that echoes that of his medieval theological forebears: God is

> an absolutely and infinitely perfect being; and it is impossible that he should do amiss. As he is eternal, and receives not his existence from any other, but exists of himself, he cannot be limited in his being, or any attribute, to any certain determinate quantity; for such a limitation necessarily supposes a cause why he is just so great, and no greater. If any thing have bounds fixed to it, there must be some cause or reason why those bounds are fixed just where they are, and not further nor nearer. Whence it will follow, that every limited thing must have some cause; and therefore that that being which has no cause must be unlimited.[27]

Although Edwards clearly does think that the arguments of natural theology have their place, in his notebooks he reflects on the fact that it is the Christian scheme of salvation that best expresses the manner of God's perfection. This nevertheless depends upon divine revelation. He writes in "Miscellanies" entry 547 that "the Christian revelation gives us a most rational account of the design of God in his providential disposition of things, a design most worthy of an infinitely wise, holy, and perfect being; and of the way and means of God's accomplishment of it."[28] Edwards sees

---

26. WJE 1:182. In another "Miscellanies" entry, no. 1340, Edwards defines reason as follows: "*Definition*. By REASON I mean that power or faculty an intelligent being has to judge of the truth of propositions, either immediately, by only looking on the propositions, which is judging by intuition and self-evidence; or by putting together several propositions which are already evident by intuition, or at least whose evidence is originally derived from intuition." See WJE 23:359.

27. WJE 50:41.

28. WJE 18:95.

nothing intellectually dubious in the use of human reason to reflect upon the perfections of the divine nature while searching out the revelation of the same divine nature in Scripture. The limitation of human reason prevents us from apprehending the divine nature basically, or without the arguments of natural theology. Such arguments do have a place in theology. But divine revelation provides for us the most rational account of the divine nature—more rational than that provided by natural theology. Presumably, it is more rational because it is provided directly by the divine intellect, rather than inferred *a posteriori*, using human reason.

## The Divine Simple Pure Act

Edwards is unequivocal about his adherence to several parts of the medieval pure act tradition. He is clear that God is an immaterial being. In fact, for Edwards, God is, strictly speaking, the only real substance, since created entities are ideal, existing as divine ideas of a sort: "God is . . . *ens entium* [that is, the being of beings]; or if there was nothing else in the world but bodies, the only real being. . . . The nearer in nature beings are to God, so much the more properly they are beings, and more substantial; and that spirits are much more properly beings, and more substantial, than bodies."[29]

Edwards also affirms the traditional idea that God is eternal, existing outside time: "The eternal duration which was before the world . . . [is] only the eternity of God's existence: which is nothing else but his immediate, perfect, and invariable possession of the whole of his unlimited life, together and at once; *vitae interminabilis, tota, simul et perfecta possessio.*"[30]

---

29. WJE 6:238. Earlier in the same passage, Edwards goes so far as to say that "bodies have no substance of their own, neither is solidity, strictly speaking, a property belonging to body . . . neither are the other properties of body, which depend upon it and are only modifications of it. So that there is neither real substance nor property belonging to bodies; but all that is real, it is immediately in the first being." Moreover, like Locke in his *Essay Concerning Human Understanding* II.23, Edwards observes that "substance" means "only 'something,' because of abstract substance we have no idea that is more particular than only existence in general" (WJE 6:378).

30. WJE 1:385–86. The Latin statement that God possesses his life perfectly, completely, and comprehensively or simultaneously is lifted straight from the influential Roman theologian Boethius.

The eternal God is also immutable:

> The notion of an infinite Eternal implies absolute immutabil-
> ity.... And this immutability, being constant from eternity, im
> plies duration without succession, is wholly mystery and seem-
> ing inconsistence. It seems as much as to say an infinitely great
> or long duration all at once, or all in a moment, which seems to
> say an infinitely great in an infinitely little, or an infinitely long
> line in a point without any length.

What is more, "if there be an absolute immutability in God, then there
never arises any new act in God or new exertion of himself—and yet
there arise new effects, which seems an utter inconsistence."[31] Yet such
apparent inconsistence can be reconciled if God is a timeless being whose
acts or act is timelessly eternal, but has numerous temporal effects, rather
like pouring a jug of water through a colander. The single jug-worth of
liquid is distributed through the holes in the colander to different areas.
Similarly, the one action of God may be distributed to different moments
in time.

Edwards also explicitly affirms his allegiance to the divine simplicity tradition of Western theology in his treatise on *Freedom of the Will*,
where he speaks of God's "perfect and absolute simplicity,"[32] as well as
in his *Religious Affections*, where, in speaking of the moral excellency
of the divine attributes, he says that "a love to God for the beauty of his
moral attributes, leads to, and necessarily causes a delight in God for
all his attributes; for his moral attributes cannot be without his natural
attributes: for infinite holiness supposes infinite wisdom, and an infinite
capacity and greatness; and *all the attributes of God do as it were imply
each other*."[33] At the very beginning of his unpublished work "Discourse
on the Trinity," he underlines much the same point, saying,

> there is no distinction to be made in God between power or
> habit and act; and with respect to God's understanding, that
> there are no such distinctions to be admitted as in ours between
> perception or idea, and reasoning and judgment—excepting

31. "Miscellanies," no. 1340, in WJE 23:371–72.
32. WJE 1:377.
33. WJE 2:256–57. Emphasis added.

what the will has to do in judgment—but that the whole of the divine understanding or wisdom consists in the mere perception or unvaried presence of his infinitely perfect idea. And with respect to the other faculty, as it is in God, there are no distinctions to be admitted of faculty, habit and act, between will, inclination and love: but that it is all one simple act.[34]

Finally, in Edwards's "Miscellanies" notebook, entry 94 endorses the idea that God is a pure act in these words: the "Holy Spirit is the act of God between the Father and the Son infinitely loving and delighting in each other." What is more, the Holy Spirit is "distinct from each of the other two [divine persons], and yet it [sic] is God; for the pure and perfect act of God is God, because God is a pure act. It appears that this is God, because that which acts perfectly is all act, and nothing but act."[35] Similarly, in the "Discourse on the Trinity," he says at one point that "the Holy Ghost is the Deity subsisting in act or the divine essence flowing out and breathed forth, in God's infinite love to and delight in himself."[36] Echoing the Reformed scholastic theologians before him, Edwards endorses the basically medieval view that God is without potentiality.[37] In his trinitarian life, God is entirely realized, as it were. The Holy Spirit is spoken of here in Augustinian language as the bond of love between the Father and the Son, but Edwards is clear that the Holy Spirit is as much a divine person as the other two, because (as we saw in the previous chapter) he also shares in the divine essence that is entirely actualized in the inner life of the Trinity. This is underlined elsewhere in his sermons, where Edwards speaks of God as a pure act in no uncertain terms. He says, "we must take heed that we han't to[o] Gross a notion of God's Immensity and Omnipresence we must not Conceive of it as part of God." He continues, "for God is not made . . .

---

34. WJE 21:113.

35. WJE 13:260.

36. WJE 21:131.

37. However, as we shall see in the next chapter, Edwards does say in his dissertation, *God's End in Creation*, "*a disposition in God, as an original property of his nature, to an emanation of his own infinite fullness, was what excited him to create the world; and so that the emanation itself was aimed at by him as a last end of creation*" (WJE 8:435; emphasis in the original). We shall see that this doesn't necessarily conflict with Edwards's doctrine of divine simplicity, though it appears to do so at first glance, causing some unwary commentators to think that his views are more revisionary than they actually are.

up of Parts for he is a simple pure act." What is more, when "we say that God is in this house," this must not be understood to mean "that Part of God is . . . in this house but God is here. 'tis not part of God that is in us but God is in us."[38]

## Complicating the Picture: The Trinity

From this brief overview we can see that Edwards had an optimistic view of the place and power of human reason, even if it is limited in its capacity to conceptualize or perceive the divine nature. He clearly thought of God as a perfect being and as a simple pure act—a matter we have already touched upon with respect to the Holy Spirit as the divine act in the previous chapter. If we draw together what we saw of Edwards's trinitarianism in the last chapter with what we have said about his doctrine of God in this chapter, it seems that his account is not without peculiarities. Although in some of his sermon outlines he is clear that God is a simple pure act, there is evidence in his "Miscellanies" and in his "Discourse on the Trinity" that Edwards thought of the Deity subsisting wholly in act as a property peculiar to the third person of the Trinity. Somehow, on Edwards's reckoning, God is a simple pure act, yet in such a manner that God's being in act is associated with the person of the Holy Spirit in particular, the divine person who is the act or bond of love between the Father and Son in the inner life of the Trinity.

In the last chapter we also noted that in the "Discourse on the Trinity," Edwards has much to say about the doctrine of perichoresis, or divine interpenetration, as well. The divine persons interpenetrate one another in a marvelous fashion, such that the Father is wholly in the Son and the Spirit, the Son is wholly in the Father and Spirit, and the Spirit is wholly in the Father and Son. Yet there are three distinct

---

38. WJE Online Vol. 42, §44, Sermon outline on Psalm 139:7–10. See also the sermon outline on Ezekiel 8:8 in WJE Online Vol. 53, §477. There, Edwards says God "is a pure act, i.e. he is nothing but mere act without any passiveness . . . he cannot be passive in any thing whatsoever." Cf. WJE 23:657, where he says much the same thing: God is "a pure act whose essence is energy; without all extension [or] bulk; indivisible; unmultipliable; one most simple; everywhere present yet not properly in place; perfectly immutable." (I have corrected the orthography given in WJE Online Vols. 42 and 53 and left ellipses where Edwards has crossed out material in the original—material that is transcribed by the editors.)

divine persons. At one point, Edwards confides, "But I don't pretend fully to explain how these things are, and I am sensible a hundred other objections may be made, and puzzling doubts and questions raised, that I can't solve. I am far from pretending to explain the Trinity so as to render it no longer a mystery. I think it to be the highest and deepest of all divine mysteries still, notwithstanding anything that I have said or conceived about it."[39]

One way of making sense of these different aspects of Edwards's trinitarian thought involves an analogy with a maxim of Western catholic theology, namely, that the external works of the Trinity are indivisible (*opera trinitatis ad extra sunt indivisa*). According to much catholic thought, at least some external works devolve upon particular divine persons. The paradigm of this is, of course, the incarnation. God the Son assumes human nature. But this is still a work of the whole Trinity, since the Father sends the Son and the Spirit enables the Son to perform his work. Perhaps Edwards has something similar in mind in his account of the internal differentiation in the Trinity. Although the individuation of the divine persons is not an external act of God in creation, nevertheless, it appears that, for Edwards, God is wholly in act and that this aspect or operation internal to the life of God is particularly associated with the Holy Spirit. But this is of a piece with his view of the divine persons as mutually indwelling and (somehow) constituting the one God, as we saw in chapter two.

## Summary

In this chapter we have seen how Edwards defends a particular ontology, namely, idealism. We have argued that his view is best understood as a species of immaterial antirealism, according to which the creation is a world of minds and their ideas that is radically dependent upon the divine mind. We have also seen that Edwards endorses a species of perfect being theology alongside his commitment to the notion that God is a simple pure act, in keeping with his Puritan and Reformed orthodox forebears as well as many of the medieval school theologians from whom the Reformed and Puritan theologians took their cue. But there are other

---

39. WJE 21:134. The discussion of perichoresis occurs immediately prior to this comment, in WJE 21:133.

aspects of Edwards's philosophical theology that appear to pull in a very different direction from this, which have led some recent interpreters to argue that Edwards departed from the Reformed tradition in which he was schooled, ending up with a doctrine of God very different from that beloved of scholastic theology. It is to these more controversial claims that we turn next.

# CHAPTER FOUR

# God and Creation

In the previous chapters we considered Edwards's doctrine of the Trinity and some of the central metaphysical claims he makes about idealism and perfect being theology. Having considered his treatment of the doctrine of God, we can turn in this chapter to a number of other characteristically Edwardsean philosophical-theological notions, focusing on his conception of the relationship between God and creation. These include discussion of the divine nature and dispositions, whether Edwards was committed to some version of panentheism (the idea that the world is somehow contained in God), his doctrine of continuous creation, his doctrine of occasionalism (the idea that God is the sole cause of all things), and, finally, his doctrine of determinism.

## Understanding Edwards on the Divine Nature and Dispositions

Where Edwards does speak about the divine nature in detail, he has some interesting things to say. Although he did not write a treatise devoted entirely to the doctrine of God, he did compose numerous "Miscellanies" entries that deal with the character of God and a dissertation entitled *Concerning the End for Which God Created the World* that has much to say about the nature of God and the relationship between the Deity and the created order.[1] In the latter work he makes a number of startling claims. Let us consider three in particular. First, that in order to be

---

1. This dissertation, commonly known by the short title *The End of Creation*, is contained in WJE 8.

exercised certain divine perfections require an act of creation: "there is included in this [creating] the exercise of God's perfections to produce a proper effect, in opposition to their lying eternally dormant and ineffectual."[2] Second, that in creating the world God "diffuses" or "emanates" himself, according to a "disposition to communicate himself or diffuse his own fullness."[3] Third, and perhaps most controversially, the divine disposition to create is an "original property" of the divine nature: *a disposition in God, as an original property of his nature, to an emanation of his own infinite fullness, was what excited him to create the world; and so that the emanation itself was aimed at by him as a last end of creation.*[4]

These assertions seem to pull in a rather different direction from the picture of Edwards's doctrine of God painted thus far. For a God who is both triune as well as a simple pure act does not seem to have metaphysical room (as it were) for dispositions—at least, dispositions that remain unactualized. Yet Edwards claims that God has dispositions. In particular, he thinks a disposition to communicate or emanate himself *ad extra*, or in the created order, is "a perfection."[5] This is a puzzle that we will need to consider carefully, since language of dispositions is an important feature of Edwards's doctrine of God, and dispositions have been the source of some controversy in recent interpretations of Edwards's thought.[6]

According to a dictionary definition, a disposition is an attribute that an entity has that describes some sort of tendency or power latent in that thing. But having a tendency or power to do a thing is not the same as performing an action that requires that power or tendency. So, if I have the power or tendency to swim a mile but live in the high desert and never encounter a large body of water in which to attempt to swim, this power or tendency will remain merely virtual or potential. That is, I have the potential to swim a mile given the right circumstances. But if those circumstances do not obtain because I am never presented with a

---

2. WJE 8:527.
3. WJE 8:433.
4. WJE 8:435. Emphasis in the original.
5. WJE 8:433.
6. See, e.g., Stephen R. Holmes, "Does Jonathan Edwards Use a Dispositional Ontology? A Response to Sang Hyun Lee," in *Jonathan Edwards: Philosophical Theologian*, ed. Paul Helm and Oliver D. Crisp (Aldershot: Ashgate, 2003), 99–114; Crisp, *Jonathan Edwards on God and Creation* (New York: Oxford University Press, 2011); and Kyle C. Strobel, *Jonathan Edwards's Theology* (London: T & T Clark, 2012).

body of water in which to swim, I cannot realize the power to swim with which I have been born.

Now, if Edwards thinks that a disposition is something like a tendency or power to do such and such a thing under certain circumstances, then it appears that there is a tension in his thinking. For it seems that his doctrine of God includes both a traditional pure act account of the divine nature, according to which there are no unrealized potentialities in God, and the claim that God's nature includes dispositions, which just are unrealized potentialities. But both of these things cannot coexist in the one divine nature; they are incompatible with each other. A being cannot be without potentiality and yet have potentiality at one and the same time. Yet (so it seems) Edwards is committed to both these claims. This seems incredible. How could a thinker as careful as Edwards fail to see that in this fundamental matter of the divine nature he held views that were muddled, or worse, incoherent?

### Four Recent Interpretations on Edwardsean Dispositions

Giving some account of Edwards's response to this question has proven controversial in recent Edwards studies. In order to get a sense of some of the most important recent attempts to make sense of what he is saying about the relationship between the divine nature and the divine disposition to emanate God's self in creation, we shall consider four recent interpretations of Edwards's views.

The first line of interpretation in recent Edwards studies has taken the view that the older, pure act language we find scattered throughout his published and unpublished writings should be tempered by what he says about divine dispositions. On this view, the dispositional language is taken to be more basic or fundamental to Edwards's thought. What references there are to a more traditional picture of the divine nature should be understood in light of the language about dispositions, not vice-versa. Some interpreters, such as Sang Lee and Amy Plantinga Pauw, have argued that the traditional language about the divine nature is a sort of theological residue left over from his intellectual formation, which should not be taken at face value.[7] They regard the scattered references we

---

7. See Sang Hyun Lee, *The Philosophical Theology of Jonathan Edwards*, expanded edition (Princeton: Princeton University Press, 2000), and Amy Plantinga Pauw, "The Su-

have to the doctrine of divine simplicity or to the claim that God is a pure act as the last vestiges of Edwards's Puritan heritage, a sort of intellectual tick that he was trying to slough off as he reconsidered the divine nature along the more dynamic lines of divine dispositions.

Others have offered a second, more moderate account, arguing that there is a place for dispositions as well as for much (though not all) of the traditional language about God in Edwards's *corpus*. On this second line of interpretation, there are tensions in Edwards's work, perhaps even contradictions, but the central claim that God has the disposition to en-large himself in creation is not obviously incoherent. However, neither of these alternatives is particularly satisfactory. If one follows Lee and Plantinga Pauw, then Edwards's works (including his published works) are internally disordered and one must make an interpretative decision to discard, or at least suppress, the traditional-sounding language about the divine nature that can be found in Edwards.

But there are significant obstacles that this interpretative model must overcome. First, there is nowhere in Edwards's work where he dis-tances himself from the tradition that formed him. He never disassociates himself from the pure act account of the divine nature; and he never dis-avows it. In fact, although the references to the traditional language about the divine nature are not a major feature of his writings, they are present throughout his published and unpublished works, including his mature works. What is more, his passing references to the doctrines that make up the traditional pure act account of the divine nature are not evidence that he held these doctrines lightly, but rather that these were uncontroversial matters in the tradition that he simply wished to affirm. It would be very odd—given what a careful, logical, and transparent thinker Edwards was in his writings—to find that he surreptitiously left one model of the divine nature behind while seeking to commend another, dispositional model to his readers without explanation or introduction. Edwards was just not that sort of person, let alone that sort of thinker, as even a passing familiarity with his biography will show. He dealt openly and directly with matters he thought controverted, and he was unafraid of taking up unusual or peculiar positions if he thought they were warranted. Where he did do this—as in his doctrines of continuous creation and occasion-alism, or in his views about the transmission of original sin in his treatise

---

preme Harmony of All": *The Trinitarian Theology of Jonathan Edwards* (Grand Rapids: Eerdmans, 2002).

of the same name—it was patently obvious from the beginning that this was what he was doing. He was no Reimarus, teaching in public doctrines that he secretly despised or rejected.[8]

The problem with the second, mediating position (according to which Edwards teaches both the traditional view plus the idea that God has dispositions) is that it is not clear how these two things are to be reconciled. John Bombaro claims that by locating the dispositions in God, Edwards preserves the uniqueness of the divine nature. But, says Bombaro, Edwards does adjust the traditional doctrine of God by adding in the claim that God enlarges himself in the created order. God is disposed to enlarge himself and (in some sense) necessarily enlarges himself. Hence, Edwards's doctrine of God makes an important qualification to the traditional view, namely, that God's relation to the created order requires a doctrine of panentheism. This, very roughly, is the idea that the world is related to God as a body to its soul: God must enlarge himself in the creation, and this helps explain the traditional and novel aspects of Edwards's doctrine of God.[9]

There is much to commend this view, and Bombaro has hit upon an important component of Edwards's doctrine in his affirmation of his doctrine of panentheism. But there are still problems with this way of thinking if explanation stops at this juncture. For it is still not clear how God can be a pure act and have dispositions on this view. In fact, introducing panentheism into the mix only complicates matters further,

8. Hermann Samuel Reimarus (1694–1768) was a German scholar of classical languages and philosophy whose public support of traditional accounts of the inspiration and authority of the Bible conflicted with his *Apology*, a work which was published posthumously, and which did much to further the rationalistic critical attack upon the authority and veracity of Scripture pursued by early practitioners of historical biblical criticism. A useful overview of his life and influence can be found in Roy A. Harrisville and Walter Sundberg, *The Bible in Modern Culture, Baruch Spinoza to Brevard Childs*, 2nd ed. (Grand Rapids: Eerdmans, 2002 [1995]), 46–61. The Communion Controversy that led to Edwards's dismissal from his pastorate in Northampton might be thought counter-evidence to the claim being made here. After all, he was accused of changing his views on the qualifications for communion that he had inherited from his grandfather, Solomon Stoddard, the previous incumbent in the pulpit. However, Edwards vigorously defended himself against these criticisms in two published works, *An Humble Inquiry* (1749) and *Misrepresentations Corrected* (1752), both of which are reprinted in WJE 12.

9. This is one of the central planks of John Bombaro's monograph *Jonathan Edwards's Vision of Reality: The Relationship of God to the World, Redemption History, and the Reprobate*, Princeton Theological Monographs Series (Eugene, OR: Pickwick Publications, 2012).

since the traditional account of the divine nature assumes God exists *a se*, that is, independently of the creation. He is free to create or refrain from creation. Yet on this way of interpreting Edwards, God does not appear to be free to refrain from creating. Nor does God appear to exist independent of the creation. In some sense he seems to need the creation in order to enlarge himself.

A third option—the one favored by the present author[10]—is to try to find a way of harmonizing these apparently antithetical aspects of Edwards's understanding of the divine nature. Let us assume that Edwards is committed to the traditional doctrine of God being a simple pure act. To this we need to add the claim from his dissertation *The End of Creation* that God is essentially disposed to "emanate himself" (as Edwards puts it), bringing about some world. This raises the following problem: if God has an "essential disposition" to generate the world, then it appears God is not a pure act because there are unrealized potentialities in the divine nature, e.g., the potential to refrain from creating or to create some other world. However, one component of the pure act view Edwards endorses is the idea that God is atemporal. He is outside time. What is innovative about Edwards's position (if it is innovative) is that God is essentially creative, or, perhaps better, essentially diffusive. It is part of the divine nature to be creative, in the diffusing of God's self. But this is not necessarily inconsistent with a pure act view, despite the language of dispositions that Edwards deploys. For, in this creative emanation, God exercises certain divine attributes that would not otherwise be exercised, including his omnipotence. Nevertheless, the disposition to diffuse himself and thereby exercise the divine attributes that would not be exercised without such a creative action is eternally realized; God is necessarily, eternally creative. This means that the divine attributes that require some act of creative emanation or diffusion in order to be exercised are necessarily eternally exercised. The disposition to generate the world and the exercise of those divine attributes that would not be exercised without this generative act, are actualized in the creation of the world.

In short, the disposition to generate a world is not inconsistent with the claim that God is a pure act if this disposition is eternally realized. In fact, this is really only a particular form of a common problem for pure act accounts of the divine nature, having to do with counterfactuals. How should possible, but not actual, states of affairs be understood if God is

10. See Crisp, *Jonathan Edwards on God and Creation.*

a pure act? How can there be unrealized possibilities in the divine mind if God lacks potentiality and if he has no distinct parts? One answer is to claim that such counterfactual states of affairs exist eternally in the divine mind as divine ideas. In one sense they are "actual" because they really do exist. It is just that they exist as ideas of what might have been. Indeed, as we saw in the previous chapter, there is nothing more real than minds and their ideas, on Edwards's way of thinking. The whole of creation is a set of stable divine ideas, nothing more. Presumably, there are an infinite number of such states of affairs since there are an infinite number of possible worlds God has chosen not to actualize. In which case, even if God is a pure act, he has an infinite number of ideas of possible, but not actualized, states of affairs of what might have been. But, since God exists atemporally, these ideas are coeternal with God, as aspects of his perfect nature.

Edwards's claim that God has an essential disposition to create or diffuse himself is related to this matter of unrealized possible states of affairs because it seems to suggest that there is some potentiality or power in God that has to be realized in action. On this charitable reading of Edwards, it turns out that there is no real conflict between these two claims in his thought. We might put it like this. According to Edwards, God has an eternal desire to create a world, and this desire is eternally realized. Usually, we think of desires as something that find their fulfillment, if they are fulfilled at all, at some point in time subsequent to our desire. I desire a cup of tea. I make the tea and drink it, thereby realizing the desire in action. But, in keeping with other classical, orthodox Christian theists, Edwards thinks that there is no such time lapse required between God's being disposed to do something and God's bringing about that thing. So divine dispositions, such as the disposition to create, do not have the same phenomenology that the dispositions of creatures do because God is not in time.

Desire and disposition, like emotion, are not to be understood anthropopathically. That is, we are not to conjure up some perfect instance of a human desire, disposition, or emotion and then project that onto the divine nature. God is significantly unlike his creatures in this respect. Not only is he a perfect being. He is also without temporal succession, according to Edwards. His thoughts really are not our thoughts or his ways our ways (Isa. 55:8). In short, even though God is essentially disposed to create, this is not obviously inconsistent with the pure act account given that a divine being who is a pure act may have dispositions that are realized eternally. This interpretation is able to make sense of even the most effusive passages in *The End of Creation*, such as this one:

> This propensity in God to diffuse himself may be considered as a propensity to have himself diffused, or to his own glory existing in its emanation. A respect to himself, or an infinite propensity to, and delight in his own glory, is that which causes him to incline to its being abundantly diffused, and to delight in the emanation of it. . . . God looks on the communication of himself, and the emanation of the infinite glory and good that are in himself to belong to the fullness and completeness of himself, as though he were not in his most complete and glorious state without it.[11]

The language of emanation is Neoplatonic and can be found in many other representatives of Reformed and, more broadly, Augustinian Christianity. His references to inclination and diffusion could be misleading taken without reference to other passages that echo the pure act tradition of thinking about the divine nature. But notice his careful qualification at the end of this passage: "as though he were." This is an important signal. Edwards uses this sort of qualification frequently in his writings when he is aware of the inadequacy of human language to capture the theological notions under scrutiny. God emanates or diffuses himself in creation, but this is an eternal act that is so fundamental to the divine being it is as if, without this effusion, God would remain incomplete. He is, then, essentially diffusive. He cannot but create a world. He must diffuse himself in action. But, since this is an eternal act that has numerous temporal effects (given Edwards's scattered endorsements of the pure act tradition), it is as an eternal pure act that God diffuses or emanates himself.[12]

---

11. WJE 8:439.

12. Compare Edwards's earlier remarks in setting up his discussion in *The End of Creation*, where he says, "no notion of God's last end in the creation of the world is agreeable to reason which would truly imply or infer any indigence, insufficiency and mutability in God; or any dependence of the Creator on the creature, for any part of his perfection or happiness." It is evident in Scripture and reason "that God is infinitely, eternally, unchangeably, and independently glorious and happy," that he needs nothing from his creatures, and that he cannot be changed "or be the subject of any sufferings or *impair* of his glory and felicity from any other being." WJE 8:420. These are important qualifiers to what he later says about the diffusion and emanation of God's nature in creation.

In the same work, Edwards also speaks of certain divine attributes that would not be realized without a creation. These include his "infinite power, wisdom, righteousness, goodness, etc." Edwards writes, "if the world had not been created, these attributes would never have had any exercise."[13] God's power would have remained dormant. His wisdom and prudence would have had no exercise in the disposal of created things. And so on. Edwards goes on to observe that God would have known he possessed these attributes even if they were never exercised, but since he esteems these attributes and thinks them valuable in and of themselves, delighting in them as divine perfections, "'tis natural to suppose that he delights in their proper exercise and expression."[14] Once again, on the face of it, the language Edwards uses here could be taken to imply his departure from the pure act tradition, since he contemplates the prospect that certain divine attributes might have never been exercised without the creation of some world.

However, on reflection, it would seem that this too is not inconsistent with a pure act account if God is atemporal. On the charitable interpretation we have been offering here, the way to understand his comments in this part of *The End of Creation* would be as follows. Suppose God is essentially creative. Then, it is part of his being to be creative; so he must create some world. And suppose that some of his attributes would only be exercised *ad extra* if he creates some world (e.g., his power and wisdom). Finally, suppose God is eternal. On these assumptions (all of which Edwards endorses, as we have seen) it is necessarily the case that God will create a world in order to exercise his divine attributes.

Is it possible that he would fail to act in this manner? No, it is not. There is a Pickwickian sense in which if God had not created a world some of his attributes would have remained unexercised—and I take it Edwards means something like this in the passage in question. But given that God is so constituted that he must create and therefore must exercise the attributes that would remain dormant without such creative activity, it is not possible that God would fail to create a world. This would be like saying, "if God were to refrain from exercising his omniscience for a moment then he might be said to be capable of forgetting who he was." This is also a Pickwickian sort of claim because God cannot cease to exercise his omniscience for even a moment without ceasing to exist.

13. WJE 8:428–29.
14. WJE 8:430.

But since God cannot cease to exist (given a widely held assumption among classical, orthodox Christian theologians that God cannot not exist) he cannot fail to be omniscient. So such a question is idle. It seems to imply some important thing that God could do were he so minded. But, in fact, it describes something that it is impossible for God to do, given that he is essentially, not merely contingently or accidentally, omniscient. In other words, being omniscient is part and parcel of who he is; it isn't something he just happens to be, though things could have been different.

I (Crisp) suggest that Edwards's remarks about God failing to exercise some of his attributes without creating a world should be taken along similar lines to this query about the nature of divine omniscience. That is, just as God cannot fail to be omniscient, though we might speculate on whether God can lack omniscience, so also God cannot fail to exercise his disposition to create the world, on this charitable interpretation of Edwards's doctrine. Nevertheless, he can speculate about what it would be like for God to not exercise his disposition to create or fail to exercise those attributes that require a creation, like his power, presence, and knowledge. This seems to be what Edwards is doing in *The End of Creation* when he speaks of God's disposition to create the world. When it is seen in this light, the apparent contradiction this presents for Edwards's doctrine of God dissipates.

There is a further twist to this aspect of Edwards's thought, however. Recall from chapter two that, according to Edwards's understanding of the Trinity, there are two real distinctions in God, corresponding to his understanding (God the Son) and his will (God the Holy Spirit). From what Edwards's says in some of his "Miscellanies" entries, it looks as if he identifies divine dispositions with the action of particular divine persons. Specifically, he closely associates the eternal exercise of God's disposition to create with his understanding and will to create—which is just to say, with the particular action in creation of the Son and the Holy Spirit. Thus, in "Miscellanies," entry 1218, Edwards writes of God "exercising his perfections" (which are, of course, his understanding and will—the Son and the Spirit). He goes on to explain that it would be improper for God to fail to exercise certain divine attributes that require some creature as the object upon whom God may lavish these attributes, such as justice, faithfulness, and wisdom. But of course, as we have already noted from *The End of Creation*, God, being eternal, has no dormant attributes. They are eternally exercised in creation. He continues,

Both these dispositions, of exerting himself and communicating himself, may be reduced to one, viz. a disposition effectually to exert himself, or to exert himself in order to an effect. That effect is the communication of himself, or himself *ad extra*, which is what is called his glory. This communication is of two sorts: the communication that consists in understanding or idea, which is summed up in the knowledge of God; and the other is in the will, consisting in love and joy, which may be summed up in the love and enjoyment of God. Thus that which proceeds from God *ad extra* is agreeable to the twofold subsistences which proceed from him *ad intra*, which is the Son and the Holy Spirit, the Son being the idea of God or the knowledge of God, and the Holy Ghost which is the love of God and joy in God.[15]

We can suggest the following reconstruction of Edwards's thinking here. First, divine dispositions that require a creation in order to be exercised cannot remain eternally dormant (for, as we have seen, God is a simple pure act). He eternally exercises these attributes in his act of creating the world. Not only that, the act of communicating himself in creation is an act of divine understanding and will, which correspond to the two divine subsistences that eternally proceed from the Father in the Godhead, that is, to the Son and the Spirit. God's disposition to create the world is the action of the second and third person, respectively. It is an action associated with their character as the divine understanding and will, and it is directed from God to bring about the creation. Thus, God's dispositions (such as they are) are directly associated with the divine persons in the divine life.[16]

Having said that, this line of reasoning in *Concerning the End of Creation* does push Edwards toward panentheism, which, as we have already noted, has not gone unnoticed in Edwardsean scholarship. In this respect Edwards does innovate within his tradition. But—importantly—this is a variation on themes and concepts within the Western theological tradition (and his Reformed branch of that tradition), not a departure from the tradition or attempt to smuggle in concepts that would undo the tradition that had formed him.

15. WJE 23:153.
16. For a fuller exposition of this particular way of thinking about the divine dispositions and the divine persons, see Strobel, *Jonathan Edwards's Theology*, 83–94.

Before turning to Edwards's panentheism in more detail, it is worth considering a fourth option on the question of the divine nature and dispositions. This too is an attempt to reconcile Edwards's apparently innovative language with his Reformed heritage, and it can be found in the work of Kyle Strobel.[17] In this way of thinking, the question of the exercise of those divine attributes that would remain dormant without some emanation of the divine *ad extra* toward his creation should be construed along the lines of God willing to exercise his attributes in emanating himself in creation in a way that is fitting but not necessary. In this connection Edwards says, "If it be fit that God's power and wisdom, etc., should be exercised and expressed in some effects, and not lie eternally dormant, then it seems proper that these exercises should appear, and not be totally hidden and unknown."[18] Edwards argues here that God cannot have a disposition to communicate himself to a creature, since that would "presuppose the existence of the object."[19] Rather, God has a disposition to emanate his own fullness, and therefore this fullness is, as Edwards puts it, "what excited him to create the world."

According to Strobel's interpretation of Edwards, God does not have to create as such (unlike Crisp's interpretation of Edwards on this point), but his emanation is fully actualized in his own life, and it is fitting that his emanation flow forth *ad extra* (therefore, God creates). If creation has to do with the bringing about of some entity other than God that is his creature, emanation has to do with God communicating himself—a sort of projection or overflow of himself in the created order. Reflecting on this theme, Edwards adopts the imagery of a fountain (God) and the stream that pours forth from it (the creation). He writes,

> The communication or external stream [that is the divine emanation in creation] may be looked upon as anything besides the fountain, so far it may be looked on as an increase of good. And if the fullness of good that is in the fountain is in itself excellent and worthy to exist, then the emanation, or that which is as it were an increase, repetition or multiplication of it, is excellent and worthy to exist.[20]

17. Strobel, *Jonathan Edwards's Theology*, 75–104.
18. WJE 8:431.
19. WJE 8:434–35.
20. WJE 8:433.

The fountain is full in itself, but if its fullness, which is good, can be communicated in streams that flow from it, then it is fitting that it do so. Moreover, it is the fullness of God that excites him to communicate himself in the act of emanation. Edwards's use of the word "excites" is key in Strobel's way of thinking. He construes it as Edwards's way of saying that it is fitting that God would create based on the nature of his fullness.

According to Strobel, Edwards is simply restating in his own language—the language of the emanation of God's fullness in creation—what the Reformed had always said about this matter. Like his Reformed forebears, Edwards affirms that God creates for his own glory.[21] It is just that Edwards links this to the language of divine fullness. This emanation language in *The End of Creation* is meant to connect, more tightly than did his immediate theological forebears, the processions within God's life (of the Son from the Father, and of the Spirit from the Father and the Son) with God's economic self-giving in the act of generation that brings about the created order.

## Evaluating the Four Interpretations of Edwards on Dispositions

Of the four different interpretations of Edwards we have canvassed, the last two in particular attempt to take seriously the fact that Edwards regarded himself as theologizing from within a particular theological tradition, that of the Reformed tradition. These two accounts also try to take Edwards at his word, attempting to understand him on his own terms rather than regarding him as conflicted in his views or as a thinker trying to move away from the tradition that had formed him. This has been a particularly lively area for discussion in recent Edwards studies because of the far-reaching implications these issues have for his thought—as we shall see going forward. Having provided some sense of the interpretive landscape on this important recent debate in the secondary literature, we return in the rest of the chapter to giving a jointly written account of Edwards's views on four other nodal issues in Edwards's understanding

21. Francis Turretin's language is similar to Edwards at this juncture. He writes, "Now when God became the Creator, he was not changed in himself (for nothing new happened to him, for from eternity he had the efficacious will of creating the world in time), but only in order to the creature (because a new relation took place with it)." *Institutes of Elenctic Theology*, vol. 1, trans. George Giger, ed. James T. Dennison Jr. (Phillipsburg, NJ: Presbyterian and Reformed, 1992), 205.

of God and creation, namely, panentheism, continuous creation, occasionalism, and determinism.

## Pure Act Panentheism?

We come to the apparently panentheistic implications of these views in Edwards's thought. Describing the views of any traditional, orthodox Christian theologian as panentheistic courts misunderstanding. In contemporary theological parlance, those who espouse panentheism are often also associated with a theologically revisionist agenda. Panentheism is, after all, distinct from theism. So we need to begin by distinguishing Edwards's brand of panentheism so as to avoid any confusion in this regard.

We take it that theism is the view that there is a God, and that God and the world he creates are distinct, separate entities such that the world depends upon God's sustenance but is not somehow "part" of God. By contrast, according to one widely used definition, panentheism is the view according to which the "being of God includes and penetrates the whole universe, so that every part exists in Him, but His Being is more than, and not exhausted by, the universe."[22] But this must be distinguished from yet another position, that is, pantheism. The pantheist believes that God and the world are identical, or at least completely overlap, rather as the marble block and the statue from which it is carved are identical, or at least occupy the same overlapping space and are composed of the same stuff. Edwards has sometimes been accused of being a pantheist. The accusation is not that he flatly declared himself a pantheist, but that various theological commitments he has imply pantheism.[23] But Edwards would have denied he was a pantheist. He did not think, nor do the deep

---

22. F. L. Cross and E. A. Livingstone, eds., *The Oxford Dictionary of the Christian Church*, 3rd ed. (New York: Oxford University Press, 1997), 1213.

23. See, e.g., the robust criticism of Edwards's doctrine in Charles Hodge, *Systematic Theology*, vol. 1, *Theology* (1871; Grand Rapids: Eerdmans, 1940), 580. Arthur Crabtree also makes this claim as part of his critique of Edwards in *Jonathan Edwards' View of Man: A Study in Eighteenth Century Calvinism* (Wallington: Religious Education Press, 1948), 17–18. Bombaro also maintains that there are elements latent in Edwards's doctrine of God that push him in the direction of pantheism, although Edwards resists this drift, settling instead for a species of panentheist view. See Bombaro, *Jonathan Edwards's Vision of Reality*, 79–83 and Appendix A. See also Oliver D. Crisp, *Jonathan Edwards among the Theologians* (Grand Rapids: Eerdmans, 2015), ch. 9.

structures of his metaphysics demand, that pantheism is true. Some have argued he was a theist. But this is also mistaken. Although Edwards does believe that God and the world are, in one sense, distinct, he also thinks that the creation exists in the mind of God as a set of what he calls stable ideas (that is, ideas God continues to hold before his mind). The world is ideal; it exists as a set of divine ideas; hence it is distinct from God. But it is sustained within the divine mind. Thus, his views imply more than theism—they commit him to panentheism.

However, since assertions do not an argument make, let us turn to the evidence for this claim. Edwards believes that God is essentially creative. It is not merely that God may create or refrain from creating. According to Edwards, it is necessary for God to create, since it is part of his nature to be creative or effusive. In *The End of Creation* he remarks, "This propensity in God to diffuse himself may be considered as a propensity to have himself diffused, or to his own glory existing in its emanation." Indeed, "God looks on the communication of himself, and the emanation of the infinite glory and good that are in himself to belong to the fullness and completeness of himself, as though he were not in his most complete and glorious state without it."[24] Later in the same work, he says,

> God would be less happy . . . if he had not that perfection of nature which consists in a *propensity of nature to diffuse of his own fullness.* And he would be less happy, *if it were possible for him to be hindered* in the exercise of his goodness and his other perfections in their proper effects. But he has complete happiness, because he has these perfections, and can't be hindered in exercising and displaying them in their proper effects.[25]

In a still later passage he says,

> God in his benevolence to his creatures, can't have his heart enlarged in such a manner as to take in beings that he finds, who are originally out of himself, distinct and independent. This can't be in an infinite being, who exists alone from eternity. But he, from his goodness, as it were enlarges himself in a more

24. WJE 8:439.
25. WJE 8:447. Emphasis added.

excellent and divine manner. This is by communicating and diffusing himself; and so instead of finding, making objects of his
benevolence: not by taking into himself what he finds distinct
from himself, and so partaking of their good, and being happy
in them; but by flowing forth, and expressing himself in them,
and making them to partake of him, and rejoicing in himself
expressed in them, and communicated to them.[26]

What is more, Edwards thinks of the creation as existing in a somewhat *attenuated* state in the divine mind as a set of stable divine ideas. In
his early philosophical notebooks, he writes the following:

> the substance of bodies at last becomes either nothing, or noth-
> ing but the Deity acting in that particular manner in those parts
> of space where he thinks fit. So that, speaking most strictly,
> there is no proper substance but God himself. . . . Since . . . so-
> lidity or body is immediately from the exercise of divine power,
> causing there to be resistance in such a part of space, it follows
> that motion also, which is the communication of body, solidity,
> or this resistance, from one part of space to another successively
> . . . is from the immediate exercise of divine power so commu-
> nicating that resistance, according to certain conditions which
> we call the laws of motion. . . . Hence we see what's that we call
> the laws of nature in bodies, to wit: the stated methods of God's
> acting with respect to bodies, and the stated conditions of the
> alteration of the manner of his acting.[27]

And again,

> the secret lies here: that which truly is the substance of all bod-
> ies is the infinitely exact and precise and perfectly stable idea
> in God's mind, together with his stable will that the same shall
> gradually be communicated to us, and to other minds, accord-
> ing to certain fixed and exact established methods and laws: or
> in somewhat different language, the infinitely exact and precise
> divine idea, together with an answerable, perfectly exact, pre-

26. WJE 8:461–62.
27. WJE 6:215–16.

cise and stable will with respect to correspondent communications to created minds, and effects on their minds.[28]

Nor is it that the creation exists across time, being somehow sustained as a set of divine ideas. Rather, "it appears, if we consider matters strictly, there is no such thing as any identity or oneness in created objects, existing at different times, but what depends on *God's sovereign constitution*. . . . it appears, that a *divine constitution* is the thing which *makes truth*, in affairs of this nature."[29]

Even from these few scattered excerpts, it is clear that Edwards's understanding of the relationship of God to his creation is rather unusual. Instead of the classical theistic language of God creating the world and then sustaining it in existence as a distinct entity, Edwards conceives of the world as in some sense the inevitable effusion of the divine power. What is more, he thinks that creation is ideal and exists as a set of divine ideas, God being the only true substance. "Here is both an *emanation* and *remanation*," he observes, at the conclusion to *The End of Creation*. "The refulgence shines upon and into the creature, and is reflected back to the luminary. The beams of glory come from God, and are something of God, and are refunded back again to their original. So that the whole is *of God*, and *in* God, and *to* God; and God is the beginning, middle and end in this affair."[30] But matters are more complicated than even this rather exotic picture of the divine-creaturely relation suggests. For his views about the non-persistence of created objects through time have important consequences for his understanding of the nature of created reality. It is this matter to which we turn next.

## Continuous Creation and Occasionalism

We have seen that Edwards's view of the relationship between God and creation was rather unusual and, in important respects, exotic. He espoused a version of idealism, according to which God is the only true substance, strictly speaking, with creatures such as human beings being

---

28. WJE 6:344.
29. WJE 3:403–4. The context of these comments is his discussion of the transmission of original sin from Adam to his progeny in his treatise on *Original Sin*.
30. WJE 8:531. Emphasis in the original.

substances only in some attenuated sense. He thought that all created reality is mind-dependent, specifically, divine mind–dependent. This is Edwards's doctrine of divine ideas, where all that exists apart from God is sustained, as it were, within the divine mind. We are literally ideas God thinks. In this way, Edwards is an immaterial antirealist. What is more, given his commitment to a traditional picture of God as a simple being who is pure act (having no distinction between what he is and what he does), Edwards thought the created order, though distinct from God in some sense, nevertheless exists in God. God is greater than the world. The two are not identical. But the world is radically dependent on God's continuing to think it in order for its ongoing existence.

However, there is a further aspect to Edwards's metaphysical vision that needs to be factored into the overall picture in order to finesse what has been said thus far. For Edwards also thought that the created world is incapable of existing for more than a moment. It cannot persist through time. God does not merely create and then sustain the world in existence. He is continuously creating worlds out of nothing. What we call "the world," meaning by this the created order, which we normally think of as having existed from the first moment at which it was called into existence by divine fiat across vast swathes of time and space until now, is really an infinite number of world-stages. These stages are numerically distinct entities that are segued together in the divine mind. The world appears to subsist according to certain physical laws. Things that happened in the past appear to cause things that happen in the present. Actions seem to occur across time, from one moment to the next. But according to Edwards these things are, strictly speaking, illusory. God is the agent that directly orders these events as he does; indeed, according to Edwards, he "makes truth in this matter." The world as we know it appears to persist through time, but in reality the apparent sequence of things across time is due solely to God's constituting things that way. This is what we may call the Edwardsean continuous creation thesis. In his treatise on *Original Sin*, he says this:

> If the existence of created *substance*, in each successive moment, be wholly the effect of God's immediate power, in *that* moment, without any dependence on prior existence, as much as the first creation out of *nothing*, then what exists at this moment, by his power, is a *new effect*; and simply and absolutely considered, not the same with any past existence, though it be

like it, and follows it according to a certain established method. And there is no identity or oneness in the case, but what depends on the *arbitrary* constitution of the Creator; who by his wise sovereign establishment so unites these successive new effects, that he *treats them as one*, by communicating to them like properties, relations and circumstances; and so leads us to regard and treat them as *one*.[31]

This is the same passage where he makes the claim that "there is no such thing as any identity or oneness in created objects, existing at different times, but what depends on *God's sovereign constitution*," for, as we noted earlier, it appears "that a *divine constitution* is what *makes truth*, in affairs of this nature."[32]

## Understanding Edwards on Continuous Creation

The argument seems to be this: God creates a particular world (that is an entire cosmos—the whole created order). But no creation has the power to persist without the immediate upholding of divine grace. The vast majority of orthodox, classical Christian theologians agree on this much. But they usually go on to say that God does uphold the cosmos from its first moment of existence until now, and will continue to do so until such time as he draws all things together in the consummation of creation at the end of time. On this way of thinking, God is said to conserve the creation in being. It is this doctrine of divine conservation that Edwards denies. He readily grants that the world cannot persist without God's conservation. But he also claims that God does not conserve the world in being after it is created out of nothing. Upon being created the world immediately ceases to exist because no created thing has power in and of itself to continue to exist, and God does not conserve it in existence beyond this first moment of existence.

Why Edwards makes this strong metaphysical claim is something of a puzzle. At least part of the reason is that he was obsessed with pre-

---

31. WJE 3, 402–3. Emphasis added.
32. WJE 3, 404. Emphasis added. These passages in *Original Sin* are discussed at greater length in Oliver D. Crisp, *Jonathan Edwards and the Metaphysics of Sin* (Aldershot: Ashgate, 2005).

serving the absolute sovereignty of God.[33] He appears to have thought that no created thing persists for more than a moment and that God does not conserve anything in being for more than a moment because he is an absolute sovereign.[34] Of course, he also believes all created things are ideal. Once the world God initially creates ceases to exist (the moment after it has been brought into existence), God creates a numerically distinct, but qualitatively identical, world in its place. This second world is almost the same as the previous one, apart from any small, incremental changes God builds into this second world, so that it appears as if action is taking place across time. This second world immediately ceases to exist, to be replaced by a third world. As before, it is numerically distinct from the second world, but qualitatively identical to it, except for those minor incremental changes built into this third world to distinguish it from the previous one, in order to preserve the appearance of change across the three worlds, from the first, through the second, to the third; and so on. Each momentary world God instantiates is an entire state of affairs created *ex nihilo* that is immediately annihilated and replaced by an entirely new world the next moment—one that appears to all intents and purposes to be just like the previous world.

So, Edwards's view entails the denial of one important aspect of a traditional understanding of divine providence. God does not create the world at the first moment of its existence and then preserve the existing world at all those moments after the first moment at which it begins to exist. Rather, God is continuously creating the world. Or, rather, God is continuously creating worlds that are run together in his mind as a series of world-stages across time.

---

33. This can be seen in the first of his youthful "Resolutions," which he vowed to make the basis of his adult spirituality, reading through them every week. The first of these reads as follows: "Resolved, that I will do whatsoever I think to be most to God's glory, and my own good, profit and pleasure, in the whole of my duration, without any consideration of the time, whether now, or never so many myriad's of ages hence. Resolved to do whatever I think to be my duty and most for the good and advantage of mankind in general. Resolved to do this, whatever difficulties I meet with, how many and how great soever." WJE 16:753.

34. However, this may not be the only reason Edwards embraced continuous creation. In "Miscellanies" 1263, to which we shall return presently, he offers the following reasoning. "'Tis nonsense to say he a[cts] upon all mediately, because in so doing w[e] go back *in infinitum* from one thing acting on another without ever coming to a prime, present agent, and yet at the same time suppose God to be such a present agent." WJE 23:201.

These are difficult matters to understand. So, in order to get some idea of what Edwards has in mind, consider the following analogy. The world-stages that are created and annihilated to be replaced by successor worlds that are annihilated in turn, and so on, are rather like the celluloid photographic stills that, taken together, form the photographic reel of a motion picture. When we go to a movie theater, we do not stop to think that the motion picture that we see on the silver screen is really a series of photographic stills run together in the projector room of the cinema and projected over our heads onto the screen in front of us. Yet that is exactly what is happening. Strictly speaking, there is no action that happens across time in a movie. Not only is the moving image itself an illusion (there are, after all, no actors in front of us, only the film recording of them being played back to us). It is also the case that the particular images we see apparently moving in front of our eyes are in fact a series of photographic stills run together.

This is very like (though, for obvious reasons, not exactly the same as) the sort of view Edwards outlines in *Original Sin*. Each world-stage God creates is like a photographic still in a motion picture. They are put together in a series that appear to follow one after another in sequence because the film director has spliced them together in this way, giving the appearance of action across time. When the world-stages are run together on the silver screen of God's mind, as it were, the result is like the illusion of the motion picture in the theater. The motion picture in this instance is the series of world-stages God continuously creates out of nothing and segues together seriatim, so that it appears that action across time obtains according to certain regular physical laws. But, in fact, all this is, strictly speaking, an illusion. God is continuously creating the world (in fact, the worlds—plural) out of nothing, moment by moment. They are run together rather like a motion picture on the silver screen of the divine mind, for all created things are merely ideal, matter being a fiction in Edwards's way of thinking. It transpires that for Edwards you, I, and the whole created universe are actually simply a photographic still in the celluloid-like motion picture of God's purposes in creation, as they are played out like a movie in the divine mind.

## Understanding Edwards on Occasionalism

This is heady stuff. But—as if this were not enough—for Edwards, God is the efficient cause of all that comes to pass; we creatures are merely the occasions of God's action. In which case, God is the only causal agent involved in each of the world stages. He is the director, the photographer, and the one who arranges the actors and their actions in the movie. It is rather like stop-frame animation. No creature brings about any action, strictly speaking, because no creature exists for long enough to bring about a given action. What we think of as causes and effects are, in Edwardsean parlance, merely the occasion of God's action. So not only is it true for Edwards that God continuously creates. He is also the only efficient cause of all that comes to pass. This is his doctrine of occasionalism. Edwards does not join up the dots between his occasionalism and his continuous creation thesis in quite the way we might like. But it is clear that he is committed to this sort of view. He thinks that the world is being continuously created (as we have already seen in his treatise *Original Sin*). But he also maintains that the mundane cause of things, like the cause of my writing these words, is God; I am merely the occasion of this divine action.

This commitment to an occasionalist account of causation can be found scattered in his writings from fairly early on in his career to its end. For instance, in "Miscellanies," entry 267, an early entry in that notebook, Edwards implies a connection between continuous creation and something like a doctrine of occasional causation: "the mere exertion of a new thought is a certain proof of a God. For certainly there is something that immediately produces and upholds that thought; here is a new thing, and there is a necessity of a cause. It is not antecedent thoughts, for they are vanished and gone; they are past, and what is past is not."[35] Further

---

35. WJE 13, 373. William Wainwright notes that Edwards explicitly distinguishes between "real" and mundane causes in places like WJE 6:350 and WJE 3:400. Real causes actually bring about their effects; mundane or ordinary causes do not, for they are spatially and/or temporally distinct from their effects. What is more, if mundane causes were sufficient to produce their effects, then God's activity would be redundant. "God alone, then, is the only real cause," he writes. "Vulgar [or mundane] causes (e.g., heating water) are simply the occasions upon which God produces effects (e.g., the water's boiling) according to 'methods and laws' which express his customary manner of acting." Wainwright, "Jonathan Edwards," §2.2, in the *Stanford Encyclopedia of Philosophy*, located at www.plato.stanford .edu (last accessed October 5, 2011). Philip Quinn gives a critical account of Edwardsean

evidence can be adduced from his short work *Some Thoughts Concerning the Revival*, published in 1743, mid-career. There he says this:

> They that are studied in logic have learned that the nature of the cause is not to be judged of by the nature of the effect, nor the nature of the effect from the nature of the cause, when the cause is only *causa sine qua non*, or an occasional cause; yea, that in such a case, oftentimes the nature of the effect is quite contrary to the nature of the cause.[36]

Similar views are expressed in his treatise *Freedom of the Will*, which was published at the end of his life. There he denies that a cause is ontologically more than an occasion. "Therefore I sometimes use the word 'cause,' in this inquiry, to signify . . . any antecedent with which a consequent event is so connected, that it truly belongs to the reason why the proposition which affirms that event is true." However, the relation between the causal antecedent and its consequent "is perhaps rather an occasion than a cause, most properly speaking."[37]

## Consequences of the Edwardsean Picture

As already mentioned, Edwards thought that his espousal of continuous creation and occasionalism was important because it preserved divine sovereignty. In fact, he thought that Scripture warranted these rather extreme metaphysical views. But few Christian theologians have been willing to follow him in this regard, not least because a consequence of Edwards's view seems to be that no created being is a moral agent, strictly speaking. For his position seems to require that no creaturely agents persist through time long enough to bring about any action for which they can be morally responsible. And even if they did persist for long enough, Edwards thinks that God is the only real causal agent. So

occasionalism in "Divine Conservation, Secondary Causes, and Occasionalism" in *Divine and Human Action*, ed. Thomas V. Morris (Ithaca: Cornell University Press, 1988), 50–73. See also Quinn, "Divine Conservation, Continuous Creation, and Human Action," in *The Existence and Nature of God*, ed. Alfred J. Freddoso (Notre Dame: University of Notre Dame Press, 1983), 55–79.

36. WJE 4:316.
37. WJE 1:180–81.

God alone is the one bringing about all that obtains in the created order. We just appear to be the causes of our own actions, the stop-frame clay models God animates, giving the appearance of agency across time. Though Edwards's desire to uphold divine sovereignty is laudable, even the most sympathetic of his admirers would be forgiven for thinking that this particular consequence of his view is a step too far. For it is very difficult indeed to see how, on the Edwardsean view, God can fail to be the agent both causally and morally responsible for everything, including evil. The corollary of this is just as unpalatable: the Edwardsean position denies real causal agency to creatures, including human creatures. It also requires a deeply counterintuitive conception of the relationship between creature and Creator, according to which no creature persists for more than a moment.[38]

It is perhaps because of these unpalatable consequences that some Edwards scholars have denied he really did espouse both continuous creation and occasionalism. Sang Lee thinks that Edwards's position is that the created order exists virtually in the divine mind as a set of dispositions and habits (i.e., dispositional properties) that God actualizes moment by moment according to a set of laws God prescribes for the created order. On this way of thinking, God's relation to the world is rather like that between the sun and the rays of sunlight emanating from it (a metaphor beloved of Edwards). God is constantly emanating his ideas of the creation outwards from himself, moment by moment, such that the created order is constantly moving from a virtual state (as a set of dispositions in God's mind) to actuality. Lee puts it like this:

> It is God who constantly preserves the established general laws and causes actual existences according to those laws. But it is not a continual *creatio ex nihilo* in a simple sense. The divinely established general laws are given a permanence, and are in a sense not created ex nihilo every moment. Edwards' view is an

---

38. Jonathan Kvanvig thinks that occasionalism includes a doctrine of conservation. He writes, "according to occasionalism, the doctrine of conservation is simply the result of generalizing the temporal account of initial creation to every moment of time, so that God is solely responsible not only for the coming into being of every contingent thing but also for every feature of every contingent thing." But this does not sound very much like a doctrine of conservation to me—at least, not as I have characterized the doctrine here. See his essay "Creation and Conservation," *Stanford Encyclopedia of Philosophy*, located at http://plato.stanford.edu/ (last accessed October 5, 2011).

occasionalism only in the sense that God moves the world from virtuality to full actuality every moment through an immediate exercise of his power. Edwards' view is not an unqualified occasionalist position, however, since the world has an abiding reality in a virtual mode.[39]

Lee's is a rather different approach to Edwards's metaphysics, as is reflected in this passage. I have argued that the combination of continuous creation and occasionalism is fundamental to Edwards's thought. But there is some evidence that would appear to count in Lee's favor. The most important example is Edwards's "Miscellanies," entry 1263, where he seems to admit that there are laws established by God by means of which the world is governed. These laws determine the shape of the world from moment to moment, and, on Lee's interpretation, give reason for thinking that Edwards is committed to this "virtual existence" of the world as it emanates at each moment from the sun of God's being.

Edwards sets up his discussion in this "Miscellanies" entry with an eye firmly fixed upon the deists. These freethinkers were happy to grant that the Deity governs the orderly cosmos, but they believed that this was brought about by God setting up the universe in its initial conditions such that certain physical constants, such as natural laws, would obtain, setting boundaries to the sort of natural operations that would exist thereafter. In other words, the deists maintained that God set the world in motion, including within it the physical constants necessary for the world to exist in the ordered manner that it does. As Edwards puts it, although "men of learning" are "compelled" to accede to such reasoning, many among them "are averse to allow that God acts any otherwise than as limiting himself by such invariable laws, fixed from the beginning of the creation, when he precisely marked out and determined the rules and paths of all his future operations, and that he never departs from those paths."[40] Such thinkers can admit God now works according to laws of nature. But they deny that God now works via what Edwards calls arbitrary operations, that is, immediate, unmediated divine action in the creation.

---

39. Lee, *The Philosophical Theology of Jonathan Edwards*, 63. See also Stephen Daniel, "Edwards' Occasionalism," in *Jonathan Edwards as Contemporary: Essays in Honor of Sang Hyun Lee*, ed. Don Schweitzer (New York: Peter Lang, 2010), 1–14, and Anri Morimoto, *Jonathan Edwards and the Catholic View of Salvation* (University Park: Pennsylvania State University Press, 1995), 56–59.

40. WJE 23:202.

In place of such deist thinking, Edwards posits two sorts of operations in the creation. The first is the arbitrary operation of God by direct and unmediated divine fiat. The second is a natural or mundane operation, whereby God brings about certain events in the created order via the laws of nature he has created.[41] It is clear that he thinks divine arbitrary operations the more fundamental. He even goes as far as to say that mundane operations must be finally resolved into arbitrary ones:

> Of the two kinds of divine operation, viz. that which is arbitrary and that which is limited by fixed laws, the former, viz. arbitrary, is the first and foundation of the other, and that which all divine operation must finally be resolved into, and which all events and divine effects whatsoever primarily depend upon. Even the fixing of the method and rules of the other kind of operation is an instance of arbitrary operation.[42]

But, though he is happy in this "Miscellanies" entry to speak in terms of natural operations, nothing he says here is inconsistent with his stated commitment to continuous creation and occasionalism. The natural operations are merely what we might think of as a framework of natural laws existing in the divine mind, according to which God fashions each world-stage so as to preserve the appearance of continuity between different stages. Just as the different stills in a motion picture display similar laws, things moving in an orderly fashion as one frame succeeds another, so God acts in such a way that his natural operations have the appearance of nomological consistency across different world-stages. For example, it would be bizarre if God created one world-stage with gravity and the next without. Such action would hardly be a fitting or suitable way for God to conduct his work, for there would be no physical order from one moment to the next. A creation that appears to be regular and orderly, though strictly speaking it is not a single entity as such but a series of world-stages lined up in a sequence determined entirely by divine fiat, would constitute a much more fitting arrangement by means

41. "When I speak of arbitrary operation, I don't mean arbitrary in opposition to an operation directed by wisdom, but in opposition to an operation confined to and limited by those fixed establishments and laws commonly called the laws of nature. The one of these I shall therefore, for want of better phrases, call *a natural operation*; the other, *an arbitrary operation*." WJE 23:202. Emphasis in the original.

42. WJE 23:202.

of which God may bring glory to himself. It is such an arrangement that Edwards opts for in this "Miscellanies" entry.[43] And such an arrangement is just what we find reflected in *Original Sin*, as we have already noted.

## Divine Determinism

The final aspect of Edwards's metaphysics we will consider here is his view of free will. Recent work in the thought of a number of post-Reformation Reformed theologians has suggested that, contrary to popular belief, many of these thinkers were not committed to a species of divine determinism that thins out human freedom.[44] Among other things, Calvinism is often thought to entail several claims. The first is that God ordains all things according to his good pleasure and will (in accordance with Eph. 1:4). The second is that human freedom is just the freedom to act in accordance with one's desires, which is consistent with God ordaining—that is determining, predestining—all that comes to pass. In this way of thinking, the human person is free provided she acts in accordance with her desires, where those desires are not frustrated, impeded, or otherwise overridden by another agent (e.g., another human, or God). This is usually called theological compatibilism because it entails a conception of human freedom that is compatible with the idea that God determines all that comes to pass.

However, on this revisionist account of the Reformed tradition, such compatibilism is somewhat wide of the mark. Instead, it is argued, many of the Reformed orthodox, that is, theologians who developed the scholastic method for Reformed theology, held that the act of making a free choice for which an individual is morally responsible involves what is called a synchronic contingency. This idea, culled from the medieval theology of John Duns Scotus, is that "for one moment of time, there is a true alternative for the state of affairs that actually occurs." Moreover, "only this

---

43. This is argued in greater detail in Crisp, *Jonathan Edwards on God and Creation*.

44. See Willem J. van Asselt, J. Martin Bac, and Roelf T. te Velde, eds., *Reformed Thought on Freedom: The Concept of Free Choice in Early Modern Reformed Thought* (Grand Rapids: Baker Academic, 2010); Oliver D. Crisp, *Deviant Calvinism: Expanding the Reformed Tradition* (Minneapolis: Fortress, 2014); Crisp, *Jonathan Edwards among the Theologians*, ch. 5; and Richard A. Muller, *Divine Will and Human Choice: Freedom, Contingency, and Necessity in Early Modern Reformed Thought* (Grand Rapids: Baker Academic, 2017).

synchronic contingency can account for real freedom of choice, both on God's part and on our part." The reason being that "without synchronic contingency there is no structural alternativity in reality, so neither can there be alternativity in acting, which is a requirement for freedom."[45] But in this way of thinking, an action can be free and an act for which the agent is morally responsible only if at the moment of choice the agent could have availed herself or himself of the alternative state of affairs. That is, Smith is free and morally responsible for choosing to hit Jones only if she could have refrained from hitting Jones at the moment of choice. If she could see that not hitting Jones would be a good thing, but was unable to bring this state of affairs about through her own choice (because, say, she had been psychologically programmed to hit Jones), then her action is not truly free and her moral responsibility is diminished accordingly. It looks as if synchronic contingency requires the presence of an alternate state of affairs to which the moral agent has access at the moment of choice. Smith must be able to hit Jones, or to not hit Jones, at the moment of choice; and that choice cannot be one that is predetermined by God or other factors if it is to be a truly free, morally responsible choice.

But Edwards denies synchronic contingency. He thinks that the sort of philosophical view in which synchronic contingency might be embedded is not merely a false account of the freedom of moral agents but is incoherent. His treatise *Freedom of the Will* is a massive attempt to refute the claim that one must be free in the sense required by synchronic contingency if one is to be morally responsible for one's actions. Edwards sets his discussion up as a refutation of what he calls "Arminianism." But this is not so much the historic theological position as it is a label for various freethinkers who deny that God's ordination of all things is consistent with his determining what comes to pass. The main point of contention is moral responsibility. The issue is what sort of freedom of will is required in order for a person to be held morally responsible for her or his action.

According to Edwards, the "Arminians" believe that I am really free, and morally responsible for my volition, only if I have a choice to do something other than I do at the point of choosing and that choice is uncaused by God or anything else. Edwards denies all this. He claims that a person always chooses according to the strongest desire at the moment of choice, which is consistent with being determined to act in this way by God. The idea that at the moment of choice a person is in a state of

45. Asselt et al., *Reformed Thought on Freedom*, 41.

moral equilibrium, having nothing that predisposes the person to choose one option rather than another, is, according to Edwards, incoherent. If it were true then no one would ever make a free choice because there would be nothing to dispose one to choose one thing rather than another. In place of this, Edwards proposes that we choose on the basis of strongest desire, choosing what seems the greatest apparent good at the moment of choice. Having alternate possibilities before us is not a requirement for a free action in Edwards's way of thinking because free will is just the ability to choose according to our strongest desires at the moment of choice. He does think that a person would have been able to do the course of action not chosen if she or he had chosen to do so; it is just that she or he has not chosen to do so. And this, he maintains, is all we mean by free will.

For Edwards this picture of free will generalizes to God as well as to creatures. For this reason, he thinks that God acts as he does in creating the world because he chooses to do so, acting according to his strongest desire (his desire to create a world). His essential creativity is a feature of his freely choosing to act as he does, but by this Edwards just means that God acts according to the moral necessity of his nature. He must act in this way because he is constituted, as it were, to act in a creative way. Yet this is a free action because God chooses according to his strongest desire, and he would have been able to do some alternative course of action if he had chosen to do so. Thus, Edwards's views about free will dovetail with his views about the necessity of creation, which we encountered earlier in the chapter.[46]

## The Upshot

We have covered a lot of ground in these last two chapters, much of which may be unfamiliar to some readers. It might be helpful to pause before continuing on to the consideration of some of the main issues in Edwards's theology to reflect on what we have considered thus far.

---

46. For further discussion of this matter, see Crisp, *Jonathan Edwards on God and Creation*; William Rowe, *Can God Be Free?* (Oxford: Oxford University Press, 2004), ch. 4; and William Wainwright, "Jonathan Edwards, William Rowe, and the Necessity of Creation," in *Faith, Freedom, and Responsibility*, ed. Jeff Jordan and Daniel Howard-Snyder (Lanham, MD: Rowman and Littlefield, 1996), ch. 9. As noted previously, in this respect the views expressed here and earlier in expounding my own position on the necessity of creation are rather different from those of several other Edwards interpreters, including Kyle Strobel.

First, we have seen that Edwards is an idealist, rather like Bishop George Berkeley. He denies that there is any such thing as a material world: the only things that exist are minds and their ideas. God is the one true substance, in the final analysis. But humans and other creatures are substances in some attenuated sense. Nevertheless, all created things exist in the mind of God as a set of stable divine ideas.

Second, Edwards holds the traditional notion, found in much medieval theology, that God is a perfect being and is both simple (without composition) and a pure act (having no distinction between his being and his action). God is also timeless. He thinks that the created order is radically dependent on its Creator, though it is the necessary product or overflow of the essential creativity of God. Not only is God so constituted that he must create a world, according to Edwards. He must create *this* world, which Edwards takes to be the best possible world, all things considered. This does not mean there are not other possible worlds God could have created. Although Edwards thinks God could have created other worlds than the actual world had he so desired, he maintains that it is morally impossible for God to have chosen to create a world other than the one he did create.

Third, we have seen that Edwards holds to the doctrine of continuous creation coupled with occasionalism. This means that the world is shorthand for that four-dimensional entity that persists through time by virtue of different world stages that God creates moment by moment, and that are annihilated, to be replaced by numerically distinct world-stages that are qualitatively identical to the previous stage, with incremental changes being built into them, so as to give the appearance of change across time. Strictly speaking, no created thing persists through time if by "persists through time" we mean "is numerically identical from one moment to the next over time." Edwards maintains that the world is really a series of momentary stages held together in the particular sequence they are in by the divine mind, in which they subsist. As if that were not enough, Edwards also claims that God is the sole causal agent of all that comes to pass. This is his occasionalism: we creatures are merely the occasions of God's action. When I will to raise my hand, it is God that causes it to obtain, not me. But this implies God is the cause of all that takes place, including evil.

Fourth, we have seen that Edwards is a theological determinist. It is not merely that he thinks there is no effect that is uncaused. He thinks it is impossible for there to be an effect without a cause or causes sufficient for the bringing about of that thing. This applies to God as well as creatures.

God is self-determined, according to Edwards. He is not determined in his actions by anything outside himself because he is independent of all created things and is not subject to them. Nevertheless, God is constrained to act as he does by his perfect nature. This constraint (if we may speak of it as such) means that God desires to act in a certain way, the way he does act. Although he was free to act in a way different from the course of action he did perform, God's nature is such that he is morally incapable of so acting. A similar distinction between moral and natural necessity is at work in Edwards's understanding of human acts of will. We are determined by God to do the things we do. But this is consistent with our having freedom, provided that means something like "acting in accordance with our strongest desires." These desires are constrained by the moral natures we have such that we are incapable of acting other than we do in many actions for which we are morally responsible as creatures. A paradigm of this sort of thing is conversion. Edwards thinks that there is no natural impediment to a fallen human being turning to God for salvation. But such humans are morally constrained by their turpitude and addiction to sin so that they will never turn to God without divine grace. In fact, for Edwards, this amounts to a moral necessity. It is necessarily the case that you and I will never turn to God independent of divine grace because of the corruptions of our human natures attendant upon original sin.

It should be clear from this chapter that Edwards was, as has sometimes been alleged, a "God intoxicated theist." He was so committed to the absolute sovereignty of God over all that God has created that he went to great lengths to preserve that sovereignty in the face of what he would have thought of as potential avenues by means of which God's exalted status might be eroded or undermined by his creatures. But the cost of Edwards's vision of God is that human agency appears to be a very meagre thing indeed, and God appears to be morally responsible for sin. For although he speaks of human moral responsibility in *Freedom of the Will*, from his other works it is clear that no creature persists from one moment to the next in order to perform any of the actions he imputes to them. Created persons are just conglomerations of instantaneous stages aggregated across time. It is very difficult to see how one can salvage a robust account of creaturely moral responsibility from a view like that. For it means that no creature exists long enough to be able to complete an action for which the creature may be held morally responsible—a matter to which we shall return in the final chapter.

# CHAPTER FIVE

# The Atonement

The big picture of Edwards's soteriology is organized around God's movement in the Son and Spirit to call his people into his own life. The actual mechanics for how God's redemptive activity works is addressed in the doctrine of the atonement. God's redemptive work as a whole centers around the Son's descent into humanity and his work on the cross—with the latter being the proper focus of his atoning work. The sending of the Son and the Spirit is an act of the divine wisdom, which leads to a specific kind of redemptive activity that honors God, addresses the depths of sin, and allows for redemption to be purchased without somehow compromising divine justice. Edwards recognizes how easy it is to ignore one of these facets of redemption, improperly reducing God's work in one direction or another. Therefore, the main focus of his account is on the nature of God (that is, how God could accept creatures who reject him), which triggers his characteristic focus on the Son and Spirit, before turning to issues concerning justice, honor, and satisfaction.

In Edwards's *History of Redemption* the centrality of Christ's redemptive work is emphasized as the great hinge of all of history:

> We have observed that all [things] that had been done before were only preparatory for what was done now, and it may also be observed that all that was done before the beginning of time in the eternal counsels of God, and that eternal transaction there was between the persons of the Trinity, chiefly respect this period.[1]

1. WJE 9:294.

Edwards asserts that, from the morning that Christ opened his eyes as a newborn infant to his first resurrected breath, everything he accomplished was for redemption.[2] This does not render the ascension meaningless; indeed it was in that movement of the Son to the Father that believers are made partakers of Christ's righteousness.[3] Nevertheless, while Christ's earthly ministry is the center of redemption history, it is not alone sufficient to account for Christ's work. Behind this ministry—fueling it—are the triune life and divine decrees. What we discover in those decrees is that Christ has "substituted himself in their [the elect's] stead *from eternity*."[4] This eternal backdrop exposes the work of redemption as a relational one between the Father, the Son, and the elect, flowing out of the *pactum salutis* (the pre-temporal covenant of redemption).[5] In light of this, Christ is now known as "the elect."[6] Christ is, "as it were, the first elect and the head of election."[7] Furthermore, "the man Christ Jesus is to be considered as the first of the elect, the head of the elect body, the foundation of the whole building,"[8] and in election "believers were from all eternity given to Jesus Christ. As believers were chosen from all eternity, so Christ was from eternity chosen and appointed to be their redeemer, and he undertook the work of redeeming them."[9] Scripture points us to the eternal depths of Christ's ministry, and so Edwards keeps these things in view as he considers the atoning work of Christ.

Building upon Edwards's notion of the Son's election, we first exposit his doctrine of atonement in connection with his discussion of God's love and wisdom. We shall see that the love and wisdom of God

---

2. WJE 9:295.

3. WJE 14:392.

4. WJE 18:451. Emphasis added.

5. Steve Holmes argues that "Edwards' concern . . . is to argue for the rationality of the atonement in personal terms. Perhaps the key point here is that it is not abstract 'Justice' or even 'Goodness' that must be satisfied, but that, for Edwards, what goes on in the life, death and resurrection of Christ must make sense as a relational event between Christ, His Father, and the elect." Stephen R. Holmes, *God of Grace and God of Glory: An Account of the Theology of Jonathan Edwards* (Edinburgh: T&T Clark, 2000), 146.

6. Jonathan Edwards, "The Wisdom of God, as display'd in the Way of Salvation by Jesus Christ, far Superior to the Wisdom of the Angels," in *The Life and Character of the Late Reverend Mr. Jonathan Edwards*, ed. Samuel Hopkins (Boston, 1765), 170.

7. WJE 23:180.

8. WJE 23:180.

9. WJE 17:282.

serve as the theological foundation upon which Edwards constructed his atonement doctrine—a view he never really articulated in a systematic fashion. From this point, we will attempt to describe how Edwards's developing thought offers a specific mechanism of the atonement and what it means that God has atoned in the way Edwards articulates.

## Atoning Love

Contrary to popular caricatures of Edwards's theology, which focus almost solely on divine wrath, what we discover instead is that God's love is the impetus for Edwards's understanding of salvation. "Everything that was contrived and done for the redemption and salvation of believers, and every benefit they have by it," Edwards avers, "is wholly and perfectly from the free, eternal, distinguishing love and infinite grace of Christ towards them."[10] Christ has loved his people from eternity. All of God's economic activity is done with redemption in mind, which means that creation is subsumed under the work of redemption (which is itself subsumed under the Father's eternal love of the Son).[11] It is because of the Father's infinite love for the Son that the elect are accepted by God, having been purchased by the Son's own love for the elect: "Because of the infinite worthiness and excellency of Christ and his dearness to the Father, the Father is willing for his sake to accept of those that have deserved infinite ill at his hands."[12]

In the eternal covenant of redemption, the Son covenants with the Father to give himself to his people in love. The incarnation is the embodiment of that love. Edwards boldly declares that "by the incarnation [God] is really become passionate to his own, so that he loves them with such a sort of love as we have. . . . Now this passionate love of Christ, by virtue of the union with the divine nature, is in a sort infinite."[13] Robert Jenson responds to this proclamation by claiming that the idea "that God, as incarnate, is *passionate* in the very way we are passionate is the heart of what theology has rarely dared say about him;

10. WJE 24:617.
11. Phillip Hussey has a helpful articulation of the ordering of these realities in his article "Jesus Christ as the 'Sum of God's Decrees': Christological Supralapsarianism in the Theology of Jonathan Edwards," *Jonathan Edwards Studies* 6 (2016).
12. WJE 13:524.
13. WJE 13:176–77.

Edwards just goes ahead and does it."[14] In light of our discussion about God's internal life, it is important to notice the affective dimension in this proclamation. The incarnation was an act of passion—an act of affection—and as such, entails an overflow of God's affectionate life within a creaturely register.[15]

The beloved Son of the Father, who has the love of God without measure, pours forth this love to his people. Ultimately, as we will see more completely below, the atoning suffering of Christ is regarded as the elect's because of their union with him. Christ is so united with the elect, in fact, that they are "justly looked upon as the same."[16] As Edwards goes on to explain, "Now there is no other way of different spirits' being thus united, but by love."[17] This love is a thorough love, a love in which the lover is willing to put himself in his lover's stead in all concerns (Christ passionately loved his people as his own).[18] This union, of course, is the work of God's Spirit, the overflowing and uniting love of God's own life. It is the Spirit that unites the Son to himself and to the elect. As Edwards explains,

> And if his [God's] love to the suffering person [Jesus] be heavy enough to counterpoise his anger to the offending [sinners], yet it will not counterpoise it unless it be laid in the balance with it to counterpoise it, unless it be put in the opposite scale; which it is not, unless the suffering person suffers for the sake of the offending and out of mere love to him, or unless his love be great enough to put him in the place of the offender.[19]

14. Robert Jenson, "Christology," in *The Princeton Companion to Jonathan Edwards*, ed. Sang Hyun Lee (Princeton: Princeton University Press, 2005), 79.

15. It is important to note that this construction is not inconsistent with the account of God's pure act that was developed above, at least not on Edwards's terms. His use of the word "passion" may be a bit loose, but it seems most likely that Edwards is locating Christ's movement toward the creature in affection, and he is doing so through the use of erotic terminology (not outside the bounds of the bridegroom imagery Edwards is fond of).

16. WJE 13:463.

17. WJE 13:463.

18. WJE 13:463, 525.

19. WJE 13:464. Edwards emphasizes the intention and inner state of Christ when he talks about the atonement. Not only did Christ have to suffer for the sake of sinners specifically, out of mere love to them, but Edwards also notes that Christ knew "that God was not angry with him personally, knew that God did not hate him, but infinitely loved him." WJE 20:329.

It is not enough that Christ suffers and dies; he must suffer and die out of a dual love: love to his Father and love to the offender.

> Now the foundation of the propriety of this imputation of righteousness seems to lie in these two things: in Christ's union with God, and his union with men. It would not be proper that the righteousness of any person should be accepted by God for another, but a person that was one with God; nor would it [be] proper that it should be accepted for any person, but only a person that he is one with.[20]

In other words, Christ must embody for humanity the love of God and love of neighbor. Edwards gives a precise analysis of this dual love in an attempt to justify how a holy God could allow himself to accept sinners into his own life. He spent the most significant space musing about these issues later in his life, and, at face value, took a new direction (or, if nothing else, utilized new imagery not used previously). But while the imagery is new, closer examination reveals that these musings follow the same trajectory he had traced from the beginning, namely, that "everything that was contrived and done for the redemption and salvation of believers, and every benefit they have by it, is wholly and perfectly from the free, eternal, distinguishing love and infinite grace of Christ towards them."[21] God has moved toward his people in love, and this is the underlying reality of Edwards's understanding of the atonement.

## Relations of Love as the Foundation of the Atonement

To advance his account, Edwards turns to the imagery of a patron, a friend of the patron, and a client: Jesus, God the Father, and the believer, respectively. To articulate this model, Edwards utilizes the category of merit.[22]

20. WJE 14:401. In this sense, imputation is simply a gloss on union. Imputation is a notion in Edwards's theology that simply explains what is meant by union. The term "imputation" simply calls out that by being one with Christ, what he has (i.e., righteousness) is given over and what you have (i.e., debt) is taken on by Christ.

21. WJE 24.1:617.

22. Edwards defines merit as "anything whatsoever in any person or being, or about him or belonging to him, which, appearing in the view of another, is a recommendation of him to that other's regard, esteem or affection." In WJE 23:486.

The key question in this scheme concerns how the patron (Jesus) covers the lack of merit in his client (believers), while still maintaining his relationship with his friend (Father).[23] For this relationship to work, the patron must have an abundance of merit, enough to cover the client's lack. Edwards explains, "'Tis not unreasonable, or against nature, or without foundation in the reason and nature of things, that respect should be shown to one on account of his relation to or union and connection with another."[24] The believer's relation with Christ and union with Christ are one in the love of the Spirit. The focus, here, concerns how union can ground respect. To keep in mind the difficulty, we need to know that, for Edwards, sin against God is an infinite transgression. The believer has lost all that makes her or him moral, holy, or good. How can Christ maintain his relationship with his Father if he receives *these people* into life with himself? To use imagery closer to Edwards's own idiom, how can the Father and Son maintain their intimate union in the event that the Son takes a prostitute as his wife? How can she be accepted into the Father-Son relationship?

In order to explain the logic of redemption, Edwards makes several assertions. First, he points out that just any old union will not do. Jesus's ability to vouch for his client—while still being accepted by the Father—depends upon the greatness of the union between Jesus and his elect people.[25] How strong must this union be between Christ and the elect in order for the Father to accept them? Edwards claims that Jesus's "heart is so united to the client that, when the client is destroyed, he from love is willing to take his destruction on himself."[26] Jesus's love is the main feature of this image, not only because Jesus loves his creatures enough to take their destruction upon himself, but also because the union between them *is* Christ's love to them. Because of the strength of this union of love, the believer's interest is Jesus's own. The believer's plight is now Jesus's plight because he has given himself so fully to the believer.[27] Second, and building on the first assertion, Edwards turns to the nature of Christ's

23. Edwards defines patron as "a person of superior dignity or merit that stands for and espouses the interest of another"—the other being the "client," whom Edwards defines as the person "whose interest the patron thus espouses, and in this manner endeavours to maintain and promote." In WJE 23:486–87.

24. WJE 23:487.

25. WJE 23:488.

26. WJE 23:488.

27. "By his own act he places his interest in the interest of the other, and so substitutes himself in the other's stead as to the affair of interest or welfare." WJE 23:489.

atoning work specifically, noting that the atonement does not simply involve paying off a debt out of his abundance (which is true); it also entails Jesus's personal suffering for the interest of the believer.[28]

Edwards's concerns can be easily detected. The apparent dilemma is this: the patron must remain friendly with his friend, but taking on a client that reeks of sin and vice may shatter the patron-friend relationship. This concern is especially important in a soteriology of participation. There are two things that need to be intact when a patron is united to an offending and unworthy client, namely, his regard for his friend (in this case, God the Father) and his regard for virtue or holiness ("For in these two things consists his merit in the eyes of his friend").[29] Edwards turns his attention, for the moment, away from God's people and focuses on Jesus's identity in relation to the Father. Christ's perfect relationship with his Father is the ground and, for Edwards, the reality of salvation. But it is not only Christ's standing before the Father, but also his standing before the blindfolded justice of virtue that is necessary for the salvation of sinful creatures. Christ must be infinitely worthy in his own life in order to secure salvation for the elect. To accept someone unsavory, the patron must be truly great, and the friend of the patron must have the deepest regard for him.[30] If the Father has a great degree of regard for Jesus's dignity, then "there is a sufficiency to countervail all the favour that the client needs."[31] In this circumstance, the lover must be willing to part with his own welfare for the sake of the beloved.[32] Jesus must regard the believer's welfare as his own and must love the believer to such a degree that it is a part of his self-love. As with all persons, Jesus's love internalizes the believer into his own self-love (something we address in chapter six). Jesus's love to himself, and, in this sense, the Father's love to him, must now include the believer.[33] "Christ loves the elect with so great and strong a love, they are so near to him, that God looks upon them as it were as parts of him."[34]

---

28. Importantly, the transaction does not only include the patron getting the client out of debt, but imputing merit as well. "It is peculiarly natural to accept the client on the account of the merit of the patron. For the merit is on his account, has its existence for the sake of the client." WJE 23:490.

29. WJE 23:491.

30. WJE 23:713.

31. WJE 23:713.

32. WJE 23:715.

33. "The love, therefore, is sufficient and equal to self-love." WJE 23:716.

34. WJE 14:403.

Now if it be inquired how much love is sufficient for that, I answer, that if Christ loves men so that when they are to be destroyed, he out of mere love is willing to take their destruction upon himself—or what is equivalent to their destruction—then is Christ's love sufficient in God's account to make them one, for this reason, because when it is so, his love is such as does as it were of itself put the love in the beloved's stead, even to the utmost and the most extreme case. That love that makes the lover willing to be in the stead of the beloved, even in the last extremity and where the beloved's utmost is concerned, even to perfect ruin and destruction, such love makes a thorough union.[35]

For Edwards's redemptive reasoning to work, the patron and client must be united together in an act of faith and love.[36] But the patron and the friend—Jesus and the Father, respectively—must be united to provide the foundation for Jesus to act on behalf of his people. Jesus can save his people, not only because he shares the nature and love of the Father, but also because he shares the nature of the saints and has loved them into union with himself (recalling that this union is in the Spirit of love).

If it be inquired how great a love it ought to be, in order to their being accepted for his sake, I answer: the love should be so great as to be justly looked upon [as] a thorough union with them, so great that Christ may be justly looked upon as making himself one with them, *such a love as is thoroughly assuming them into union with himself.*[37]

Furthermore, because Jesus has taken on the sinners' cause as his own, suffering all that was needed for their full redemption, they can know true salvation in him. The role of the clients, simply enough, is to be clients—to cleave to Christ and trust that he, their patron, will do all that is needed in recommending them to the Father. It is here that Edwards's patron-client imagery gives way to his prior and more fundamental metaphor for the relation of the elect to Christ—that of bride and groom. The uniting of faith

---

35. WJE 14:403–4.
36. WJE 23:716.
37. WJE 13:524–25. Emphasis added.

is the uniting of marriage, not only between the church and Christ, but also between the individual soul and Christ. In this union, the bridegroom has made his bride's interest his own. In this marriage, not only has her incredible debt been cast away, but she has also received Christ's merit as her own (i.e., double imputation). In this she is ushered into the household of God and shares Christ's standing before the Father. What grounds this atoning work, from beginning to end, is love. Put another way, the logic of the atonement is discovered in love-in-relation; the atonement works because of the love that the Father and Son share, as well as the love that Christ has for his people. This point does not yet explain the mechanism of the atonement; nevertheless, whatever else Edwards says about the atonement should be interpreted through the lens of this particular insight.

## Atoning Wisdom[38]

Whereas the assumptions of Edwards's position are grounded in divine love, the structure of his account is determined by the divine wisdom. The divine wisdom determines how the work of redemption should be accomplished.

> It hardly carries a right idea with it, to say that God is obliged in justice to punish sin. 'Tis a mere act of justice to punish sin; yet if he did not punish it nobody could charge God with any wrong. It seems to me to exhibit the thing more properly to say that God is obliged in holiness and in wisdom to punish sin. It would not be a prudent, decent and beautiful thing for a being of infinite glory and majesty, and the sovereign of the world, to let an infinite evil go unpunished. And as God's nature inclines him [to] order all things beautifully, properly and decently, so it was necessary that sin should be punished.[39]

Whereas the Son's love for the creature was the focus of the last section, here the focus is on the Son as wisdom. Once again, the cosmic

38. Aspects of this section were developed in a chapter cowritten with Adam J. Johnson entitled, "Atoning Wisdom: The Wisdom of God in the Way of Salvation," in *Locating Atonement: Explorations in Constructive Dogmatics*, ed. Oliver D. Crisp and Fred Sanders (Grand Rapids: Zondervan, 2015), 89–100.

39. WJE 13:391.

dimensions of Edwards's Christology are on the surface. Edwards knows that "from him [Christ] and through him and to him are all things" (Rom. 11:36), and that "by him all things were created" (Col. 1:16), but his detailed exegetical eye also discerns that Jesus is the wisdom of God (1 Cor. 1:30; compare also Matt. 23:34 with Luke 11:49). Edwards narrates a summary of his doctrine in this manner:

> But yet the wisdom of God has truly accomplished each of these things. He has accomplished, that though men are sinners, yet they should be without guilt, in that he has found out a way that the threatenings of the law should truly and properly be fulfilled, and punishment be executed on sin, and yet not on the sinner. The sufferings of Christ do answer the demands of the law, with respect to the sins of those who believe in Christ; and justice is truly fulfilled and satisfied thereby. And the law is fulfilled and answered by the obedience of Christ, so that his righteousness should properly be our righteousness. Though not performed by us, yet it is properly and reasonably accepted for us, as much as if we had performed it ourselves. Divine wisdom has so contrived, that such an interchanging of sin and righteousness should be consistent, and most agreeable with reason, with the law, and his own holy attributes. And that because Jesus Christ has so united himself to us, and us to him, as to make himself ours—to make himself our head. He has united himself to the elect by his dying love. The love of Christ to the elect is so great, that God the Father looks upon it proper and suitable to account Christ and the elect as one; and accordingly to account what Christ does and suffers, as if they did and suffered it.[40]

The notion of wisdom is important here. According to Edwards, human wisdom could never have conceived such a salvation. Thus, he believes that his understanding of the atonement upholds all of God's attributes as glorified and honored—along with the law of God—while allowing for the paradox that an elect creature's sin only glorifies God more greatly.[41]

40. Edwards, "The Wisdom of God," 211–12.
41. Edwards, "The Wisdom of God," 210–22.

Wisdom appears in appointing the way how he should perform this work. Should be incarnate. Should be a sacrifice for sin. Wisdom of God appears by the glorious ends obtained. The glory of God secured and advanced. Each person of the Trinity glorified. All manner of good obtained for men. Peace with God. Justice satisfied. The law answered.[42]

In this, God has undermined the power of sin and uses it for his own glory.[43] Here Edwards is not merely concerned that God should be glorified in the abstract. Edwards asserts more specifically that God must be glorified in his wisdom, power, justice, holiness, truth, mercy, and love, and the work of redemption must glorify God according to each of these attributes.[44] It is an act of the divine wisdom that created *this* world needing *this* kind of redemption, and therefore wisdom provides the specific scheme for grasping the logic of redemption. Furthermore, Edwards argues that each person of the Trinity must be glorified in the work of redemption: "In this work every distinct person has his distinct parts and offices assigned him. Each one has his particular and distinct concern in it, agreeable to their distinct, personal properties, relations, and economical offices."[45] The divine wisdom is able to conceive an act of redemption that glorifies God in his three persons as well as his attributes. But Edwards does not stop there. The divine wisdom designs a way of redemption that uniquely supplies the creature with every necessary provision. The creature needs peace with God, the appeasement of divine wrath, pardon from sin, deliverance from Hell, happiness and enjoyment, as well as "every sort of good" that people crave. Furthermore, the creature needs to be given what is good for body and soul, ultimately culminating in eternal blessedness and perfect holiness.[46] In his wisdom, God devises a plan to accomplish all of this.

By mooring the atonement in the divine wisdom and love, Edwards focuses on the life history of Jesus—from birth to resurrection—as

---

42. Jonathan Edwards, "Jesus Christ Is the Shining Forth of the Father's Glory," in *The Glory and Honor of God: Volume 2 of the Previously Unpublished Sermons of Jonathan Edwards*, ed. Michael D. McMullen (Nashville: Broadman & Holman Publishers, 2004), 235.

43. Edwards, "Jesus Christ Is the Shining Forth of the Father's Glory," 209–10.

44. Edwards, "The Wisdom of God," 181–84.

45. Edwards, "The Wisdom of God," 185 (alterations made for readability).

46. Edwards, "The Wisdom of God," 186–94.

the singular act that refracts in multiform ways. This is why Edwards's doctrine can be so confusing. His employment of the divine wisdom is meant to refocus the doctrine of the atonement on the person of Christ and the manifold nature of Christ's work. Edwards claims, "The contrivance is so manifold that one may spend an eternity in discovering more of the excellent ends and designs accomplished by it, and the multitude and vast variety of things that are, by divine contrivance, brought to conspire to the bringing about those ends."[47] Instead of pitting one aspect of the biblical data against others, Edwards constructs an account that shows how Christ has fulfilled, satisfied, honored, and earned all things necessary for human salvation in a way that could never have been anticipated.

### The Form of Redemption

The Son's economic mission as the wisdom of God and the Spirit of love flowing forth to his people is what grounds Edwards's doctrine of atonement. Beneath this view—funding it—is the Son's eternal substitution for his people and his unwavering love for his elect, which is ultimately grounded upon the pure actuality of God's life of religious affection as Father, Son, and Spirit. With this eternal background in mind, it is within the historical narrative of Jesus's life and ministry that we encounter satisfaction and merit as the overarching category of the purchase of redemption. The price that Christ paid accomplishes two things: "it pays our debt and so it satisfies by its intrinsic value between the Father and the Son," and it also "procures a title for us to happiness and so it merits."[48] Edwards's brief summary is that "the satisfaction of Christ is to free us from misery, and the merit of Christ is to purchase happiness for us."[49] In this affirmation, Edwards argues that Christ himself can assume the punishment for our sin. He can also offer us his own happiness. In short, Edwards asserts that the Father will accept people on the Son's behalf.

As part of the divine wisdom, moreover, Christ's act to pay the debt and merit happiness for the elect complies with the "mutual free

---

47. Edwards, "The Wisdom of God," 285.
48. WJE 9:304.
49. WJE 9:304.

agreement" and *pactum salutis*, and therefore each aspect of redemption concerns God's honor. In the mutual free agreement between the persons of the Trinity prior to creation, it is decided that the Father "holds to the rights of the Godhead" and so holds on to the offense against the Godhead.[50] The Son accepts the role as mediator and it is decided that the Son and Spirit will be subordinated to the Father in the economy of salvation. In this subordination, the Son freely enters into a covenant with the Father to take on the sins of the world, debasing himself through the incarnation and work of redemption—acts driven by love for his people. "The Son acts altogether freely, and as in his own right, in undertaking the great and difficult and self-abasing work of our redemption, and that he becomes obliged to the Father with respect to it by voluntary covenant engagements, and not by any establishment prior thereto."[51] Prior to this covenant (keeping in mind that discussions of eternity aim to address logical priorities rather than temporal ones), the Father determines to redeem for himself a people.[52] After the mutual agreement among the persons concerning their economic roles, but prior to the covenant of redemption, the Father determines to accomplish a redemption that will occur in the form determined by the mutual free agreement. The form of this redemption, therefore, must comport with the reality that the Father's "majesty and authority as supreme rector, legislator and judge" has been scorned.[53] The Father is the "first mover" in the act of redemption, electing the Son to this work, and therefore the Father's honor is tied to the whole of redemption history.[54] The form of this redemption is set by the divine wisdom, such that the majesty and authority of God are supremely honored.

In the love and wisdom of God, Christ takes on the work of redemption so that in him the Father may receive the elect into his life by the Spirit.

> Christ unites mankind with the Father, by being the bond of
> union between them . . . by making sinful men one with himself,
> as he does by three things, viz. by substituting himself in their
> stead from eternity, and by taking on their nature, and bringing

50. Edwards, "The Wisdom of God," 172.
51. WJE 20:436.
52. WJE 20:433.
53. WJE 20:433.
54. WJE 20:436.

them home to an union of hearts, and vital union: I say, by thus bringing them to himself he unites them to the Father.[55]

As mediator, Christ becomes the "bond of union" between the Father and believers (the friend and his client). In Christ's person, therefore, redemption is accomplished in full; Christ, the head of the church, is judged, justified, and glorified. Christ does not act simply for his own sake, but to purchase salvation through his obedience for the elect. It is by being united to this new Adam that believers are saved, and it is through the purchase made on their behalf that they are found to be truly in him.[56] Therefore, Edwards can preach: "Consider, will God reject his own Son, in whom his infinite delight is, and has been, from all eternity, and that is so united to him, that if he should reject him he would reject himself?"[57]

### Receiving Sinners

The preceding allows us to speak more specifically about the work Christ accomplished in order to make redemption possible. On Edwards's understanding, there are two interconnected beliefs that are logically, but not actually, distinct. First is the idea that sin against God's law requires punishment by death. Second, if God is going to redeem, the Father has to be honored and glorified in the kind of redemption that occurs. Edwards states,

> He that is entrusted with the rights and honor of the majesty and authority of the whole Trinity, surely will not forgive sin without a perfect satisfaction [and] a perfect obedience. Therefore, [we] presume not to go to him in our own righteousness. If he should bestow salvation upon you in any other way, he would not only injure the honor of his majesty and justice, but

55. WJE 18:451.

56. S. Mark Hamilton addresses the metaphysical depths and the various distinctions Edwards draws between the unions the believer has with Christ in his article, "Jonathan Edwards on the Atonement," *International Journal of Systematic Theology* 15 (2013): 394–415.

57. WJE 19:585. Moreover, Edwards writes, "For there is doubtless an infinite intimacy between the Father and the Son. . . . And saints being in him, shall, in their measure and manner, partake with him in it, and the blessedness of it." WJE 19:593.

he would disparage his own wisdom [and] oppose all that he has done in the great things he has contrived and approved and brought to pass to reproach [sin and evil].[58]

In identifying both satisfaction and obedience as central to Christ's work, Edwards argues, "God gave us a law that we might have opportunity to honor God by obeying of it; and God now insists upon satisfaction, that his law and authority may not go without its honor."[59] God (as well as his law and authority) must be honored. But for redemption to take place, God must also be satisfied. God's honor is tied to his law, and his law is "the fixed and established rule of all transactions between God and us, that all mankind are under."[60] Therefore, as transgressors of the law, humankind is in debt to God. By being united to Christ, "the debt was crossed out that was in the sinner's account and was set on Christ's account."[61] Christ's death alone would simply secure forgiveness for sinners, but it would not grant them the positive righteousness necessary to share in God's life.[62] Only Christ's active obedience, which purchases happiness, preserves God's honor.

Edwards offers a brief summary of his argument, noting that the death of Christ was necessary for human salvation on three accounts. First, it was necessary because it manifested the sufficiency of God's love for his people in his uniting himself to his elect, upon which basis he accepts the elect. Second, Christ's death was necessary for the expiation of sin, whereby Christ could ascend into the true Holy of Holies, entering by his own blood.[63] Finally, Christ's death was necessary because it was the "main instance of Christ's obedience."[64] Christ took the place of his

---

58. WJE 25:154.

59. WJE 14:398.

60. WJE 14:404.

61. WJE 14:396.

62. This positive righteousness stems from Christ's active obedience. This active obedience is necessary, Edwards argues, because (1) the law is not answered without it; (2) without it, God's authority would not be sufficiently honored; and (3) it is plainly taught in Scripture (e.g., Rom. 5:17–19). See WJE 14:397–99.

63. WJE 18:153.

64. WJE 13:526–27. Later in the same passage he writes, "We are saved by Christ's death as much as it was an act of obedience, as it was a propitiation. For as it was not the only act of obedience that merited, so neither was it the only suffering that was propitiatory: all his sufferings from the beginning were propitiatory, as every act of obedience was meritorious. Indeed this was his principal suffering, and it was as much his principal act of obedience." WJE 13:539–40.

people, substituted himself for them, and provided a means for their participation in the benefits of his substitution. Furthermore, it is important to keep the eternal backdrop to Christ's saving work in mind. In eternity, Christ entered into a covenant with the Father (the *pactum salutis*). The Holy Spirit was not asked to debase himself, but only the Son was asked to freely enter into humiliation, and therefore only the Son needed to covenant with the Father for this work.[65] This eternal background to Christ's work of obedience shows how Christ's work to honor the Father through his humiliation was established before creation.

### Substitution, Satisfaction, and Merit

One of the common missteps in attempting to interpret Edwards's understanding of redemption concerns the notion of forgiveness and justification. The key question for Edwards's account is not, how are unrighteous sinners declared justified or forgiven? Rather, for Edwards, the main question concerns how believers can be seen to be one with Christ (in whom justification and forgiveness reside). His view represents a kind of substitution, in the sense that Christ's satisfaction of the law and righteousness can be the believer's own. But, according to Edwards, Christ does not hand over satisfaction to the elect *per se*. Rather, Christ's satisfaction and merit are his own, and it is only as believers become a part of him that they come to share in these benefits. Edwards holds this view especially because he wants to affirm, in the highest possible way, the unwavering nature of God's justice. Notice the focus of Edwards's claim: "Hereby he [God] shew'd himself unappeasable to sin. And that it was impossible for him to be at peace with it."[66] In this we see the main problem of sin: God is unappeasable. His retributive justice cannot be relaxed if his holiness is to be maintained.[67] This drives Edwards to construct his particular account of justification (see the discussion in chapter six). Edwards's soteriology demands that sinners become a part of Christ, the redeemed human, and only by being in Christ do they know redemption. Edwards further spells this out, stating,

65. WJE 20:441–42. But this covenant should not be seen as a mere contractual agreement, which would be a misunderstanding of the nature of God's covenanting activity. Rather, for Christ to atone, the driving motive must be Christ's love for the Father. I appreciate S. Mark Hamilton's insights in this regard.
66. Edwards, "The Wisdom of God," 183.
67. Edwards, "The Wisdom of God," 183.

God is so strictly and immutably just, that he would not spare his Son when he took upon him the guilt of men's sins, and was substituted in the room of sinners; he spared him not at all. He would not abate him the least mite of that debt which justice demanded. Justice should take place, though it cost his infinite dear Son his precious blood; and his enduring such extraordinary reproach and pain and death in its most dreadful form. Such was God's justice, that his love to his own Son would not influence him to abate the least of what justice required.[68]

God's justice requires that he punish sin; thus God wields his justice without flinching, even if his Son becomes the eventual target of his just wrath (keeping in mind that these roles are appropriated). For the sake of redemption, Christ unites himself to his elect and accepts their guilt as his own, "but not in any blameable sense."[69] Christ displayed his love for the elect on the cross by fully recognizing the heinous nature of the sin of the elect, and, as it were, with a "readiness to bear their guilt himself and suffer their punishment."[70] This action was required. Christ could not just die; he had to die *for us*. But die he must—justice would allow no other way.

It was but fair, and what justice required, that seeing Christ would so unite himself by love to sinners that had deserved wrath, that they might be partakers of the Father's love to him and so they be screened and sheltered, that he himself should receive the Father's wrath to them. That love of Christ which united him to sinners, assumed their guilt upon himself. So that Christ's death and sufferings were absolutely necessary, in order [to] our being delivered from destruction for the sake of Christ's worthiness and excellency, and through the love of God to him that loved us.[71]

---

68. Edwards, "The Wisdom of God," 183 (with alterations).

69. WJE 13:526.

70. WJE 13:526. Edwards even saw the pillar of cloud in the wilderness as a type of Christ's work in this manner. The pillar of cloud "defended the children of Israel from the sunbeams in that parched wilderness," which is a type of Christ, "defending his church from the wrath of God." WJE 20:180. In being united to Christ, the wrath still rains down, but Christ is the shelter who has fulfilled the law through his perfect obedience.

71. WJE 13:526. Edwards argues that Christ's suffering was necessary, but note what

Christ, in atoning for humankind's sin and disobedience, put himself in the way of the wrath of God by taking the sinner's guilt upon himself. Furthermore, "Christ never so eminently appeared for divine justice, and yet never suffered so much from divine justice, as when he offered up himself a sacrifice for our sins."[72] Sacrifice was, for Edwards, a helpful and important image for what Christ had accomplished on the cross.[73] The sacrificial system provided a backdrop for how Edwards understood Christ's work and its necessity. Because of the honor and status of the one who was sinned against, "a sacrifice of infinite value was necessary, . . . for an atonement that bears no proportion to the offense is no atonement."[74] Christ is the lamb God provided for our sacrifice as our substitution—our scapegoat—who takes our guilt and punishment upon himself, giving God his due honor. Edwards the preacher was hoping to instill a deeply affective sense of what Christ accomplished in our stead. Just as Christ's infinite highness and lowness collide together to refract the beauty of God as "the excellency of Christ," our own affections need to be struck by the infinite debt of our sin in order to grasp the beauty of Christ's infinite payment. In Edwards's thought, therefore, it was impossible to overstate the punishment poured out upon Christ. The more one emphasized the punishment, the more redemption shined forth. It is in this vein that Edwards states,

> Christ was the mark of the vindictive expressions of that very justice of God. Revenging justice then spent all its force upon him, on the account of our guilt that was laid upon him; he was not spared at all; but God spent the arrows of his vengeance upon him. . . . For when he had undertaken for sinners, and had substituted himself in their room, divine justice could have its due honor, no other way than by his suffering its revenges.[75]

---

makes this suffering efficacious: "This love of God to the Son gives an infinite value to Christ's sufferings and actions in God's account. If it were not for this, let Christ suffer never so much for sinners, it would not appease God's anger against them." "So 'tis God's love to Christ that gives that value in God's account to his positive righteousness." WJE 14:402.

72. WJE 19:577.

73. For more on sacrifice, see WJE 2:123; WJE 3:415; WJE 5:131; WJE 7:432; WJE 18:490–91; WJE 19:362; and WJE 20:66.

74. WJE 20:164.

75. WJE 19:578.

## The Example of Christ

Edwards further holds that Christ must be more, not less, than a penal substitute. He must also be a penal example. Edwards's location of atonement in the divine wisdom is important because it heightens the aesthetic and, therefore, moral component to his doctrine of salvation. In the same balance with God's law and attributes being honored and glorified, Edwards believes that creatures must be affected deeply by what God has done. There is no deeper affection for Edwards than to see one's sin set upon Christ, and to witness Christ give himself to death on the cross.[76] As Edwards prodded his congregation, Christ's

> admirable conjunction of excellencies remarkably appears, in his offering up himself [as] a sacrifice for sinners in his last sufferings. As this was the greatest thing in all the works of redemption, the greatest act of Christ in that work; so in this act especially does there appear that admirable conjunction of excellencies, that has been spoken of. Christ never so much appeared as a lamb, as when he was slain: he came like "a lamb to the slaughter" (Isa. 53:7).[77]

For their part, the elect partake of the Father's love to Christ, and so are "screened and sheltered" from God's wrath.[78] But this act was also an act of love:

> That love of Christ which united him to sinners, assumed their guilt upon himself. So that Christ's death and sufferings were absolutely necessary, in order [to] our being delivered from destruction for the sake of Christ's worthiness and excellency, and through the love of God to him that loved us.[79]

In line with Edwards's focus on the atoning love and wisdom of God, the means by which Christ achieves atonement must also honor God and his authority. Furthermore, this work must be beautiful, highlight-

---

76. See, for instance, WJE 19:585–86.
77. WJE 19:576.
78. WJE 13:526.
79. WJE 13:526.

ing Christ's excellencies, so that believers' affections are aroused in witnessing—by faith—Christ's self-giving unto death. For Edwards, only the "admirable conjunction" of Christ's work could refract the divine glory and beauty into creation to awaken the depth of affection necessary for creatures to love Christ above all.

This is why the means of salvation was so important to Edwards. It was in Christ's greatest humiliation that his divine glory is most manifest.[80] Christ turned evil on its head and used it to glorify himself. In this act of taking death upon himself, Christ's excellencies shine forth to those with eyes to see. To know God is to see him by faith and see who he is for you in his sacrificial death. For the Christian, this means seeing the act of the cross as an act of beauty—the dual love between Father and Son, and between the Son and his bride—and, importantly, recognizing the moral imperatives inherent in this act. Edwards says,

> Christ by his death also has laid a foundation for peace and love among enemies, in that therein he has done two things; first, in setting the most marvelous, affecting example of love to enemies, an example in an instance wherein we are most nearly concerned, for we ourselves are those enemies that he has manifested such love to. And second, he has done the greatest thing to engage us to love him, and so to follow his example, for the examples of such as we have a strong love to have a most powerful influence upon us.[81]

Christ's work of atonement, as a work of wisdom, necessarily affects the contours of Edwards's moral theology. Furthermore, as a work of love, it should not surprise us to discover the fundamental role love plays in Edwards's thought as the sum of all Christian virtue. (We will discuss Edwards's moral theology and beauty in chapter seven.)

---

80. WJE 19:576. Moreover, "In this the diverse excellencies that met in the person of Christ appeared, viz. his infinite regard to God's justice, and such love to those that have exposed themselves to it, as induced him thus to yield himself a sacrifice to it." WJE 19:578.

81. WJE 18:451.

## Mechanism of the Atonement

By way of conclusion, it proves helpful to recapitulate the preceding overview by focusing on the mechanism of the atonement on Edwards's view.
In other words, this conclusion seeks to answer the question, how does
Christ's work reconcile us to God?[82] What should be clear from the above
treatment is that Edwards's account will not easily be narrowed to a single
model. This is because Edwards's discussion of the atonement always
takes the entirety of Christ's life into account, not simply Christ's work
on the cross. Therefore, following the salvation-historical orientation of
Edwards's doctrine, at the very least it seems fitting to say that the following conditions are requisite for an atonement to be made.

First, because of the nature of the mutual free agreement and the
*pactum salutis*, the entire framing of redemption needs to honor the
Father who has been dishonored by sin.[83] This helps explain Edwards's
robust emphasis on rectoral justice.[84] For the sake of evaluation here,
"*rectoral justice* is that aspect of divine justice whereby God rightly governs the cosmos in accordance with his moral law. *Retributive justice* is
that aspect of divine justice whereby God's wrath is meted out to those
creatures who transgress the divine law."[85] In Edwards's account, these

82. The focus on the mechanism of the atonement is helpfully addressed by Oliver D. Crisp in "Methodological Issues in Approaching the Atonement," in *T&T Clark
Companion to the Atonement*, ed. Adam Johnson (London: Bloomsbury T&T Clark, 2017),
ch. 17, and Oliver D. Crisp, "Is Ransom Enough?," *Journal of Analytic Theology* 3 (2015):
1–16.

83. S. Mark Hamilton helpfully clarifies how these images and metaphors in Ed-
wards's thought have wrongly led to scholars thinking that Edwards held to some sort of
Anselmic satisfaction model. See his "Jonathan Edwards: Anselmic Satisfaction and God's
Moral Government," *International Journal of Systematic Theology* 17 (2015): 46–68.

84. For a similar point, see Oliver D. Crisp, "The Moral Government of God: Jonathan Edwards and Joseph Bellamy on the Atonement," in *After Jonathan Edwards: The
Courses of New England Theology*, ed. Oliver D. Crisp and Douglas A. Sweeney (New York:
Oxford University Press, 2012), 82. Crisp's article does a good job of narrating how Edwards's development of the atonement ends up being developed into the account of the
New Divinity. Mark Hamilton claims that there is an "emerging consensus" that Edwards's
view is a version of penal substitution. Along with his own work, Hamilton also cites Mi-
chael J. McClymond and Gerald R. McDermott, eds., *The Theology of Jonathan Edwards*
(New York: Oxford University Press, 2011), 251; Crisp, "The Moral Government of God";
and Hamilton, "Jonathan Edwards on the Atonement." See Hamilton, "Jonathan Edwards:
Anselmic Satisfaction and God's Moral Government," 46n1.

85. These definitions are from Oliver D. Crisp, "Penal Non-Substitution," in *A Reader*

two forms of justice require an act of divine wisdom to be satisfied (and a divine person to do so based on the covenant of redemption).[86]

Second, God's retributive justice needs to be satisfied, which necessarily entails Christ performing a work of penal substitution. Christ does not substitute for a people apart from himself, but becomes their substitute insofar as he unites them to himself in love. The divine wisdom is the form by which the divine love is victorious. Christ's love to his people is not just any love; it is such a great love that "Christ may justly be looked upon as making himself one with them," and this love assumes "them into union with himself."[87] Christ's love for his people has to be great enough to allow for a "just" union between himself and his people. But the only love that can atone is the kind of love whereby Christ puts himself "in the beloved's stead even in the total loss of himself, and in his perfect destruction, that may be looked upon as perfectly or thoroughly uniting."[88] This is the "dying love of Christ" addressed above, and only this love allows Christ to substitute for his people in a just manner.

Third, it is important to distinguish between Christ's work of satisfaction and his work of merit. The Son's work to pay the price of the sinner's debt is a work of satisfaction, whereas the Son's work to obtain happiness (which is the life of God—God's blessedness) is deemed a work of merit.[89] In this sense, all the suffering and humiliation that Christ endured (starting with his incarnation) was for satisfaction, whereas all of his obedience and righteousness merited happiness. Importantly, there are two different legal issues at play here:

> The satisfaction of Christ consists in his answering those demands that the law laid on man that were consequent on the breach of the law, which was suffering the penalty of the law.

in Contemporary Philosophical Theology, ed. Oliver D. Crisp (London: T&T Clark, 2009), 303–4.

86. In a recent paper, Hamilton has suggested that Edwards's two focal points cannot be brought together into one cohesive view, and therefore he denies his earlier assessment that Edwards holds to a version of penal substitution. As will be seen, I think that Edwards is able to hold these together once the "mechanism" of the atonement is seen in a broader historical-redemptive context. See Hamilton, "For What Does Christ Die? Jonathan Edwards on Divine Justice and Atonement," presented at the Annual Conference of the Evangelical Theological Society, San Antonio, TX, November 2016.

87. WJE 13:524–25.
88. WJE 13:525.
89. WJE 9:304.

The merit of Christ consisted in what he did to answer those demands of the law that were prior to man's breach of the law, or to fulfill what the law demanded before man sinned, which was obedience.[90]

Christ's work satisfies the demands of the law by receiving the law's penalty, while also meriting the righteousness that the law originally required. Furthermore, Edwards states, "The end of that negative righteousness which Christ procured by his suffering is only to deliver from guilt and from punishment, but gives no title to heaven." The cross only procures the forgiveness of sins. But it does not provide a full account of atonement, according to the Edwardsean system. "But Christ's active righteousness is the price of happiness," Edwards goes on to add, claiming that "Christ's passion delivers from the obligation and leaves the sinner in a state of indifference, but Christ's active righteousness purchases heaven."[91]

According to Edwards's interpretation of the atonement in a salvation-historical framework, everything that Christ accomplished— from his incarnation to his resurrection—was for his people. Edwards's view assumes a form of penal substitution. Nevertheless, although Christ's work as a penal substitute on the cross is a necessary feature of salvation, it is not sufficient for the kind of redemption from sin that God offers. To "purchase heaven," Edwards avers, is to purchase the Spirit and communion in the life of God. This means that full redemption also requires a kind of "reparative substitution" to "fulfill what the law demanded before man sinned," as was just noted.[92] Unlike Anselmic satisfaction, the focus on this reparative substitution is not to diffuse God's retributive justice but functions alongside of Christ's penal substitution.[93] Christ's work of obedience is still a substitution, as much as penal substitution is, but on

90. WJE 9:305.
91. WJE 14:396. See also WJE 14:397–98 and WJE 24:1011.
92. I am utilizing Hamilton's language of "reparative substitution" here. See Hamilton, "Jonathan Edwards: Anselmic Satisfaction and God's Moral Government."
93. While I am following Hamilton's use of the term "reparative substitution" and his exposition of Anselmic satisfaction, I am changing one key element for the sake of Edwards's view. Unlike a reparative model of the atonement, Edwards does not believe that this kind of satisfaction would diffuse retributive justice. While his overarching view is reparative, therefore, he nonetheless still believes it is necessary to have a penal substitute. See Hamilton, "Jonathan Edwards: Anselmic Satisfaction and God's Moral Government," 48.

Edwards's system both are necessary for the believer to receive the full reward of Christ's work.[94]

Because of the nature of divine wisdom, according to Edwards, the mechanism of the atonement is the entirety of Christ's life (rather than simply the cross), and this work is grounded in eternity in the *pactum salutis* and continues all the way down into Christ's death.

> Christ did [not] only make satisfaction by proper suffering, but by whatsoever had the nature of humiliation and abasement of circumstances. Thus Christ made satisfaction for sin by continuing under the power of death after his lying buried in the grave, though neither his body nor soul properly endured any suffering after he was dead.[95]

Therefore, Edwards's doctrine of atonement focuses on two realities: first, the original commands of the law for obtaining heaven, which Christ's active righteousness and merit purchase for the believer; and second, the reception of God's wrath in Christ's penal substitution. At the heart of Edwards's account is God's honor, which serves as an overarching category for the whole scheme.[96] The only way for Christ to honor God and save creatures was to enact redemption in the way he did, which was why his atoning work was an act of divine wisdom. But punishment of sin was also necessary; God's holiness and wisdom demanded it, and therefore a penal substitute was still necessary. Clearly, some kind of penal substitution model is at work in Edwards's account, even if this model does not exhaust the full breadth of his project. Moreover, since redemption is about purchasing happiness (the Spirit),[97] according to Edwards, merit

94. Hamilton similarly suggests that one might "say that Christ dies in order to satisfy retributive justice qua (in the capacity of) penal substitution and rectoral justice qua penal non-substitution." He furthermore suggests that this approach would seem to "entail more than one mechanism for the atonement. While this does not necessarily present any obvious problems, no such qualifications readily appear in Edwards's discussion of the atonement." Rather, what we are suggesting is that this is precisely the case. Hamilton, "Jonathan Edwards, Anselmic Satisfaction and God's Moral Government," 54. The mechanism is singular, however, or can be considered so, because Christ's person and work ground the whole within himself.

95. WJE 9:305.

96. This is why it was out of regard for "the honor of God's majesty: that Christ was willing to endure suffering." WJE 18:410.

97. "What Christ does for men in the office of a mediator between God and men is

was required because of sinful creatures' lack of obedience. Christ's active obedience repairs what was broken through a reparative substitution. Both of these features of Edwards's account are governed by God's honor, and both are ordered by the eternal covenant of redemption.

In Edwards's understanding of the atonement, Christ defeated sin by bearing its guilt and penalty unto death. At the ascension, Christ reveals himself to be the redeemed, justified, and glorified one, who can grant salvation to his people through union with him. All of the various elements of redemption, as outlined above, are organized by the love and wisdom of God in Christ, who gave himself in life and in death to the Father for his people. Building on this account of the atonement, we turn now to some remaining features of Edwards's soteriology. The following sketch reveals how *theōsis*—the overarching structure of Edwards's soteriology—orients his understanding of God's redemptive work. Specifically, we will see how Edwards's decisions concerning the atonement—most specifically the point that God's justice is unappeasable—help to orient his understanding of justification.

---

to procure the Holy Ghost for man and bestow it upon him, *and the whole may be summed up in that.*" Jonathan Edwards, "Jesus Christ Is the Shining Forth of the Father's Glory," 316. Emphasis added.

# CHAPTER SIX

# Salvation as Participation

We have approached the theological material thus far with a specific kind of order, from God's life *in se* to the movement of God's self-giving *ad extra*. From there, we've attended to Edwards's doctrine of the atonement, seeing how the atonement flows through the wisdom and love of God. To explicate the self-giving and communication of God more fully, we turn our attention to Edwards's soteriology of participation. In short, in Edwards's way of thinking, the economic work of the Son and the Spirit are the organizing factors of salvation. While this claim might seem trite at first glance, what follows is an exposition of Edwards's soteriology revealing how important of a point this really is.

In developing a soteriology whose contours are shaped by the economic work of Son and Spirit, Edwards advances a Reformed doctrine of *theōsis*, or participation in the divine life.[1] By focusing on God's economic activity, i.e., by orienting redemption around the purchase of the Spirit by Christ from the Father, Edwards emphasizes God's self-giving. A proper grammar of redemption, therefore, arises by attending to the acts of Word

---

1. For the most relevant material for Edwards on *theōsis*, see Michael McClymond, "Salvation as Divinization: Jonathan Edwards, Gregory Palamas and the Theological Uses of Neoplatonism," in *Jonathan Edwards: Philosophical Theologian*, ed. Oliver Crisp and Paul Helm (Aldershot: Ashgate, 2004), 139–60; and Kyle Strobel, "Jonathan Edwards and the Polemics of *Theosis*," *Harvard Theological Review* 105, no. 3 (July 2012): 259–79; Kyle Strobel, "Jonathan Edwards's Reformed Doctrine of *Theosis*," *Harvard Theological Review* 109, no. 3 (2016): 370–98; and Crisp, *Jonathan Edwards on God and Creation* (New York: Oxford University Press, 2011), 275–85.

and Spirit.[2] This is in contrast to an account driven by benefits procured by Word and Spirit. In other words, redemption broadly, and justification specifically, are oriented by the Son's unwavering love for the saints, a love that drives the work of redemption and, ultimately, unites believers to Christ's own life. John Webster, navigating the theological location of soteriology, states that "soteriology is a derivative doctrine, and no derivative doctrine may occupy the material place which is properly reserved for the Christian doctrine of God, from which alone all other doctrines derive."[3] In Edwards, we find this exact impulse.

To reveal how Edwards's soteriology is constructed, this chapter proceeds in three progressive movements. First, recalling our development of the persons of God, we show how Edwards's doctrine of God lays the groundwork for his schema of redemption. Second, building on his development of the triune persons, we focus on the incarnation as the doctrine that ultimately organizes soteriology along its specific trajectory of *theōsis*. Last, we show how this account establishes Edwards's understanding of regeneration and justification. Our focus, therefore, is on the broad contours of salvation, building upon our exposition of the atonement and then advancing this discussion to address more specific inquiries. This approach should help reveal the emphasis of Edwards's soteriology and should guide our exposition of regeneration and justification. This approach, furthermore, makes sure that God is the focus of soteriology and that polemical issues and inquiries do not overtake this theocentrism.

## Personhood, Participation, and *Theōsis*

It is helpful to begin with a brief reflection on the term *theōsis*. This is important for two reasons.

First, the term *theōsis* is often misunderstood. *Theōsis* is synonymous with deification and divinization, both of which sound unfortunate (if not heretical!) to Protestant ears. Furthermore, in the modern retrieval of *theōsis* in the West, many have mistakenly come to believe that *theōsis*

2. "He by his Word and Spirit, as it were, does the part of an intercessor between them" (WJE 18:451).

3. John Webster, "'It Was the Will of the Lord to Bruise Him': Soteriology and the Doctrine of God," in *God of Salvation: Soteriology in Theological Perspective*, ed. Ivor J. Davidson (Aldershot: Ashgate, 2011), 16.

is somehow a distinctively Eastern doctrine.[4] This neglects the breadth of the doctrine and how it has uniquely developed in every stream of the Christian tradition. It also fails to attend to how distinctively Protestant forms of *theōsis* developed, and it ignores the role the doctrine played in the theology of the Reformed. Calvin, for instance, does not hesitate to say, in commentary on 2 Peter 1:4, that Peter's description is a "kind of de-ification."[5] Carl Mosser provides a helpful definition of *theōsis*, claiming, "Succinctly, *theōsis* is for believers to become by grace what the Son of God is by nature and to receive the blessings that are his by rights as un-deserved gifts. Most boldly, *theōsis* is described as a transforming union of the believer with God and Christ usually, if inadequately, translated as 'divinization' or 'deification.'"[6] The type of *theōsis* will depend on how any given thinker develops these concepts.

Second, and maybe more directly relevant, Edwards never used the terms *theōsis*, deification, or divinization, but instead spoke about participation, sharing in God's fullness, and partaking of God's nature. Even though Edwards does not utilize the technical terminology from the tradition, we still choose to use the term *theōsis* since it represents the standard Christian soteriology, even if that "standard" entails a wide spectrum. Keeping in mind the breadth of the interpretive options con-cerning *theōsis*, it proves helpful to narrow down the tradition into two broad strands. Rowan Williams argues that the tradition bequeaths two distinct trajectories of *theōsis*, one focusing on the communication of the divine attributes, and the other offering a view of salvation based on the participation among the divine persons.[7] Whereas the East has focused more on the communicable nature of the divine attributes through the

4. For an explanation of this mistake see Carl Mosser, "An Exotic Flower: Calvin and the Patristic Doctrine of Deification," in *Reformation Faith: Exegesis and Theology in the Protestant Reformations*, ed. Michael Parsons (Milton Keynes: Paternoster, 2014), 38–56.

5. John Calvin, *Calvin's New Testament Commentaries*, vol. 12, *Hebrews and 1 and 2 Peter* (Grand Rapids: Eerdmans, 1994), 330. For Calvin on *theōsis*, see Carl Mosser, "The Greatest Possible Blessing: Calvin and Deification," *Scottish Journal of Theology* 55 (2002): 36–57, and J. Todd Billings, "United to God through Christ: Assessing Calvin on the Ques-tion of Deification," *Harvard Theological Review* 98 (2005): 313–34.

6. Mosser, "The Greatest Possible Blessing," 36.

7. Rowan Williams, "Deification," in *The Westminster Dictionary of Christian Spir-ituality*, ed. Gordon S. Wakefield (Philadelphia: Westminster, 1983), 106. I build on Wil-liams's historical development and argue that, while the Reformed always land on the relational side of the spectrum, Edwards can uniquely bridge the two strands; see Strobel, "Jonathan Edwards's Reformed Doctrine of *Theosis*," 370–98.

"divine energies" (following Palamas's theological construct), Western theologians have tended to reject this particular notion. Rather, the general orientation of Western accounts, particularly all Reformed accounts of *theōsis*, is on partaking in the Sonship of the Son, which therefore articulates the relational side of the spectrum. Christian depictions of *theōsis* can never entail "becoming God," if this is understood as partaking in the divine essence. Rather, Christian *theōsis* is sharing by grace what is Christ's by nature.[8] The kind of doctrine of *theōsis* one espouses will depend on what one means by nature.

Building on our foundation of God in himself and God for us set forth in earlier chapters, we continue by focusing on how Edwards's doctrine of the Trinity organizes his soteriology. Two key points ground our analysis: first, Edwards's understanding of personhood; and, second, Edwards's development of the nature of the triune persons. Edwards is clear that a person, divine or human, is a being with both understanding and will, and that the processions of the divine essence are best articulated through this framework. For the divine understanding and will to be persons, however, they have to interpenetrate each other. On this notion of personhood, individuality is not the highest priority. The Father has personhood only insofar as he has the Son and the Spirit—understanding and will, respectively. Likewise, the Father and Spirit are necessary for the Son's personhood, and the Spirit needs both the Father and the Son in the same way.[9] Similarly, the vision of salvation Edwards propounds is focused on union, communion, and participation, such that he will say,

> What insight I have of the nature of minds, I am convinced that there is no guessing what kind of union and mixtion, by consciousness or otherwise, there may be between them. So that all difficulty is removed in believing what the Scripture declares about spiritual unions—of the persons of the Trinity, of the two natures of Christ, of Christ and the minds of saints.[10]

8. *Theōsis* is not, it should be noted, a type of doctrine of justification or sanctification but is something of a meta-doctrine that governs soteriology in its entirety. Andrew Louth makes this point in his chapter "The Place of *Theosis* in Orthodox Theology," in *Partakers of the Divine Nature: The History and Development of Deification in the Christian Traditions*, ed. Michael J. Christensen and Jeffery A. Wittung (Grand Rapids: Baker Academic, 2007), 32–45.

9. WJE 21:133.

10. WJE 13:330.

Whereas in the life of God personhood is established through the interpenetration of the divine subsistences, for regenerate human persons the Spirit is infused into their beings, and Christ is now united to their minds. To receive God, and that is the only possible salvation, is to receive him in Son and Spirit. The Son reveals and offers the life of God in his person and work, and the Spirit illumines and unites to Christ. The Spirit, likewise, as the love, holiness, and beauty of God, brings communion in the love, holiness, and beauty of God. This leads to a twofold reality. First, the human being is taken up into God's personal existence, in a participation in God's own life. Second, the Spirit, with his particular nature (i.e., love, holiness, peace, beauty, etc.) is infused into the human person, functioning in the regenerate as a disposition of love and holiness, and illumining Christ as the image of the invisible God.

In this first aspect of salvation, human persons are taken up into the life of God by participating in the divine fullness. This fullness is the overflow of God's life to the creature in Son and Spirit and is received and rebounded as the creature knows and loves God from within his self-knowing and self-loving. This is the only true knowledge of God because knowledge of God entails a participation in his self-knowledge. Furthermore, since God's knowledge is affectionate knowledge, all knowledge of God must also share in that affection. This, for Edwards, is the nature of grace, and grace "is something divine."[11] In explaining his use of the word "divine," Edwards explains that it is not a partaking of the divine essence, "for the essence of God is not divisible nor communicable."[12] Other usages of the term "divine," such as with grace, "are said to be divine as they are a supernatural communication of something of that good which God himself possesses. It is not a communication of God's essence, but it is a communication of that which the scripture calls God's fellowship, as in Ephesians 3:17–19."[13] Therefore, "Grace is a communication or a participation of God's own good, . . . a partaking in some sort of his own bounty and happiness. 'Tis a supernatural communication of God's fullness of that good that God possesses in himself, and so is divine in a sense beyond other gifts of God."[14] Grace is God's self-giving. To receive grace

---

11. Jonathan Edwards, WJE Online Sermon Series II, 1738. Alterations have been made to all quotations from this sermon for readability and clarity.

12. Edwards, WJE Online Sermon Series II, 1738.

13. Edwards, WJE Online Sermon Series II, 1738.

14. Edwards, WJE Online Sermon Series II, 1738.

is to receive God in Christ Jesus by his Spirit, such that one becomes a partaker of the divine fullness.

Edwards's focus on participation, what he also calls fellowship, led some to think he was positing a radical notion of divinization (one where creatures participate in the essence of God). Even though Edwards is clear in the statement above, his polemical opponents were attempting to link him to more radical thought. In his *Religious Affections*, Edwards emphasizes this point, claiming,

> There is no work so high and excellent; for there is no work wherein God does so much communicate himself, and wherein the mere creature hath, in so high a sense, a participation of God; so that it is expressed in Scripture by the saints being made "partakers of the divine nature" (II Pet. 1:4). . . . Not that we are made partakers of the essence of God, and so are "God-ded" with God, and "Christed" with Christ, according to the abominable and blasphemous language and notions of some heretics; but, to use the Scripture phrase, they are made partakers of God's fullness (Eph. 3:17–19; John 1:16), that is, of God's beauty and happiness . . . for so it is evident the word "fullness" signifies in Scripture language.[15]

Edwards had in mind a variety of heretical groups, particularly the familists, a cult that had transplanted to the colonies from Britain.[16] To partake in God's essence would be to become God and would run contrary to any Christian notion of *theōsis*. Rather, in keeping with a Reformed understanding of *theōsis*, Edwards's focus is not the divine essence but the divine nature (second point below).[17] Here, it is important to note that Edwards argues for the creature's participation in God, partaking of the divine nature, as what it means to share in the divine fullness. This, furthermore, is to partake in God's beauty and happiness and is a sharing in the divine nature through the work of Son and Spirit to unite the creature to God's own life.

15. WJE 2:203.

16. One of the most neglected aspects of Edwards's doctrine of *theōsis* is the polemical context of his development. In the generation preceding Edwards, there were several heretical groups claiming that salvation entailed a participation in the divine essence. See Strobel, "Jonathan Edwards and the Polemics of *Theosis*," 259–79.

17. For more on the nature of a distinctively Reformed account of *theōsis*, see Strobel, "Jonathan Edwards's Reformed Doctrine of *Theosis*."

This leads to the second feature of salvation we are highlighting here, that the divine persons communicate a feature of the divine *nature* based on their procession in the inner life of God. As highlighted in chapter 2, the Son and the Spirit have communicable natures (understanding and will, respectively), established through Edwards's development of the psychological analogy, and are persons only as they exist in mutual interpenetration. Within this mutual interpenetration (i.e., perichoresis), each member of the Trinity has the divine nature in full. But in the economy, based on the mutual free agreement and *pactum salutis*, the triune persons find it fitting to carry over their natures (i.e., God's understanding and will) to creatures.[18] It is noteworthy that Edwards's use of the word "nature" is idiosyncratic.[19] Following the same line of interpretation as Calvin, but seeing it through his unique understanding of the divine nature in the economy, Edwards states,

> I think holiness may, without absurdity, be said to be the *proper nature* of the Holy Spirit on two accounts: (1) As 'tis his peculiar beauty and glory and so may in a special manner be called *his nature*, as brightness may in a peculiar manner be said to be the nature of the sun, and [as] that which is in a peculiar manner the nature of honey is its sweetness. (2) 'Tis the proper character of the Spirit above all other things, in that office and work of his wherein we are concerned with him. . . . And this is that *in his nature* which he communicates something of to the saints, and therefore is called by divines in general a communicable attribute; and the saints are made partakers of his holiness, as the Scripture expressly declares (Heb. 12:10), and that without imparting to them his essence.[20]

Here, Edwards's use of the word "nature" focuses on the particular attributes and character of the Spirit. Edwards notes that "spirit" is used in reference, not to ontology, but to disposition, inclination, or temper.[21] To

18. See WJE 21:124.

19. When someone pressed Edwards on his use of the term "nature," he wrote a letter back, claiming, "I confess, my skill in the English tongue does not extend so far as to discern the great impropriety of the word as I have used it. The word 'nature' is not used only to signify the essence of a thing, but is used very variously." WJE 8:639.

20. WJE 8:639. Emphasis added.

21. See WJE 21:122.

highlight this point, he quotes Numbers 14:24 where Caleb is said to be of "another spirit." Therefore, the Holy Spirit is the disposition of holiness inherent in the Godhead, which is the Spirit's proper nature. With many patristic scholars, Edwards utilizes the image of the sun to show how God can communicate his nature (or, with Eastern accounts that follow Palamas, his "energies") without communicating his essence.[22] The natures of the divine persons are communicable as *their* natures and are offered to the elect in redemption. In redeeming humankind, God gives himself in the Son and Spirit so that believers can participate in God's nature of self-understanding and self-love (i.e., the Son and Spirit, respectively, as the "fullness" of God).[23]

Edwards's account of the Trinity offers a way to talk about personhood through participation and God's communicable nature without succumbing to some form of radical divinization where God communicates his essence. Just as in Edwards's doctrine of the Trinity, personhood is central. The focus of Edwards's account of life with God is not that we come to share in God's metaphysical status (becoming "godded with god"), but that we come to share in the divine life. While it is true that God is omniscient, omnipotent, etc., what is most fundamentally true about God is that he is the infinite actuality of love and delight flowing forth between the Father and the Son as the Holy Spirit. That is who God is, and, therefore, this is who orients soteriology. By employing the term "nature" in his peculiar way, furthermore, Edwards can utilize 2 Peter 1:4, where Peter claims that believers partake in the divine nature as a central text for his overarching soteriology (which is, historically, a key text in constructions of *theōsis*). But notice what this does. Edwards's understanding of partaking in the divine nature makes two realities foundational: first, believers partake relationally among the divine persons; and second, believers partake in the divine fullness and therefore have the same divine nature that defines God's life infused into their being. Rather than being "godded with god," which would entail that believers partake of the divine essence, the divine nature is relational, so that partaking

22. There are two studies, to my knowledge, that focus on Edwards in relation to Palamas. See Michael McClymond, "Salvation as Divinization: Jonathan Edwards, Gregory Palamas and the Theological Uses of Neoplatonism," in *Jonathan Edwards: Philosophical Theologian*; and Richard B. Steele, "Transfiguring Light: The Moral Beauty of the Christian Life According to Gregory Palamas and Jonathan Edwards," *St. Vladimir's Theological Quarterly* 52 (2008): 403–39.

23. See WJE 8:528 for an exposition of this reality.

in this divine nature is partaking in the divine knowledge and love (in a creaturely, and therefore finite, way). In union with the Son and by the infusion and illumination of the Spirit, believers truly partake by grace what is God's by nature.

## Incarnation: Unity in the Spirit

Edwards's doctrine of the incarnation offers the theological blueprint upon which he builds his soteriology. In his sermon on Canticles 1:3, he claims, "We shall in a sort be partakers of his [Christ's] relation to the Father or his communion with him in his Sonship. We shall not only be the sons of God by regeneration but a kind of participation of the Sonship of the eternal Son."[24] Along similar lines, Edwards states,

> This was the design of Christ, to bring it to pass, that he, and his Father, and his people, might all be united in one . . . that those that the Father has given him, should be brought into the household of God; that he, and his Father, and his people, should be as it were one society, one family; that the church should be as it were admitted into the society of the blessed Trinity.[25]

Believers are not merely children of God by regeneration, but by a true participation in the sonship of the Son. This is relational all the way down. God's own life of beauty and delight is broken open in the Son in his role as mediator. Turning to the mechanics of the incarnation, we attend to how his doctrine functions within the *telos* noted above. How do believers, in other words, come to partake in God's own life?[26]

---

24. Jonathan Edwards, "Thy Name Is as Ointment Poured Forth," in *The Blessing of God: Previously Unpublished Sermons of Jonathan Edwards*, ed. Michael D. McMullen (Nashville: Broadman & Holman, 2003), 177. Furthermore, Edwards states, "For there is doubtless an infinite intimacy between the Father and the Son. . . . And saints being in him, shall, in their measure and manner, partake with him in it, and the blessedness of it" (WJE 19:593).

25. WJE 19:593.

26. Edwards claims, "this seems to be one glorious end of the union of the human to the divine nature, to bring God near to us; that even our God, the infinite Being, might be made as one of us; that his terrible majesty might not make us afraid; that Jehovah, who is infinitely distant from us, might become familiar to us" (WJE 13:248).

## Spirit Christology

Following the work of John Owen, Edwards advanced a Spirit Christology, where the Spirit serves as the bond of union between the two natures of Christ.[27] This union is based on a pattern found in God's inner life, where the Father and Son are bound together in the love of the Spirit. Following this pattern in the economy, we discover that the man Jesus stands in the same relation to the Father in the Spirit: the Father looks upon Jesus as his Son with love flowing forth between them. Jesus is the Son, in part, because the Father knows him and sees him as such. The Father's grasping Jesus as the Son in the love of the Spirit is what makes Jesus, in part, the God-man. In Edwards's words, "The man Christ is united to the Logos these two ways: first, by the respect which God hath to this human nature. God hath respect to this man and loveth him as his own Son; this man hath communication with the Logos, in the love which the Father hath to him as his only begotten Son. Now the love of God is the Holy Ghost."[28] The Spirit, as the love of God, is how God unites himself to creatures. Along these lines Edwards claims, "Perhaps there is no other way of God's dwelling in a creature but by his Spirit."[29] In God's life, the bond of union is the Spirit of love, and this archetypal union becomes the pattern in Edwards's theological system. Furthermore, Edwards explains that Christ "has the same spirit or disposition towards the Father; not as believers have a filial spirit . . . but he has the Spirit of the only begotten of the Father."[30] This union of the two natures in Christ is a personal union by the Spirit and is *sui generis*. On the other hand, as

27. Although Edwards did not publish his notes on Christology, it is clear that he is compiling arguments for his view rather than addressing their adequacy. I would agree with Robert W. Caldwell III when he states, "Because we see him [Edwards] not only developing this view, but bringing theological and exegetical clarity to it throughout these entries, we can be fairly certain that it was his mature position." Caldwell, *Communion in the Spirit: The Holy Spirit as the Bond of Union in the Theology of Jonathan Edwards*, Studies in Evangelical History and Thought (Milton Keynes: Paternoster, 2006), 85.

28. WJE 13:529.

29. WJE 13:528. In "Miscellanies," entry 183, Edwards writes, "Such was the love of the Son of God to the human nature, that he desired a most near and close union with it, something like the union in the persons of the Trinity, nearer than there can be between any two distinct [beings]" (WJE 13:329). It becomes clear in Edwards's notes that his assumed position is that the Spirit is in fact this union. See "Miscellanies," entries 513, 624, 709, 764b, 766, 958, 1043; WJE 15:87, 575, and 244.

30. WJE 13:529.

an economic act of the Spirit it has a parallel in creaturely redemption. The redemption of the elect follows the pattern found in the incarnation of the Son: "There is a likeness in the manner of God's dwelling in the man Christ, and in believers."[31] Edwards's development of the incarnation by the Spirit parallels Christ's sending of the Spirit to pull creatures into the life of God. Likewise, the Spirit's work to unite the Father and Son in love, the two natures in the person of Christ, believers to the life of God in Christ, and the community of believers together are all acts of God's own uniting love, even if they are distinct.[32]

The Son of God takes on flesh and dwells among creatures through the action of the Spirit to personally unite a human nature to the divine in the person of Christ. The redemptive parallel to this action is Christ sending his Spirit to unite with human persons for participation in his sonship before the Father:

> He came into this world and brought God or divinity down with him to us; and then he ascended to God and carried up humanity or man with him to God. And from heaven he sent down the Holy Spirit, whereby he gives God to man, and hereby he draws them to give up themselves to God.[33]

The parallel Edwards draws with the incarnation is the sending of the Spirit. The ascension of Christ to God, now justified, sanctified, and glorified, is held in parallel to the saints ascending to God in Christ by the Spirit. Therefore, to trace this parallel, just as the Son knows the Father in communion and love, so glorified believers come to ascend within that very relationship. "The saints shall enjoy God as partaking with Christ *of his* enjoyment of God."[34] Similarly, the regenerate are partakers of God's holiness "not only as they partake of holiness that God gives, *but partake of that holiness by which he himself is holy*."[35] The saints' access to God is through the person of Christ alone, and in the Spirit they partake of the holiness by which he himself is holy. This view of *theōsis* is a "participation of God," Edwards claims, where "God put his own beauty, i.e. his beau-

---

31. WJE 13:528.

32. Caldwell, *Communion in the Spirit*, 87.

33. WJE 18:422.

34. Unpublished Sermon, Romans 2:10, Jonathan Edwards Center Transcriptions #373 [L.44v] (hereafter Romans 2:10 with leaf number). Emphasis added.

35. WJE 21:195. Emphasis added.

tiful likeness, upon their souls."[36] This partaking in Christ by the uniting activity and indwelling holiness of the Spirit is the *telos* of Edwards's soteriology. It is in this sense that he claims,

> As the new nature is from God, so it tends to God as its center; and as that which tends to its center is not quiet and at rest, till it has got quite to the very center, so the new nature that is in the saints never will it be at rest, till there is a perfect union with God and conformity to him, and so no separation, or alienation, or enmity remaining. The holy nature in the saints tends to the fountain whence it proceeds, and never will be at rest, till the soul is fully brought to that fountain, and all swallowed up in it.[37]

God is the new center for the Christian. The Father sends Christ as the mediator in response to the sinfulness of humanity. Christ is the only possible entry point of salvation, because believers come to the Father in the person of Christ. The new nature received from the Spirit's infused presence focuses the entirety of the human person on Christ and his beauty. The Spirit, furthermore, harmonizes the person with Christ through union, communion, and participation with his person. The trajectory of Edwards's theotic soteriology is an ascension, not simply to God, but in God; this is not a metaphysical merging with the divine, but is a relational ascent within the person of the Son. Edwards claims, "The way in which the saints will come to an intimate full enjoyment of the Father is not by the Father's majesty . . . but by their ascending to him by their union with Christ's person."[38] This notion of a relational ascent may be an aspect of the *Reformed* nature of Edwards's thought. Julie Canlis, in her book on Calvin's notion of ascent and ascension, writes, "But in disciplining ascent specifically to the Son, both Irenaeus and Calvin preserve the Creator-creature distinction vital to their conceptions of participation. Ascent is into *sonship*, but never as *the Son*." This is also the core idea of Edwards's doctrine of *theōsis*. She continues,

> Yet it is clear that for neither theologian is this adoptive ascent something that has to do with some abstract divinization of

36. WJE 17:208.
37. WJE 19:692.
38. WJE 18:375.

nature; rather, it is ascent into deeper *koinōnia* with God and his benefits. Everything depends on their theology of the Spirit, as both the one who preserves the contingency of creation and the one who ensures that this is the personal activity of God on and within humanity.[39]

Maintaining his emphasis on personhood and delight, the ascent of the glorified saints is an ascent "within" Christ's person to the Father, where they participate finitely in the infinite delight of God. The mediated immediacy of God's blessedness is known only in the person of the Son by the ecstatic delight of the Spirit.

The centripetal force of God's love will draw the saints into a full union with himself, a union that increases eternally. God's own life is an infinite fountain of knowledge and love, what Edwards refers to as the communicative nature of God, and this flows forth fully *ad intra*, and then overflows *ad extra* to the creation. It is the receiving of this knowledge and love—a participation in God's nature—that begins in regeneration and awaits perfection in glory. Human persons are actualized in the overflow of God's love and knowledge, partaking of the life of God, awaiting the fullness of their life in glory. Far from being static, therefore, eternity is inherently dynamic, an interplay of persons uniting in love, knowledge, and participation in one another.[40] "Thus they shall eat and drink abundantly, and swim in the ocean of love, and be eternally swallowed up in the infinitely bright, and infinitely mild and sweet beams of divine love," Edwards proclaims, "eternally receiving that light, eternally full of it, and eternally compassed round with

---

39. Julie Canlis, *Calvin's Ladder: A Spiritual Theology of Ascent and Ascension* (Grand Rapids: Eerdmans, 2010), 237–38. Canlis's book helpfully exposes an underappreciated theme among Reformed writers. Much of what she reveals in Calvin's thought could easily be said of Edwards as well. In one such case she claims, "In subtly shifting Aquinas's *exitus-reditus* scheme from anthropology to Christ, Calvin challenges Aquinas's attempt at theocentrism as not going far enough. It is not Christ who fits into the procrustean bed of anthropology but we who are fitted to Christ and his ascent. In him and by his Spirit, we ascend to the Father" (44). Furthermore, "The mystical ascent is this deeper and deeper burrowing into Christ (always pneumatologically conceived), not our effort to do so. His ascent is our path and goal. His narrative has become our own" (51). This is precisely what we see in Edwards's doctrine of *theōsis*.

40. "The soul shall not be an inactive spectator but shall be most active, shall be in the most ardent exercise of love towards the object seen. The soul shall be, as it were, all eye to behold, and yet all act to love." Romans 2:10 [L.45v].

it, and everlastingly reflecting it back again to the fountain of it."[41] It would be a mistake to read the potentially depersonalizing language of light reflecting as anything other than a deeply relational participation in the divine life. Believers "eternally receive light" as they have eyes to see the beauty and glory of God; believers "become bright" as they are actualized by love.

The meta-narrative of Edwards's soteriology is God revealing himself to believers so that they will partake in the Son's relationship to the Father. Edwards's vision of redemption works hard to constantly refocus our sight around the economic activity of Son and Spirit. He recognized the subtle error of shifting the benefits of redemption to the center, displacing Christ and the Spirit as the central defining aspects of the gospel. As an account of redemption based on participation in the sonship of the Son, Edwards develops the biblical image of the bride and bridegroom as his main metaphor for redemption. This imagery parallels adoption as another important biblical metaphor of salvation. In both, the issue of redemption is a family matter, something achievable only by the Son. Therefore, Edwards can state, "It seems by this to have been God's design to admit man as it were to the inmost fellowship with the deity," claiming there is "an eternal society or family in the Godhead in the Trinity of persons."[42] This language allows for both adoption and marital imagery, but Edwards shows his preference when he claims, "It seems to be God's design to admit the church into the divine family as his son's wife."[43] Edwards understood that the deep questions of soteriology must orbit around a participation in the life of God in Christ. This life is closed off to humanity because of sin and is only available by being united to the person of Christ. The goal of soteriology, therefore, is a greater and greater communion with God in Christ by the Spirit. To answer how humankind could become united to the life of God, Edwards turns to union by the Spirit in Christ as the logic of redemption. Whereas this is the broad picture, we need to mine the specific mechanics of redemption. To do so, we turn to Edwards's doctrines of regeneration and justification. These provide us with the heart of Edwards's soteriology and will further illumine his Christocentric account of redemption.

41. WJE 25:233.
42. WJE 18:367.
43. WJE 18:367.

## Regeneration and Justification

Edwards's focus on Son and Spirit as the axis upon which redemption turns pushes the themes of union and participation to the fore. By emphasizing union and participation, justification is located within Christ himself. The elect are united to God in Christ as a bride is united to her groom in marriage; they are truly one. Giving over the Spirit to believers is parallel to God sending the Spirit to unite a human nature to the Logos. By being united to Christ the elect are made new. This union is the "real" that grounds the forensic declaration; believers are deemed holy and righteous because they partake in the holiness and righteousness of Christ.[44]

### *The Regenerating Spirit*

For persons to partake in the life of God, they must undergo regeneration. Regeneration is, in the words of Richard Muller, "the rebirth of mind and will accomplished by the gracious work of the Holy Spirit at the outset of the *ordo salutis*."[45] Whereas justification will focus primarily on Christ and his work to redeem, regeneration emphasizes the Spirit's work to apply that redemption.[46] In regeneration, the believer has been given the Holy Spirit who awakens faith in the person, but, in doing so, the Spirit has brought the presence of God in the soul. "The Holy Spirit is given through Christ, whereby the soul is sanctified and a principle of spiritual life is infused, and the nature is renewed after the image of God."[47] In regeneration "habits of true virtue and holiness" are obtained and believers "come to have the character of true Christians."[48] The "habit" and "character" are nothing less than the habit and character of God's own

---

44. WJE 19:158

45. Richard A. Muller, "Regeneratio," in *Dictionary of Latin and Greek Theological Terms: Drawn Principally from Protestant Scholastic Theology* (Grand Rapids: Baker Academic, 1985), 259.

46. This section is necessarily thin in development because of the nature of the debates concerning justification, its relation to regeneration, and the question concerning Edwards's relation to the Reformed. I address these questions in detail in "By Word and Spirit: Jonathan Edwards on Redemption, Justification, and Regeneration," in *Jonathan Edwards and Justification*, ed. Josh Moody (Wheaton, IL: Crossway, 2012), 45–69.

47. WJE 17:135.

48. WJE 3:363.

life—the Holy Spirit—or the indwelling of God's holiness itself. Christ loves the elect to such a degree that the Spirit of love binds believers to Christ's own life; Christ, "through his great power, does but speak the powerful word and it is done, he does but call and the heart of the sinner immediately comes."[49] This call is efficacious because of the work of the Spirit to illumine Christ, and it is by this illumination that the person can "close" with Christ in faith:

> one glimpse of the moral and spiritual glory of God, and supreme amiableness of Jesus Christ, shining into the heart, overcomes and abolishes this opposition, and inclines the soul to Christ, as it were, by an omnipotent power: so that now, not only the understanding, but the will, and the whole soul receives and embraces the Savior. This is most certainly the discovery, which is the first internal foundation of a saving faith in Christ. . . . The sense of divine beauty, is the first thing in the actual change made in the soul, in true conversion, and is the foundation of everything else belonging to that change; as it evident by those words of the Apostle, II Cor. 3:18, "But we all with open face, beholding as in a glass, the glory of the Lord, are changed into the same image, from glory to glory, even as by the Spirit of the Lord."[50]

Illumination is the foundation for the other features of regeneration, because in illumination the believer is able to have faith and thereby incline to Christ. But illumination is not the only aspect of the Spirit's work. God infuses the Spirit into persons so that they know true holiness in their own life. "God's Spirit, or his love, doth but as it were come and dwell in our hearts and act there as a vital principle," as infused holiness, "and we become the living temples of the Holy Ghost; and when men are regenerated and sanctified, God pours forth of his Spirit upon them,

49. WJE 21:161–62.
50. WJE 25:635–36. Elsewhere, Edwards remarks, "Indeed the first act of the Spirit of God, or the first that this divine temper exerts itself in, is in spiritual understanding, or in the sense of the mind, its perception of glory and excellency, etc. in the ideas it has of divine things; and this is before any proper acts of the will. Indeed, the inclination of the soul is as immediately exercised in that sense of the mind which is called spiritual understanding, as the intellect. For it is not only the mere presence of ideas in the mind, but it is the mind's sense of their excellency, glory and delightfulness." WJE 13:463.

and they have fellowship or, which is the same thing, are made partakers with the Father and Son of their good, i.e. of their love, joy and beauty."[51] On this account of regeneration, it would be easy to push the weight of Edwards's discussion on the indwelling of the Spirit. In this sense, the emphasis is on God's handing over holiness and grace rather than pulling creatures into his own life. As the quote above testifies, this is mistaken. In giving the Spirit, creatures are pulled within God's own life because the Spirit is the bond of union that unites them to Christ.[52] Christ is where salvation is found, and therefore the Spirit's work is to unite the believer to Christ. In doing so, the Spirit functions as both the union of love and the nature of holiness given to believers (i.e., the "vital principle"). The Spirit is the "principle laid" in the regenerate, bringing God's holiness, grace, beauty, etc., into the soul. This work of illumination and infusion allows creatures to become alive to God and know him truly, and therefore it is only through the Spirit's presence that human persons can have faith. In faith, or the grasping of Christ by the Spirit, believers partake in the life of God and come to understand their own identity as child in the sonship of the Son.

Within this account of regeneration, the Spirit unites believers to Christ, acts as the principle of holiness within them, and illuminates Christ as God's self-revelation of goodness, truth, and beauty. Illumination opens creatures to God's own life through a vivification of their whole person. The Spirit is the divine light that makes the person of God known. It is "a true sense of the divine excellency of the things revealed in the Word of God, and a conviction of the truth and reality of them, thence arising."[53] Knowing the God of beauty entails more than knowledge about God, but it entails a relationship with him such that the creature grasps his true nature as beautiful. "He that is spiritually enlightened truly apprehends and sees it, or has a sense of it. He don't merely rationally believe that God is glorious, but he has a sense of the gloriousness of God in his heart."[54] This "sense of the heart" is the result of the new foundation laid in the soul through the infusion of the Spirit that allows the believer to function according to a new nature. This sense is not a new faculty of the

51. WJE 21:124.
52. S. Mark Hamilton exposits Edwards's theology of union as a fivefold union. See S. Mark Hamilton, "Jonathan Edwards on the Atonement," *International Journal of Systematic Theology* 15, no. 4 (2013): 404–12.
53. WJE 17:413.
54. WJE 17:413.

soul, which is not possible on Edwards's understanding of personhood, but is the new nature received by the Spirit.

Conversion, therefore, can be understood as the moment a person grasps Christ as beautiful (or excellent, to use Edwards's preferred aesthetic term for Christ).

> When a person is converted, then the day dawns and the day-star arises in his heart. There is a beam of divine light let into the soul, but this light always brings love into the heart. The soul the same moment that 'tis filled with spiritual light 'tis also filled with divine love. The heart immediately goes out after God and the Lord Jesus Christ. . . . When light and love go together, they show the truth of one another, they evidence the divinity of each.[55]

The Spirit's vivifying activity in regeneration turns the believer to Christ so that she receives him. This act of receiving, on the believer's part, is faith. Faith, therefore, is based upon the real work of the Spirit in the life of a believer, and yet righteousness remains alien because only Christ is truly righteous. Any righteousness in the believer is righteousness received from Christ.

> There is a two-fold righteousness that the saints have: an imputed righteousness, and 'tis this only that avails anything to justification; and an inherent righteousness, that is, that holiness and grace which is in the hearts and lives of the saints. This is Christ's righteousness as well as imputed righteousness: imputed righteousness is Christ's righteousness accepted for them, inherent holiness is Christ's righteousness communicated to them. They derive their holiness from Christ as the fountain of it.[56]

This raises an important question: If the believer obtains faith and holiness in the act of regeneration, and faith embraces Christ who is

---

55. Jonathan Edwards, "The Spirit of the True Saints Is a Spirit of Divine Love (1 John 4:16)," in *The Glory and Honor of God: Volume 2 of the Previously Unpublished Sermons of Jonathan Edwards*, ed. Michael McMullen (Nashville: Broadman & Holman, 2004), 312.

56. WJE 14:340.

the location of our salvation, then what place is there for a doctrine of justification?

## The Justified Christ

In the environment of High-Orthodox Reformed theology, the Catholic critique against Protestant accounts of justification, that they were mere "legal fictions," was being felt to a much greater degree than previously. In response, Edwards comes out strongly in the other direction, asserting that "God neither will nor can justify a person without a righteousness . . . if a person should be justified without a righteousness, the judgment would not be according to truth." Moreover, "the sentence of justification would be a false sentence, unless there be a righteousness performed that is by the judge properly looked upon as his."[57] Justification is, according to Edwards's account, truly legal, and therefore necessitates a right pronouncement by a judge. For the judge to be honorable and righteous, the believer must be actually righteous to be declared so (as in the atonement, the "honor" of God is fundamental). In this vein Edwards states, "what is real in the union between Christ and his people, is the foundation of what is legal; that is, it is something really in them, and between them, uniting them, that is the ground of the suitableness of their being accounted as one by the Judge."[58] Christ, as the fulfiller of the law, is the only person justified before God on his own account. The elect are not justified apart from Christ's justification, but are justified as they are one with Christ who is the justified One. God the Judge justifies Christ by raising him from the dead, and, Edwards emphasizes, "The justification of a believer *is not other* than his being admitted to communion in, or participation of the justification of this head."[59] What Edwards's doctrine of justification seeks to explain is how the believer can be found righteous when only Christ is. Edwards focuses on Christ as the location of justification, positing that only Christ is truly justified in himself. *He* is righteousness for the believer because he is the one who walked perfectly before God in

57. WJE 19:188.

58. WJE 19:158. Brandon Withrow has shown that Edwards's doctrines of justification and original sin parallel each other with this use of "real." See Brandon G. Withrow, *Becoming Divine: Jonathan Edwards's Incarnational Spirituality within the Christian Tradition* (Eugene, OR: Pickwick Publications, 2011), 163–68.

59. WJE 19:151. Emphasis added.

faithfulness. If we recall that God's commitment to the fulfillment of the law is uncompromising, what Edwards's account of justification explains is how creatures can be seen as righteous when they have sinned against God and his law. To maintain the legal aspect of salvation, Edwards turns to Christ as the justified One in whom believers come to be justified. The logic of the atonement determined that the love of the Father and the Son was infinite, and the love of the Son upon his people was infinite, so as to unite them to himself, and therefore as they are one with Christ they share by grace what he has both by nature and through faithful obedience.

Justification, as with righteousness, is found only in Christ, and therefore justification is obtained through union and participation. Union and participation, we should recall, are personal realities. To be united to God in Christ by the Spirit, one must be "harmonized" with Christ through one's understanding and will. Ultimately, this is the reality of faith. Edwards's own summary of this activity will suffice:

> Therefore saving, justifying faith in Christ, don't consist merely in the assent of the understanding, nor only in the consent of the will; but 'tis harmonizing of the whole soul with Jesus Christ, as he is revealed and held forth in the gospel. . . . Faith is no other than that harmony in the soul towards Christ that has been spoken of in its most direct act. And it may be defined [as] the soul's entirely uniting and closing with Christ for his Savior, acquiescing in his reality and goodness as a Savior, as the gospel reveals him. And hence it is that by faith that we are justified, not as commending us to God by its excellency as a qualification in us, but as uniting us to Christ.[60]

By becoming incarnate, God unites himself to the human condition. At Pentecost, Christ sends the Spirit to dwell in believers to unite them to his life. In Christ the Father is known, and by the Spirit Christ is illumined. Edwards's account of justification posits a participation in the life of the justified One so that his status is counted for the elect. This, in Edwards's understanding, is not suspect bookkeeping on God's part but is grounded in the reality that the elect are truly one with the Son through communion with his Spirit. The goal of salvation is participation in the life of God, and justification takes care of the legal realities that must be addressed for

60. WJE 19:448.

creatures to have access to the Father in Christ by the Spirit (Eph. 2:18). Justification is by faith alone, because faith is necessary for the person to receive Christ. But faith is not oriented to justification; that would center soteriology on the benefits of Christ rather than Christ himself. Rather, faith is the necessary condition by which the whole soul is harmonized with Christ, and the first reality of that union with Christ is receiving Christ's righteousness and justification as one's own. Faith is not, therefore, the instrumental cause of justification with the Westminster Confession but the instrument by which we receive Christ—the proper center of salvation.

The Westminster Confession of Faith states, "Faith, thus receiving and resting on Christ and His righteousness, is the alone instrument of justification: yet it is not alone in the person justified, but is ever accompanied with all other saving graces, and is no dead faith, but works by love."[61] At first glance this seems like a suitable overview of Edwards's position, but he does raise some concern about this kind of construction. In particular, Edwards is concerned with accounts that see faith as the instrument to receive justification.

Edwards has two worries. First, he is worried that this language is ambiguous. This had become a point of contention and confusion concerning justification in Edwards's day, and he wants to bring greater clarity to the issue. Second, Edwards is worried that this terminology misorients the doctrine. Faith is not the instrument by which we receive justification, Edwards will argue, but faith is the instrument by which we receive Christ. Richard Muller helpfully articulates this concern: "Since justification is viewed by the Protestant orthodox as a counting righteous rather than a making righteous, it rests not merely on the merit of Christ, but upon the union of the believer with Christ by grace through faith. An individual is counted righteous because he is *in Christo*, in Christ, covered as it were by the righteousness of Christ."[62] Edwards is not concerned with undermining the notion that faith is an instrumental cause (although this kind of causality is not usually employed at this point); he is simply worried that believers seek Christ's benefits over Christ himself. This becomes clear right after Edwards seems to, at first glance, undermine the instrumentality of faith. He clarifies his point by saying, "if faith be an

61. Westminster Confession of Faith (1647), XI.2, in *Reformed Confessions Harmonized: With an Annotated Bibliography of Reformed Doctrinal Works*, ed. Joel R. Beeke and Sinclair B. Ferguson (Grand Rapids: Baker Books, 1999), 99.

62. Richard Muller, "Iustificatio," in *Dictionary of Latin and Greek Theological Terms*, 162.

instrument, 'tis more properly the instrument by which we receive Christ, than the instrument by which we receive justification."[63] His turn is to focus faith on receiving Christ, and, in our reception of Christ, receiving justification as we partake in Christ's justification.

In Edwards's soteriology, the Spirit-filled Son is the justified One, and the Spirit-overflowing Son sends his Spirit to unite the elect to his own life. Through the Son, believers are united to God, and in glorification they come to see the infinite God according to their finite capacity.[64] Sanctification, therefore, is the work of the Spirit in the hearts of the saints to mortify the flesh and vivify their spirits. Just like justification, sanctification is a participation in the Son since Christ is the sanctification of the believer (1 Cor. 1:30). This participation is the engine of mortification and vivification, a work that continues the transformation begun in regeneration. Edwards's soteriology does not rotate around a singular doctrinal locus (e.g., justification) but finds its orbit in the person and work of Christ and the person and work of the Spirit. *Theōsis*, and its grammar of participation, forms Edwards's soteriology and orients it to its ultimate goal—an increasing union, communion, and participation with God in Christ for eternity. Sounding like Basil the Great, Edwards claims,

> As God delights in his own beauty, he must necessarily delight in the creature's holiness; which is a conformity to, and participation of it, as truly as the brightness of a jewel, held in the sun's beams, is a participation, or derivation of the sun's brightness, though immensely less in degree.[65]

Notice how similar this is to Basil the Great, who states,

> Shining upon those that are cleansed from every spot, He makes them spiritual by fellowship with Himself. Just as when

---

63. WJE 19:153.

64. See Kyle Strobel, "Jonathan Edwards's Reformed Doctrine of the Beatific Vision," in *Jonathan Edwards and Scotland*, ed. Kenneth Minkema, Adriaan Neale, and Kelly van Andel (Edinburgh: Dunedin Academic Press, 2011), 237–65.

65. WJE 8:442. Elsewhere, he writes "'Tis rational to suppose that this blessing should be immediately from God; for there is no gift or benefit that is in itself so nearly related to the divine nature, there is nothing the creature receives that is so much of God, of his nature, so much a participation of the Deity: 'tis a kind of emanation of God's beauty, and is related to God as the light is to the sun" (WJE 17:422).

a sunbeam falls on bright and transparent bodies, they themselves become brilliant too, and shed forth a fresh brightness
from themselves, so souls wherein the Spirit dwells, illuminated
by the Spirit, themselves become spiritual, and send forth their
grace to others.[66]

Whereas the atonement explains how the Son, in wisdom and love,
redeems believers and maintains his relationship with the Father—hon-
oring and glorifying him in all things—justification is a much more narrow doctrine. For Edwards, justification explains how it is that God can
declare a believer righteous when only Christ is. This is not done by a
declarative speech-act that justifies in itself but is done in Christ. The
declaration that believers are forgiven and deemed righteous, therefore,
mirrors the pastor who declares a couple husband and wife. The declaration names a reality that is already true but is now being recognized
publicly. God's declaration that the sinner is righteous is his declaration
that Christ has won his bride, not based on her beauty, purity, or righteousness, but based on his wisdom and love for her, a love that unites her
to himself, making her beautiful, pure, and righteous in his own beauty,
purity, and righteousness.

## Taking Stock

The overall picture of Edwards's soteriology is that God desires to call
creatures into his life, and so the Father sends the Son to find a bride,
that in union with him by the Spirit creatures become partakers of the
divine nature. As an ascent within the person of the Son, Edwards's doctrine of *theōsis* entails a relational participation among the divine persons
within the person of the Son and a sharing in the divine nature known
in the Son and Spirit as the understanding and love of the Father. This is
why Edwards can say, "the saints are exalted to glorious dignity, even to
union and fellowship with God him[self], to be in some respects *divine* in
glory and happiness."[67] In this scheme, Christ has sanctified space for the
creature within the life of God within himself, and therefore Edwards's

66. Basil, *On the Spirit* 9.23, in *A Select Library of Nicene and Post-Nicene Fathers
of the Christian Church*, vol. 8 (Grand Rapids: Eerdmans, 1978), 15.
67. WJE 18:241. Emphasis added.

account focuses on what it means to share in Christ's life. Sharing in the life of the Son, and seeing him by faith in the illuminating presence of the Spirit, affectionately draws the believer away from selfishness to long for God in his beauty. In short, the creature now knows that he or she is called to be beautiful as Christ has revealed his beauty within his person and work. This beauty is the moral reality of life in Christ, who has revealed in himself the deep wisdom of God and offered his people a participation in beauty itself.

# CHAPTER SEVEN

# Becoming Beautiful

In the previous chapter we saw that salvation is a participation in God's life. In God's self-giving we come to partake in the Father-Son relationship as we ascend in the person of the Son to the Father. This is not simply an intellectual ascent, as if the Christian life were simply abstract speculation. Rather, salvation is a harmonizing of the whole soul to God in Christ by the Spirit. In believers' union with Christ they are justified, because Christ is the justified One. In this depiction of salvation, both in its initial moment of conversion and its continual reality in sanctification, the focal point is God's movement in Son and Spirit, and the secondary feature is the participation of the Christian in that movement.

In this chapter we turn to three key features of regenerate existence. We begin with Edwards's theological anthropology, what I have referred to elsewhere as a theotic-anthropology.[1] From there we turn to participation, glory, and religious affection to reveal the nature of the affectionate life. To conclude, we address how these features provide the contours for Edwards's notion of the ethical life as a life of beauty. The overall picture of regenerate Christian existence we are depicting here is the person captivated by beauty, and, as such, the person becoming beautiful.

---

1. For a more in-depth analysis of this, see Kyle Strobel, "Being Seen and Being Known: Jonathan Edwards's Theological Anthropology," in *The Global Edwards: Papers from the Jonathan Edwards Conference Held in Melbourne, August 2015*, Australian College of Theology Monograph Series, ed. Rhys Bezzant (Eugene, OR: Wipf & Stock, 2017), 158–78.

## Anthropology

Edwards's anthropology begins and ends with God because it is theologically ordered by participation within the life of God. The creature is constituted by God for the purpose of mirroring and participating in his own life, so that God's economic overflow can be received and rebounded back to him. This anthropology can be called a theotic-anthropology, because the human person is created in participation (in the garden of Eden) and for participation in the life of God. Edwards's anthropology is set up for *theōsis* as the category within which we think about human flourishing (even though the terms Edwards utilizes for this are terms such as "grace," "glory," "holiness," and "beauty"). This section expounds the nature of his theological anthropology with an eye toward the moral features of regenerate human existence.

In his "Discourse on the Trinity," Edwards makes the bold declaration that "though the divine nature be vastly different from that of created spirits, yet our souls are made in the image of God: we have understanding and will, idea and love, as God hath, and the difference is only in the perfection of degree and manner."[2] Edwards often starts his discussion of human personhood with divine personhood, focusing more on the likeness between them than the difference. The notion that a person is a being with understanding and will is the structure that Edwards employs both in his doctrine of God and in his understanding of human personhood. To explain this similarity, we can say that the structure of personhood remains the same across the Creator/creature divide. The claim that "God the Father is a person," for instance, is, to some degree, univocally related to the structure of human personhood. While the overall structure of personhood is the same, the degree and manner by which God is personal differ categorically from human personhood. (Edwards often invokes the qualifier "infinite" to describe divine in contrast with human personhood.) For Edwards, the human person was created to mirror the divine life, however finitely, and to have the capacity to partake in that divine life and remanate it back to God.[3]

---

2. WJE 21:113.

3. Edwards does qualify this, claiming, "Words were first formed to express external things; and those that are applied to express things internal and spiritual, are almost all borrowed, and used in a sort of figurative sense. Whence they are most of 'em attended with a great deal of ambiguity and unfixedness in their signification, occasioning innumerable doubts, difficulties and confusions in inquiries and controversies about things of this

Edwards's belief that a person is a being with understanding and will does not entail that a person has a will, as if only a part (i.e., "faculty") of the soul willed. Rather, the person wills. On Edwards's account, he continues to employ the term "faculties," but now they are simply modes by which the human person engages reality, either through perception and cognition or inclination or repulsion. In his *Freedom of the Will*, Edwards states, "For the will itself is not an agent that has a will: the power of choosing, itself, has not a power of choosing. That which has the power of volition or choice is the man or the soul, and not the power of volition itself."[4] "To be free," Edwards continues, "is the property of an agent."[5] It is true that Edwards's description of the human person focuses on the faculties rather than the self behind the faculties. But Edwards is clear that the self is the agent who understands and wills, and it is not the faculties of the person. In this sense, Edwards's discussion of the human person mirrors, once again, his discourse concerning God. God the Father receives the least amount of attention, whereas the Son and the Spirit dominate his thought as the understanding and will of God. This is paralleled with the human agent, where the fundamental self is addressed by talking about her understanding and her will, the features of the self engaging and perceiving reality.

### Twofold Image of God

By mooring the structure of human personhood to God's own life, Edwards's account of human being is oriented by participation within that life. The biblical category for this is the *imago dei*. Edwards draws a distinction between the natural image and the supernatural image of God.

> The case with man was plainly this: when God made man at first, he implanted in him two kinds of principles. There was an *inferior* kind, which may be called *natural*, being the principles of mere human nature; such as self-love, with those natural

---

nature. But language is much less adapted to express things in the mind of the incomprehensible Deity, precisely as they are." WJE 1:376. Therefore, this language of personhood needs to be understood in light of these claims.

4. WJE 1:163.

5. WJE 1:163. See Paul Ramsey's remarks on how Edwards follows John Locke here. WJE 1:47–65.

appetites and passions, which belong to the nature of man, in which his love to his own liberty, honor and pleasure, were exercised: these when alone, and left to themselves, are what the Scriptures sometimes call *flesh*. Besides these, there were *superior* principles, that were spiritual, holy and divine, summarily comprehended in divine love; wherein consisted the spiritual image of God, and man's righteousness and true holiness; which are called in Scripture the *divine nature*.[6]

The natural image is focused on the intellectual capacities of human persons. "Man's reason," Edwards states, "is that wherein mainly consists the natural image of God. It is the noblest faculty of man; 'tis that which ought to bear rule over the other powers. It was given for that end, to govern in the soul."[7] The supernatural image is the Holy Spirit residing within the human person, communicating the divine nature and communion with God. This is the supernatural image because it is the Holy Spirit and is, as such, beyond the natural, but also because a human person can still be human without the Spirit's indwelling presence.

Those may be called supernatural, because they are no part of human nature. They don't belong to the nature of man as man, nor do they naturally and necessarily flow from the faculties and properties of that nature. Man can be man without 'em. They did not flow from anything in the human nature, but from the Spirit of God dwelling in man, and exerting itself by man's faculties as a principle of action.[8]

Nonetheless, the supernatural image was supposed to be a regular feature of normal life. Had Adam and Eve never sinned they would have retained the Holy Spirit within them, but with the act of sin the Spirit and his principles of holiness vacated entirely.

Man's entire nature in his primitive state was constituted of flesh and Spirit. That part of his entire nature that consists in the principles of the mean human nature, or that is the human

6. WJE 3:381.
7. WJE 17:67.
8. WJE 24:1086.

nature in its present animal state, simply and absolutely considered, is flesh. The human nature, or humanity in that animal state in which it is in this world, is often called flesh in Scripture (*Genesis 6:12; Psalms 65:2; Isaiah 40:5–6,* and *Isaiah 49:26,* and *Isaiah 66:16; Matthew 24:22; John 1:14*).[9]

Humankind was left with only the base principles, having lost the superior principles known in the Spirit's infusion. Therefore, in humanity's "natural" state, man and woman had both a natural and a supernatural image of God.

Prior to sin entering creation, "these superior principles were given to possess the throne, and maintain an absolute dominion in the heart: the other, to be wholly subordinate and subservient. And while things continued thus, all things were in excellent order, peace and beautiful harmony, and in their proper and perfect state."[10] For this order to be maintained the Spirit's presence in the soul is required, but with the entrance of sin the Spirit fled, leaving only the flesh. On this kind of account, the flesh is not intrinsically evil, but left by itself it can only be sinful; without the Spirit's presence the soul is inevitably disordered and disordering. The human person was created to live within the presence of God and to have the indwelling presence of God as a principle of holiness in the soul. Autonomy, as a result of the fall, is losing the natural (i.e., natural and supernatural combination) state of human persons in the primeval garden, descending into brokenness apart from God. So while the flesh is not evil when it is ordered by the supernatural presence of the Spirit, on its own it is humankind turned inward, willing selfishly and rejecting Christ.

> Man's natural principles, or those principles of humanity that man had, were in his primitive state very good, because that man's spiritual principles that he had were to that degree as the Spirit dwelt and acted in him, to that degree that the natural principles were entirely subordinate to them. Then the flesh did not lust against the Spirit. These two natures or two sorts of principles were by an entire, an absolute, subordination of one to t'other united, so as to be as it were one nature. The spiritual principles have absolute rule.[11]

9. WJE 3:382.
10. WJE 24:1087.
11. WJE 24:1087.

Edwards claims:

> Therefore immediately the superior divine principles wholly ceased; so light ceases in a room, when the candle is withdrawn: and thus man was left in a state of darkness, woeful corruption and ruin; nothing but flesh, without spirit. The inferior principles of self-love and natural appetite, which were given only to serve, being alone, and left to themselves, of course became reigning principles; having no superior principles to regulate or control them, they became absolute masters of the heart.[12]

In the fallen human heart, selfishness reigns. "Immediately upon the Fall the mind of man shrunk from its primitive greatness and extensiveness into an exceeding diminution and confinedness."[13] In sin the human collapses inward, such that love of God and neighbor is choked out by humankind's inherent selfishness.

> And man lost that which was his highest excellency and the proper glory of human nature, viz. his original righteousness and the spiritual image of God. And herein he lost his spiritual peace and comfort. This ceased to shine; there was a total eclipse of it in his mind, and the gloom of a guilty conscience and the darkness of sin began to fill his mind.[14]

But the *telos* of human personhood calls the creature to something greater. Rather, those made in the image of God are called to love in the manner of God's loving, which entails that their self-love enlarges to pull others within.[15] To love God and neighbor, persons cannot shrink inward, closing out God's love and their own ability to love, but must, in the Spirit, have a love that is caught up to God and a self that enlarges to internalize other human beings. This is the only way of love. Edwards explains,

12. WJE 3:382.
13. WJE 8:253.
14. WJE 17:334–33.
15. Whereas sin and selfishness confine the heart to oneself and collapse the heart inwardly, love does the opposite. "A man's self is as it were extended and enlarged by love. Others so far as beloved do, as it were, become parts of himself." WJE 8:263.

whereas before his soul was under the government of that noble principle of divine love whereby it was, as it were, enlarged to a kind of comprehension of all his fellow creatures; and not only so, but was not confined within such strait limits as the bounds of the creation but was extended to the Creator, and dispersed itself abroad in that infinite ocean of good and was, as it were, swallowed up by it, and become one with it. But as soon as he had transgressed, those nobler principles were immediately lost and all this excellent enlargedness of his soul was gone and he thenceforward shrunk into a little point, circumscribed and closely shut up within itself to the exclusion of others. God was forsaken and fellow creatures forsaken, and man retired within himself and became wholly governed by narrow, selfish principles. Self-love became absolute master of his soul, the more noble and spiritual principles having taken warning and fled. But God hath in mercy to miserable man contrived in the work of redemption, and by the glorious gospel of his Son, to bring the soul of man out of its confinement, and again to infuse those noble and divine principles by which it was governed at first.[16]

Humankind was created to have a soul capable of enlargement, such that in loving God the soul increases in elasticity to pull others within in love. The relation of love to others is internal to the human self.

I have observed from time to time that in pure love to others (i.e. love not arising from self-love) there's a union of the heart with others; a kind of enlargement of the mind, whereby it so extends itself as to take others into a man's self: and therefore it implies a disposition to feel, to desire, and to act as though others were one with ourselves.[17]

This, once again, parallels God's movement of love. As Edwards conceives of human personhood he looks to the structure of God's own self, as an agent with understanding and will, and then to the economy of redemption where God gives himself ("enlarges himself") in Son and Spirit such that the human person becomes internal to his own life in the Son by the

16. WJE 8:253–54.
17. WJE 8:589.

Spirit.[18] God's enlargement is not an expansion of God's being but is a relational opening of his life to another in the union of love to incorporate a finite being into the infinite plenitude of his own glory.

We have seen that God so fully gives himself to his creatures that it could be looked upon as though God were incomplete.[19] While it is important to lean heavily on Edwards's qualification "as though," he is, nonetheless, pushing the boundaries of God's self-giving. Edwards claims that God takes the interest of human persons into his own interest, so that they are united in his self-giving.

> Those elect creatures which must be looked upon as the end of all the rest of the creation, considered with respect to the whole of their eternal duration, and as such made God's end, must be viewed as being, as it were, one with God. They were respected as brought home to him, united with him, centering most perfectly in him, and as it were swallowed up in him: so that his respect to them finally coincides and becomes one and the same with respect to himself. The interest of the creature is, as it were, God's own interest, in proportion to the degree of their relation and union to God.[20]

This is the *telos* or goal available to the regenerate, to be caught up in the life of God such that one is internal to God's life in Christ (Col. 3:3) and has internalized the love of God in the Spirit (Col. 1:27; John 17:26).

### Created for Glory

Glory is one of the key theological constructs Edwards utilizes to talk about the human creature in the economic movement of God's life. This

---

18. Edwards states, "In some sense, the most benevolent generous person in the world seeks his own happiness in doing good to others, because he places his happiness in their good. His mind is so enlarged as to take them, as it were, into himself. Thus when they are happy he feels it, he partakes with them, and is happy in their happiness." WJE 8:461. God, Edwards argues, being infinite, does not enlarge *per se*, but flows forth and expresses himself to creatures, "making them to partake of him, and rejoicing in himself expressed in them, and communicated to them." WJE 8:462.

19. WJE 8:439–40.

20. WJE 8:443.

is true, in part, because glory was God's end in creating the world. By the time Edwards was writing his work *The End for Which God Created the World*, it was an accepted axiom of Reformed theology that God created for his own glory. Edwards accepted this axiom but put it to a precision unknown in the Reformed tradition before him. Broadly speaking, we can say that God's perfections—the excellency and fullness of his being—are able to be communicated. In God's own life of love, God is an infinite fountain in himself, the pouring forth of love between the Father and Son in the Spirit. In other words, God's life is communicative *in se*, and therefore it is good and fitting that God would overflow and communicate that fullness to another.[21] God's economic diffusion is the communication of his understanding and his will, the image of his triune processions.[22] It is both fit and desirable for God's glory to be known, i.e., God's understanding and will to be communicated to the creature, so that the creature will be conformed to his image. In Edwards's idiom, God's external life is emanation seeking remanation; the elect receive knowledge of who God is and incline to God as the fundamental beauty. This is why Edwards's anthropology must mirror the inner life of God, because God's economic existence is an image of the immanent, and God's self-revelation overflows as Son and Spirit, understanding and love, respectively. It is only as a human person has both the natural and supernatural image of God that she can receive a knowledge of God as God knows himself, in the Spirit of holiness, love, and beauty.

To outline how his teleological vision of glory works, Edwards delineates between chief ends, ultimate ends, and subordinate ends. One's

---

21. Edwards's discussion of this is much more in depth (and confusing!) than stated here, but the main idea sketched above is adequate for our purposes. Edwards employs unique and, at times, muddled language in talking about God's act of creation, including a disposition in God to create, that can be misunderstood. In short, a close reading of the *End for Which God Created the World* makes it clear that Edwards is simply wanting to affirm the Reformed notion that God created for his own glory, but he also wants to spell that out specifically. This is not to say that Edwards's doctrine is without idiosyncrasy. Edwards's approach in answering this question is entirely unique, but the answer, ultimately, is the same. For an in-depth reading of this work, see Kyle Strobel, *Jonathan Edwards's Theology* (London: T&T Clark, 2012), 75–102.

22. In Holmes's words, "For Edwards, the economic Trinity is not so much identical with the immanent Trinity as coherent, or harmonious: it is a relationship of order and beauty, rather than identity (always remembering that beauty is a key category of ontology)." Stephen R. Holmes, *God of Grace and God of Glory: An Account of the Theology of Jonathan Edwards* (Edinburgh: T&T Clark, 2000), 134.

actions stem from a chain of ends (i.e., an overall teleology): subordinate ends, ultimate ends (what may be called terminal ends), and chief ends (the end in which all other ends find their purpose). A subordinate end is an end chosen for another purpose; it is not sought for its own sake, in contrast to an ultimate end, which is sought for its own sake.

> Some ends are subordinate ends not only as they are subordi-
> nated to an ultimate end, but also to another end that is itself
> but a subordinate end: yea, there may be a succession or chain
> of many subordinate ends, one dependent on another, one
> sought for another: the first for the next; and that for the sake
> of the next to that, and so on in a long series before you come
> to anything that the agent aims at and seeks for its own sake.[23]

A chief end, furthermore, is what Edwards deems a "highest end" and is the primary ultimate end.

> A chief end is opposite to an inferior end; an ultimate end is
> opposite to a subordinate end. A subordinate end is something
> that an agent seeks and aims at in what he does; but yet don't
> seek it, or regard it at all upon its own account, but wholly on
> the account of a further end, or in order to some other thing
> which it is considered as a means of. . . . An ultimate end is that
> which the agent seeks in what he does for its own sake; that he
> has respect to, as what he loves, values and takes pleasure in on
> its own account, and not merely as a means of a further end.[24]

A chief end has within it, therefore, an overarching teleology in which all other ends find their purpose: "The chief end is an end that is most valued; and therefore most sought after by the agent in what he does."[25] Furthermore, in discussing God's end in creating the world, Edwards claims it is an original ultimate end, and as such, independent of creatures or circumstance (and, therefore, solely dependent upon God's own life).[26]

23. WJE 8:405–6.
24. WJE 8:405.
25. WJE 8:407.
26. Edwards's use of "original" to qualify the kind of ultimate end employed is in contrast to "consequential" and "dependent." A consequential or dependent ultimate end presupposes the existence of what it is qualifying. For instance, in God's creation of the

This original ultimate end is the grounding factor of all circumstantial or consequential ultimate ends (ends dependent on God's prior original end).

The focal point of Edwards's analysis is that God must, somehow, will himself in his creation of the world. By "delighting in the expressions of his perfections . . . he manifests a delight in himself; and in making these expressions of his own perfections his end, *he makes himself his end.*"[27] No end could be more ultimate than God's own perfect life. It would be a mistake, on his account, to think that God creates out of some need or lack. Rather, with the thrust of the Christian tradition behind him, Edwards grounds creation in God's fullness. It is out of the infinite actuality of God's life of love that God shares himself with another. Only God's own life has the scope and perfection to ground the whole *telos* of creation.[28] By focusing on himself, and creating through an economic overflow of his internal life of understanding and will, God creates and relates to his creation without destroying its own internal legitimacy. Edwards states,

> Here God's acting for himself, or making himself his last end, and his acting for their sake [the believers'], are not to be set in opposition; or to be considered as the opposite parts of a disjunction: they are rather to be considered as coinciding one with the other, and implied one in the other. But yet God is to be considered as first and original in his regard; and the creature is the object of God's regard consequentially and by implication as being as it were comprehended in God.[29]

By focusing on God's end as himself and his own glory, Edwards is at pains to show that this does not somehow undermine the creature, as if God's seeking himself and God's seeking the creature were set in opposition. Rather, the category of glory orders God's relation to the believer such that, in seeking himself, God seeks believers as well (more on this in the final chapter). This, as noted above, is central to how Edwards

---

world, he himself is the end. Based on this original ultimate end, the consequential ultimate ends of the creation are ordered.

27. WJE 8:437. Emphasis in the original.

28. Edwards makes six points concerning why God would create that are obvious to "reason" itself. WJE 8:419–20.

29. WJE 8:440–41.

conceives of the life of the Christian. Christians are no longer extrinsic to God but are internal to him as his love is to them. He has given himself in the Son and Spirit, and, as they have received the Son and Spirit, they are now participants in the glory of God, the end for which God created the world. God's chief end in creating the world, therefore, is his own glory, known in his inner life, diffused in the economy, and reflected back to him in remanation. It is as if the architecture of Edwards's theology were a gloss on Romans 11:36, "For from Him and through Him and to Him are all things. To Him be the glory forever. Amen."

Helpfully, Edwards breaks down three stages of glory that narrate how God wills himself and the creature simultaneously. To do so, he exposits the Hebrew word *kabod* and the Greek word *doxa*, both meaning "glory," describing a threefold overflow that parallels his account of God's end in creating: first, glory is "used to signify what is internal, what is within the being or person, inherent in the subject"; second, it is used "for emanation, exhibition or communication of this internal glory"; last, it is used "for the knowledge or sense, or effect of these, in those who behold it, to whom the exhibition or communication is made; or an expression of this knowledge or sense or effect."[30] Glory signifies God's own internal life of affectionate self-knowledge, eternally proceeding as knowledge and will. Upon willing creation, this life overflows as the second stage of glory, which is an emanation and communication of that primary glory itself. The third stage of glory reveals how God can be for the creature by being for himself. God created the creature with the capacity to receive his life, which is the greatest possible good. By creating with his own overflow as the *telos* of creation (i.e., glory), God is able to be for his own glory and for the good of the creature at the same time because God's glory and the creature's good are identical. God is the greatest possible good. Glorifying God simply is partaking in God's glory and therefore receiving the emanation of God's overflow and remanating it back to him in religious affection. This is why religious affection is imperative in the Christian life, because Christians are those who partake in God's glory and fullness and therefore in God's own affectionate self-knowing.

Because the teleology of the creation is the glory of God, Edwards's anthropology is particularly structured so that the creature can partake in this glory. God's willing himself and the overflow of his life of perfection are the grounds of God's creation, but God does not communicate him-

---

30. WJE 8:513. See also WJE 8:529.

self for no purpose, except for emanation and return: "In the creature's knowing, esteeming, loving, rejoicing in, and praising God, the glory of God is both exhibited and acknowledged; his fullness is received and returned."[31] Without the creature, the economic emanation of God's glory could not remanate. God has so given himself to his creation that he is, in a qualified sense, no longer complete without their response in affection.[32] Employing other imagery Edwards is fond of, since God is light the creature is capable of becoming luminous, but only through a participation in God's radiance. The creature "reflects" God, but this is not a subhuman refraction of something extrinsic to humanity's created ends. It is the affectionate knowledge of God that comes from being a creature in his or her natural state (recalling that our natural state included the supernatural). Reflecting God's glory is seeing God in Christ by the Spirit and recognizing God as beauty and the beautiful; it is to see and flow forth in love, mirroring the eternal beatific life of God. In heaven, Edwards claims, the saint is "transformed into love, dissolved into joy, become[s] activity itself, [and is] changed into mere ecstasy."[33] This is religious affection in perfection, where the clear sight of God enflames the soul to flow out of itself into this beauty and love. There, in the "World of Love," as Edwards calls it, God will be present and visible in a way unknown prior, "for God is the fountain of love, as the sun is the fountain of light. And therefore the glorious presence of God in heaven fills heaven with love, as the sun placed in the midst of the hemisphere in a clear day fills the world with light."[34] Likewise,

> This very manifestation that God will make of himself that will cause the beatifical vision will be an act of love in God. It will be from the exceeding love of God to them that he will give them this vision which will add an immense sweetness to it. . . . They shall see that he is their Father and that they are his children. They shall see God gloriously present with them; God with them and God in them and they in God. . . . Therefore they shall see God as their own God, when they behold this transcendent glory.[35]

31. WJE 8:531.
32. WJE 8:439–40.
33. WJE 13:260–61.
34. WJE 13:369.
35. JEC, Unpublished Sermon, Romans 2:10, #373 [L. 44r.–L.44v.].

It is here that we see Edwards's theotic-anthropology coming into fruition. The beatific vision of God is not an external gazing on a God great but transcendent. It is the sight of God within an act of love *for me* (*pro me*). God is seen as our own God, just as the Son sees the Father as his own.[36] Believers ascend to the Father, in the Son, by the Spirit. The glorified saints are internal to this knowledge and love, even though their participation is always a finite participation within an infinite life. Nonetheless, "this glorious God is manifested and shines forth in full glory, in beams of love," Edwards suggests; "there the fountain overflows in streams and rivers of love and delight, enough for all to drink at, and to swim in, yea, so as to overflow the world as it were with a deluge of love."[37] Glorified creaturely existence is a participation in God's eternal delight, and as such, is "an increasing knowledge *of* God, love *to* him, and joy *in* him."[38]

## Religious Affection

Edwards's anthropology is derived from God's personal existence as the archetype of both personhood and personal knowledge. The natural image of God in human persons is the structural principle for participation in God's life, and the spiritual image (the indwelling Spirit) is the supernatural foundation for this participation. With the indwelling Spirit, believers partake in God's affectionate self-knowledge. Just as God gazes upon his image and pours forth in love, so too do believers gaze upon God's image and pour forth in affection. To see God, therefore—to really see him—is to see him as beautiful.

The Christian life is a life of affection because God's life is the affectionate life. The divine beatitude provides the moorings for human flourishing, such that Edwards writes:

> Intellectual pleasure consists in beholding of spiritual excellencies and beauties; but the glorious excellency and beauty of God, they are by far the greatest. God's excellence is the su-

36. "He that has a blessed-making sight of God, he not only has a view of God's glory and excellency, but he views it as having a propriety in it. They also see God's love to them." WJE 17:64.

37. WJE 13:370.

38. WJE 8:443. Emphasis added.

preme excellence; when the understanding of the reasonable
creature dwells here, it dwells at the fountain and swims in a
boundless and bottomless ocean.[39]

This description articulates Christian existence as a movement of love
in the soul to see and know God as beautiful. "The love of so glorious
a Being is infinitely valuable," Edwards claims, "and the discoveries of it
are capable of ravishing the soul above all other loves."[40] This movement
of the soul is a mirroring of the divine life and blessedness. Therefore,
"when it [the soul] actually exercises delight in God, it is its most noble
and exalted exercise that it's capable of."[41]

### Nature and Role of Religious Affections

The ravishing and delight of the soul that sees God in Christ by the Spirit
are best understood, in Edwards's thought, as religious affections. It is
helpful to begin by defining affection as such. Affections are "no other,
than the more vigorous and sensible exercises of the inclination and will
of the soul."[42] Edwards believes that affections are a specific movement
of the will, rather than a distinct faculty of the soul, claiming, "The will,
and the affections of the soul, are not two faculties; the affections are
not essentially distinct from the will, nor do they differ from the mere
actings of the will and inclination of the soul, but only in the liveli-
ness and sensibleness of exercise."[43] For an affection to be religious, it
must be based on God's self-revelation. Religious affections are obtained
through spiritual sight in illumination and are efficaciously applied to
the heart by the Spirit, or, in other words, are the regenerate human
response to witnessing the beauty and glory of God. True religious affection entails knowledge (understanding) of God and love (willing)
to God. This knowledge is not merely speculative (i.e., "notional") but
entails apprehension by the sense of the heart. This dual aspect of the
soul in understanding (reception) and willing (inclination) mirrors the

39. WJE 17:67.
40. WJE 17:67.
41. WJE 17:68.
42. WJE 2:96.
43. WJE 2:97.

inner life of God and is the actualization of the twofold image of God in the regenerate believer.[44]

Prior to glorification, the sight of God is through a "glass darkly" (1 Cor. 13:12), and therefore the affections are limited and muffled. Even so, true religion is never substantially different from the "religion" in heaven, but only differs in circumstance and capacity. Regenerate believers see through the dark glass of faith and are inhibited by their sinful flesh, whereas glorified believers have a pure sight of God without sin to darken their sight. In Edwards's words, "that principle of true religion which is in them, is a communication of the religion of heaven; their grace is the dawn of glory; and God fits them for that world by conforming them to it."[45] Likewise,

> The knowledge which the saints have of God's beauty and glory in this world, and those holy affections that arise from it, are of the same nature and kind with what the saints are the subjects of in heaven, differing only in degree and circumstances: what God gives them here, is a foretaste of heavenly happiness, and an earnest of their future inheritance.[46]

When the Spirit of love is infused into the believer, the life of heaven—the very life of God—is given to them, and as such, they are now on a continuum of harmony that will be perfected in eternity.[47]

Religious affection is the anthropological mirroring of the immanent life of God. Just as the inner-triune life of God is the dynamic interplay of knowledge and love, a life revealed in the economic activity of Son and Spirit, so too the life of the believer is activated by the perception and actualization of this knowledge and love. Being awakened to true beauty—God himself—the believer now truly images God. Without re-

---

44. WJE 2:97.

45. WJE 2:114. Edwards, again invoking the image of the sun, notes that where there is light (understanding) there must be heat (affections), to claim that "if the great things of religion are rightly understood, they will affect the heart." WJE 2:120. The reason offered as to why some people are not affected is blindness. Here Edwards offers his attack on those who "cry down all religious affections," claiming that while there may be affections without true religion, there is no true religion, no real seeing of God, without them (WJE 2:121).

46. WJE 2:133.

47. This is why Edwards claims, "The end of the doctrines and precepts of Christianity, is to bring about this sweet harmony between the soul and Jesus Christ." WJE 19:447.

ligious affection there is no salvation because without religious affection there is no participation. Religious affection marks the movement of the soul in remanation as a response to the emanating revelation of God.

## Imitatio Dei

As an imitation of God (*imitatio Dei*), Christian existence mirrors the inner life of God by partaking of the divine nature in the economic activity of Son and Spirit. The God of beauty calls his creatures into harmony with himself such that they become beautiful. Becoming beautiful is not obtaining virtue through acts of ascesis (although discipline and obtaining virtue will be necessary) but is available only through a participation in God's own beauty (i.e., being "harmonized" to God's life in Christ by the Spirit).[48] As God gives the Son and the Spirit, and therefore his own self-understanding and self-willing, the creature becomes beautiful, holy, and glorious. This is what it means to be excellent and happy. Creaturely persons are truly analogous to the personhood of God, but it is only in sharing the same object of beauty—Christ—that creatures come to imitate God's life in their own.[49] The saints' "visual" object in conversion corresponds with the Father's—both gazing upon the Son—and their delight is the same, the Holy Spirit of God. Religious affection entails sensible knowledge, and not mere speculation, because it partakes in how God knows himself.[50] Likewise, as the elect behold God in Christ, their

48. Elizabeth Agnew Cochran's book helpfully engages this notion by focusing on the "receptive" nature of the virtues in Edwards's thought. In her words, "For Edwards, we acquire the virtues by receiving them." Elizabeth Agnew Cochran, *Receptive Human Virtues: A New Reading of Jonathan Edwards's Ethics* (University Park: Penn State Press, 2011), 167. This is exactly right.

49. Christ's excellency, therefore, is the model for this imitation of God. Cochran rightly notes, "Christ serves as the moral exemplar and perfect embodiment both of the true virtue that is proper to God and of those virtuous qualities that Edwards deems 'proper excellencies of created natures.' Edwards explains that qualities such as humility and meekness are legitimately considered 'virtues' even though they cannot be attributed to the divine being as divine being; in the case of these virtues as well as true virtue, however, the incarnate Jesus Christ is able to practice and embody them perfectly." Cochran, *Receptive Human Virtues*, 62.

50. "By spiritual good I mean all true moral good, all real moral beauty and excellency, and all those acts of the will, or that sense of the heart, that relates to it." WJE 18:461–62.

knowledge is affectionate—it causes love, joy, and happiness to emanate to Christ through the Spirit uniting them to Christ. By the sense of the heart, "the mind don't only speculate and behold, but relishes and feels."[51] Speculative knowledge, in other words, fails to fully actualize the soul. But when the mind is both beholding and relishing, both understanding and willing, the mind is functioning toward its full and proper end. Knowing God is knowing him as beautiful and becoming beautiful in harmony with him.

Redemption is the movement of God to pull creatures into his own life, and Edwards's anthropology delineates how this is possible. By participating in the sonship of the Son by the Spirit, believers become beloved of God. They are harmonized with him and are now attuned to the way of eternity defined by love. As they are upheld by God in love, internalized into his own self-loving, the glorified creature will be able to love in freedom. Participation in God's life does not take the creature away from others but frees the creatures to be for the other. This movement of union and participation continues for eternity because finite creatures never fully obtain the communicative overflow of the infinite God. The economic movement of God to save through participation emphasizes both a sight of God as beautiful and a partaking of that beauty. In becoming beloved, creatures become beautiful. While the creature cannot, through self-effort in obtaining virtue, somehow earn or achieve this beauty—it is only given in grace—virtue is intrinsically connected to it. Tied together with anthropology and affection for Edwards are beauty and morality, and therefore it is necessary to conclude this chapter with a brief look at Edwards's moral theology.[52] Along these lines, Edwards claims,

> When the true beauty and amiableness of the holiness or true moral good that is in divine things, is discovered to the soul, it as it were opens a new world to its view. This shows the glory of all the perfections of God, and of everything appertaining to the divine being: for, as was observed before, the beauty of all arises from God's moral perfection. . . . He that sees the beauty of holiness, or true moral good, sees the greatest and most im-

51. WJE 2:272.

52. In my estimation, the two most important works on Edwards's moral thought are Stephen A. Wilson, *Virtue Reformed: Rereading Jonathan Edwards's Ethics* (Leiden: Brill, 2005), and Cochran, *Receptive Human Virtues*.

portant thing in the world, which is the fullness of all things, without which all the world is empty, no better than nothing, yea, worse than nothing. Unless this is seen, nothing is seen, that is worth the seeing: for there is no other true excellency or beauty. Unless this be understood, nothing is understood, that is worthy of the exercise of the noble faculty of understanding. This is the beauty of the Godhead, and the divinity of Divinity (if I may so speak), the good of the infinite Fountain of Good; without which God himself (if that were possible to be) would be an infinite evil: without which, we ourselves had better never have been; and without which there had better have been no being. He therefore in effect knows nothing, that knows not this: his knowledge is but the shadow of knowledge, or the form of knowledge, as the Apostle calls it.[53]

## Moral Theology

Edwards views the Christian life as a participation, or fellowship, with God.[54] In this fellowship, Christians become beautiful because "God put his own beauty, i.e. his beautiful likeness, upon their souls."[55] Therefore, partaking in God's life of beauty, and becoming beautiful through that participation, is the grounding of Edwards's ethical thought.[56] Because of this, moral theology is a natural corollary to anthropology and religious affection.[57] A life that partakes in God's nature is necessarily a life of vir-

53. WJE 2:273–74.

54. See WJE 21:124.

55. WJE 17:208.

56. Cochran notes, "God communicates himself to creatures so that they may know and participate in God's love. . . . Through this divine communication, creatures participate in God's virtue and become conformed to the likeness of God, who is virtue itself." Cochran, *Receptive Human Virtues*, 49.

57. In choosing to use "moral theology" instead of Christian ethics, I am following the insights of D. Stephen Long in his *John Wesley's Moral Theology: The Quest for God and Goodness* (Nashville: Kingswood Books, 2005), and his essay "Moral Theology," in *The Oxford Handbook of Systematic Theology*, ed. John Webster, Kathryn Tanner, and Iain Torrance (Oxford: Oxford University Press, 2007), 456–75. In his "Moral Theology" essay, Long addresses the assumption that Christian ethics is a primarily Protestant category whereas moral theology is Roman Catholic, claiming, "While there is some truth to such an assumption, the Catholic tradition has generated its fair share of ethics of obligation,

tue and beauty. To account for God's action to make believers beautiful is to address the dogmatic contours of moral theology and therefore the "moral field," where, in the words of John Webster, "moral action and reflection on that action take place."[58] God created the world for his own glory, and therefore moral theology exposits how the creature receives and partakes in that glory. This is not, somehow, outside of beauty but is an intrinsic aspect of what it means to "become beautiful."

Edwards begins his work on virtue with the claim, "Whatever controversies and variety of opinion there are about the nature of virtue, yet all . . . mean by it something *beautiful*, or rather some kind of *beauty* or excellency."[59] Edwards continues by qualifying this initial claim, "'Tis not *all* beauty that is called virtue; for instance, not the beauty of a building, of a flower, or of the rainbow: but some beauty belonging to beings that have *perception* and *will*."[60] Once again we are confronted with Edwards's anthropology, whose origins are discovered in the divine processions, the overflow of which God willfully emanates to his creatures as a communication of himself. As we saw with religious affections, creatures remanate God's self-communication, coming to know God only as they perceive him and will him accordingly. Edwards's ethics follow these same contours. For something to be virtuous, it has to be a person, which Edwards glosses as a being with understanding and will ("intelligent being"). Virtue "is the beauty of those qualities and acts of the mind that are of a *moral* nature, i.e. such as are attended with desert or worthiness of *praise* or *blame*." "Things of this sort," Edwards continues, "are not anything belonging merely to speculation; but to the *disposition* and *will*, or . . . to the 'heart.'"[61] Once again we see Edwards refusing to posit "faculties" that have a life of their own. A person does not have a willing faculty or a thinking faculty; only persons will, and only persons think. Virtue, like affection, cannot be pushed into an isolated register of intellection or

---

and Protestants such as John Wesley and Jonathan Edwards clearly described the Christian moral life on the basis of the vision of God" (what Long believes is the starting point for moral theology) (460).

58. John Webster, *Word and Church: Essays in Christian Dogmatics* (London: T&T Clark, 2001), 233. While Webster's account of the contours of moral theology is more robust than our own here, his general framework is very similar to that developed by Edwards in his account of glory, beauty, and affection.

59. WJE 8:539.

60. WJE 8:539.

61. WJE 8:539.

volition because human persons are integrated creatures. To be virtuous, in this sense, is to be beautiful, because it entails a harmony of the whole self to God.

Far from a subjective notion, true beauty, what Edwards also calls "general beauty," is "viewed most perfectly, comprehensively and universally."[62] In other words, particular beauty is beauty in relation to a limited sphere of options, whereas universal beauty is beauty in relation to all things, and most importantly to God himself. In this sense, true virtue is "that consent, propensity and union of heart to Being in general," namely God, and it "is immediately exercised in a general good will."[63] When a person's heart is aligned and united to God, first and foremost, then that person will have a general good will to creation. Persons become virtuous through the love of God—a love that they partake in—so that they can love others. To love God with one's heart entails, for Edwards, that one stands in a relation of love to others as well (which, of course, is the argument of 1 John). To be virtuous, therefore, one must be in harmony with God. To be harmonized with God's life is to be a person of love, and if love is the undergirding tune of one's heart, then it is possible for one to act virtuously. While God is not the sole object in acts of virtue, love of God is the prevailing disposition that makes an act virtuous. This stems from the reality of "divine virtue," which, Edwards states, "must consist primarily in *love to himself*" (God's self) or "in the mutual love and friendship which subsists eternally and necessarily between the several persons in the Godhead."[64] To love others in a virtuous way depends, therefore, on an orientation to true virtue that is first and foremost God himself ("Being in general"). In this sense, loving others must "arise from the temper of mind wherein consists a disposition to love God supremely."[65] Once again, the divine life is the archetype from which the creature mirrors ectypally. This form of love is oriented not only by God's eternal life but in anticipation of God's presence in heaven. There, just as in God's life, the Son receives the Father's love without measure, and in the Son the glorified creatures partake in this love. "Infinite love is infinitely exercised toward [Christ]," Edwards explains, and "love flows out from him towards

---

62. WJE 8:540.

63. WJE 8:540.

64. WJE 8:557.

65. WJE 8:557. For more on true virtue consisting of love to "Being in general," see WJE 8:540–41.

all the inhabitants of heaven."[66] As it is in eternity by sight, so it is now by faith. God is the goal of our love, and as we partake in God's love we mirror his life of overflowing to others.

Because the scope of virtue entails a harmony with God and creation, true virtue must be ordered appropriately. The primary ground of virtue is the love of God, the foundational feature of Edwards's moral theology. Edwards's ethical thought is theocentric in a maximal kind of way because God is goodness, love, beauty, and virtue itself.[67] This is not simply true abstractly, but his fullness defines the pure actuality of goodness, love, beauty, and virtue from which all particular concrete realities discover their meaning. Because of this, the Christian life of virtue entails that creatures have God as their primary object of desire and affection. However, this is not an isolating impulse but a universalizing one. To love God primarily is to enlarge as a self to love others—love of God and love of neighbor are always intertwined. In particular, the person of virtue will be inclined toward those who are virtuous, and to all for the sake of their becoming virtuous.[68] Edwards's moral theology, which describes a movement of the heart, brings together both intellection and affection. Because of this, he addresses the internal movements of the heart as well as the external: "spiritual beauty consists wholly in this, and the various qualities and exercises of mind which proceed from it, and the external actions which proceed from these internal qualities and exercises. And in these things consists all true *virtue*, viz. in this love of Being, and the qualities and acts which arise from it."[69] True virtue is intrinsically bound to the notion of harmony—with God, creation, and others—and as such, entails internal movements of the heart in love that overflow into a life of love.

> This is the general notion, not that principles derive their goodness from actions, but that actions derive their goodness from the principles whence they proceed; and so that the act

66. WJE 8:373.

67. Therefore, in the words of Cochran, "'The most proper evidence' that we are practicing love in a manner consistent with true virtue lies in the degree to which our loves coincide with God's.... For Edwards, then, charity is fundamentally a love to God that gives rise to love to creatures, and Edwards's development of this argument shows the continuity between true virtue in God and human charity." Cochran, *Receptive Human Virtues*, 43.

68. What Edwards calls love of complacence and love of benevolence, respectively. See WJE 8:542–43.

69. WJE 8:548. Emphasis added.

of choosing that which is good, is no further virtuous than it proceeds from a good principle, or virtuous disposition of mind. . . . There can, according to our natural notions, be no virtue in a choice which proceeds from no virtuous principle, but from mere self-love, ambition, or some animal appetite. And therefore a virtuous temper of mind may be before a good act of choice, as a tree may be before the fruit, and the fountain before the stream which proceeds from it.[70]

For human persons to be moral—for creatures to become beautiful in God's beauty—they must have a principle or virtuous disposition of mind. This is nothing other than the indwelling Spirit, infused into the regenerate. In infusion, the Spirit works internally to the person, such that Edwards can say, "We are not merely passive in it, nor yet does God do some and we do the rest, but God does all and we do all. God produces all and we act all. For that is what he produces, our own acts."[71] This means that the life of virtue is not simply habituating virtuous practices, because virtue derives from the life of God (i.e., holiness). This is why infusion is necessary for *true* virtue. Edwards argues,

The nature of virtue being a positive thing, can proceed from nothing but God's immediate influence, and must take its rise from creation or infusion by God. For it must be either from that, or from our own choice and production, either at once, or gradually, by diligent culture. But it cannot begin, or take its rise from the latter, viz. our choice, or voluntary diligence. For if there exist nothing at all of the nature of virtue before, it cannot come from cultivation; for by the supposition there is nothing of the nature of virtue to cultivate, it cannot be by repeated and multiplied acts of virtuous choice, till it becomes an habit. For there can be no one virtuous choice, unless God immediately gives it.[72]

While Edwards's moral theology certainly has room to talk about a kind of virtue in the unregenerate (i.e., "natural goodness"), *true* virtue de-

70. WJE 3:224.
71. WJE 21:251.
72. Jonathan Edwards, *Documents on the Trinity, Grace and Faith* (The Jonathan Edwards Center at Yale University), WJE Online Vol. 37, $43.

pends upon God's movement to infuse the Spirit in the soul of a person, to relocate the center of their existence in Christ.[73] In regeneration, the believer is not only internal to God, but God is so internal to the human being that God's action produces creaturely freedom. The action of God in the soul is holiness, love, beauty, and affection—in short, blessedness. The creature partakes in the divine blessedness and, therefore, lives the blessed life. This is why the term "happiness" is spread so fully through Edwards's corpus.

## Recapitulation: Love, the Sum of All

By way of conclusion, we take the above analysis and focus it upon love. The goal is not to reduce Edwards's thought down to one element but to utilize love as a central and somewhat underappreciated feature of his thought. We have seen that the Christian life is a mirror image of God's life and that Christian living is an imitation of God. Furthermore, rather than mere imitation, the Christian life is a participation in the divine life, such that God's own Spirit of holiness is infused in the regenerate, creating a principle of virtue at the foundation of the human person. Bound together in this account are love, beauty, glory, and virtue, and they are all united in God's life and accessed through union and communion with him. But when Edwards is pressed to name this single divine principle in the soul from which all others derive, he claims, "That principle in the soul of the saints, which is the grand Christian virtue, and which is the soul and essence and summary comprehension of all grace, is a principle of divine love."[74] Love is the sum, Edwards argues, of all that God requires of his people. In case the reader tries to qualify Edwards's claims, he reasserts himself:

> This argument does fully and irrefragably prove that all grace, and every Christian disposition and habit of mind and heart, especially as to that which is primarily holy and divine in it, does summarily consist in divine love, and may be resolved into it; however, with respect to its kinds and manner of exercise and its appendages, it may be diversified.[75]

73. See Cochran, *Receptive Human Virtues*, 124–66, for a characteristically thoughtful analysis of this aspect of Edwards's thought.
74. WJE 21:166.
75. WJE 21:168.

Love summarizes the nature of the Christian life. Again, Edwards is not shy in his exclamation: "The very quintessence of religion, the very thing wherein lies summarily the sincerity, spirituality and divinity of religion. And that, the Apostle teaches us, is love."[76]

Whereas glory and beauty have become the dominant features of how Edwards is often understood, we would be remiss to talk about these outside of the divine love. Even in Edwards's corpus, the ethical material is often thought to be encompassed by *Freedom of the Will*, *True Virtue*, and *Religious Affections*, but *Charity and Its Fruits*, Edwards's biblical theology of love, is often left aside. But love, as we've highlighted in this volume, is absolutely foundational for everything Edwards does, and this, of course, derives from his doctrine of God:

> And therefore seeing he is an infinite Being, it follows that he is an infinite fountain of love. Seeing he is an all-sufficient Being, it follows that he is a full and overflowing and an inexhaustible fountain of love. Seeing he is an unchanging and eternal Being, he is an unchangeable and eternal source of love.[77]

We are created to receive love from this fountain of love and, as we are loved, to love our neighbors as ourselves. To be captivated by God is to be captivated by love.

In *Charity and Its Fruits*, Edwards's sermon series on 1 Corinthians 13, he makes a distinction between extraordinary (i.e., miraculous) and ordinary gifts of the Spirit. Ordinary gifts are only ordinary because they are in accord with the typical working of the Spirit. Extraordinary gifts are just that, on Edwards's view: not ordinary. Importantly, for our discussion of love, Edwards also makes the distinction between common and special gifts of the Spirit. Extraordinary gifts of the Spirit, such as gifts of prophecy, tongues, etc., are both extraordinary (Edwards did not believe these were normal workings of the Spirit) and common. Someone who is not a Christian could have a common gift of the Spirit. "Many bad men had these gifts," Edwards claims. "Many will say at the last day, 'Lord, Lord, have we not prophesied in thy name?'"[78] (Matt. 7:22). While Edwards's distinction is interesting, the reason he employs it is more so. He affirms

---

76. WJE 21:169.
77. WJE 8:369.
78. WJE 8:154.

that it is a great privilege to have miraculous gifts, but he notes that God does not have to instill the person with his true nature for them to enact miracles, only with his power. God certainly is powerful, but power does not define who God fundamentally is. God is love. So while the saint does "delight in every divine perfection; the contemplation of the infinite greatness, power and knowledge . . . their love to God for his holiness is what is most fundamental and essential in their love."[79] To know God is not to know what God is, namely deity, but to know who God is, namely love and holiness; loving the Father, in the Son, by the Spirit is the call of the Christian:

> Extraordinary gifts are nothing properly inherent in the man. . . . They are excellent things; but they are not properly excellencies in the nature of the subject, any more than the garments are which he wears. Extraordinary gifts of the Spirit are, as it were, precious jewels, which a man carries about him. But true grace in the heart is, as it were, the preciousness of the heart, by which it becomes precious or excellent; by which the very soul itself becomes a precious jewel.[80]

The Spirit of God can give us power, but in doing so he is not giving himself to us. To give himself, God gives us the Son and Spirit, that we can see and know the Son in the very love that is the Spirit. This is why the spiritual gifts discussion of 1 Corinthians 12 ends with a look at the greater gift of love in 1 Corinthians 13. In the ordinary and saving work of the Spirit, the Spirit communicates "himself in his own proper nature to the man." This is how the Spirit becomes "an indwelling vital principle in the soul" and how the person comes to have "the holy nature of the Spirit of God imparted to the soul."[81] As the Spirit communicates his nature of holiness and love as a disposition within the regenerate creature, love to God is the primary teleology. However, this does not somehow narrow the scope of the ethical life, as noted above, but broadens it to include a love to all:

> A Christian love to God, and Christian love to men, are not properly two distinct principles in the heart. These varieties

79. WJE 2:256.
80. WJE 8:158.
81. WJE 8:158.

are radically the same: the same principle flowing forth towards different objects, according to the order of their existence. God is the first cause of all things, and the fountain and source of all good; and men are derived from him, having something of his image, and are the objects of his mercy.[82]

Love does not narrow in Edwards's vision, but it refracts into something multiform. This is how love can be the sum of all. In the believer, love starts with God, since "the Spirit infuses love to God" in regeneration;[83] but also "all things which are loved with a truly holy love are loved from some respects to God. Love to God is the foundation of a gracious love to men."[84] The love of God enlarges the soul to take others within, giving freedom to the Christian to love others without using them. The love of God gives breadth of soul to the creature to love others, but this is only available through the "divine temper which is wrought in the heart."[85] As a work of the Spirit in his proper nature, this love mirrors the love internal to God's life, one that flows forth freely and unites in beauty. With this principle in the heart, the believer flows forth to others in love and has a foundation from which all other virtue comes.

Because the graces of Christianity are all found in one Spirit, they are, in Edwards's language, "concatenated" together. The divine nature, in other words, is a movement of love that refracts through the creature into various movements of heart and life we call virtue. Since they all share the same root of the knowledge and love of divine excellency, they share the same teleology: "God, his glory, and our happiness in him."[86] "Love," Edwards continues, "is the fulfilling of them all." Edwards is attentive to the apostle Paul's claim that "Faith, hope and love abide these three, but the greatest of these is love" (1 Cor. 13:13). Love is the greatest because it is the nature of God's own life, but also because it is the nature of eternity. Whereas both faith and hope dissolve upon sight (2 Cor. 5:7; Rom. 8:25), love continues to eternity. Heaven is a world of love, Edwards avers, because the God of love dwells there: "And this renders heaven a world of love; for God is the fountain of love, as the sun is the fountain of light. . . . And therefore seeing he is an infinite Being, it follows that he

82. WJE 21:172.
83. WJE 8:132.
84. WJE 8:133.
85. WJE 8:133.
86. WJE 8:333.

is an infinite fountain of love."[87] This is a vision of the place where God's people will know in full what it means to become beautiful. Because of this, the Christian life is ordered in such a way as to have this vision as the believer's great end. This life of love serves as the engine that drives the ethical vision of Christian existence in the world, because it is the goal of God's created reality. The God of love has opened his life to pull creatures in, to partake of love, beauty, and happiness that they may glorify God through their own love in the world. Becoming beautiful, or shining with the light of God, is becoming a fountain of love—not of oneself—but from, to, and for God.

Edwards was captivated by the love of God as given and revealed in Christ Jesus. Edwards's conception of human personhood is humankind fully alive within the glory, love, and holiness of God. As creatures are received and embraced by God, and as they receive and embrace him in faith, they are now on the positive side of God seeking his glory (as opposed to the damned, who still may glorify God, but not in a positive sense). The elect are ushered into the fullness of the human condition, coming to comprehend the truth of themselves in God and enlarging in love to internalize others by giving themselves to them freely. This is possible only because of God's self-giving, upholding the Christian in his love and providing the freedom that God's love and presence bring. Heaven is a world of love; therefore the Christian and the church are to be examples of this love here and now. Edwards's moral theology is driven by a vision of this kind of moral field—where the Christian in the freedom of the love of God and others overflows to a world needing love.

---

87. WJE 8:369.

# CHAPTER EIGHT

# Becoming Edwardsean

One could be forgiven for getting the sense that we have introduced two different figures called Jonathan Edwards to you, or, if nothing else, two versions of Edwards's persona: a Jekyll and a Hyde (deciding which is which would depend on one's own interests and assumptions). For most of our readers, we assume, Edwards "the theologian" rings a bit more true than Edwards "the philosopher." Whereas occasionalism, continuous creation, idealism, and panentheism were slightly less radical in Edwards's day, at least in certain circles, they seem downright unhinged to many of us. Throughout this volume we have offered only minimal critical engagement with Edwards's thought, asking questions when issues arose and naming concerns when we deemed appropriate; but our attention focused on presenting an accurate portrayal of Edwards's views. Our primary intention, in other words, has not been on evaluating Edwards's thought as much as simply expositing it well.

By way of concluding, we turn now to a slightly more critical kind of assessment. The goal is not to move away from a generous reading to criticism for its own sake, as if scholarly work necessitates criticism in order to justify itself. Instead, our goal in this concluding chapter is to read Edwards as a theologian of the church and not simply a former theologian of the church. To do so, we first address what a distinctively churchly reading of Edwards might entail, turning once again to the God-world relation as a test case for this kind of interpretation. The God-world relation provides a major doctrinal issue in Edwards's thought where his more radical ideology leads him into several unfortunate conclusions. To further parse out the implications of Edwards's views, we consider the topic of freedom and then conclude with a look at the issue of evil.

In short, we suggest that "becoming Edwardsean" will entail retrieving a central feature of Edwards's theological impulse against radical features of his thought on the topic of the God-world relation for the sake of constructive theology today.

## A Churchly Reading

The attempt to provide a faithful representation of Edwards's thought, is, of course, laudable in its own right. But there is another way to read a historical figure, a more churchly reading. A churchly reading of a historical figure recognizes that this person is a part of the church and therefore a part of the church's living witness.[1] Because of this, a churchly reading always entails solid historical work, even though historical accuracy itself is not the ultimate goal. The goal is faithfulness. The goal is to sit at the feet of the tradition, as it were, to attend more faithfully and fruitfully to God now (without bringing forward unhelpful ways the thinker was beholden to his or her context). This has become known as a theology of retrieval. A theology of retrieval seeks to be historically grounded and accurate; but, at the same time, in the words of Kent Eilers and David Buschart, "'retrieval' names a *mode or style of theological discernment* that looks back in order to move forward."[2] They develop this notion by adding, "The role of theology is to be in dialogue with previous eras of Christian faith in order to allow the past to be in conversation with the present. Theology helps the church to adapt to the present by enabling her to be interrogated by the past."[3] In this conclusion, we seek to raise these kinds of issues for our inquiry into Edwards's thought. Here, we want to ask: What does it mean to become Edwardsean today? Is it faithful to Edwards to simply repeat what he said? Or, rather, does faithfulness to Edwards entail following the contours and ends of his thought, even if it requires rejecting certain conclusions? Perhaps somewhat provocatively, we suggest that we should

1. Another way to think about this is that Edwards is a kind of church father. Not every historical figure can be seen this way, simply by being a thinker in the history of the church. Rather, since the church has judged Edwards, and has judged Edwards worthy of consideration, Edwards is placed in a register of thinkers to be wrestled with and discerned (instead of simply parroted). James Merrick's insights have been helpful in this matter.

2. W. David Buschart and Kent D. Eilers, *Theology as Retrieval: Receiving the Past, Renewing the Church* (Downers Grove: IVP Academic, 2015), 12. Emphasis in the original.

3. Buschart and Eilers, *Theology as Retrieval*, 26.

answer this last question in the affirmative. To read Edwards's theology for the proclamation of the church today we must reconsider and, in fact, reject at least one key portion of it.

To give a full analysis of what it might mean to become Edwardsean is beyond the constraints of this conclusion. But to begin the conversation about being Edwardsean today, we return to one of the foundational themes of Edwards's theological system, which we have already encountered in chapters three and four, namely, the God-world relation. This is not an arbitrary theme but one that is core to his thought and core to the intellectual climate of his day. Fidelity to Edwards presses us to consider how we might learn from both his brilliance and his negligence, and this issue serves as a helpful place to do that. Our hope is that the movement of this book has modeled the kind of initial patience and exposition necessary to read Edwards for retrieval today, where careful attention can and should be followed by critical and constructive engagement. The goal is not to call into question Edwards's greatness; time has weighed Edwards and he has been found worthy of serious consideration.[4] Rather, by engaging in theological retrieval, we seek to take the theology developed thus far and advance it in a way that reveals a deep engagement with his views but also an inclination to push beyond the more troubling features of his account.

## The Transcendence of God

If we wish to be faithful to Edwards, we have to accept who he was in light of what was happening around him. Edwards lived in an intellectual time not unlike our own. The world was flipped upside-down with new access to other religions, astonishing advances in science, the rise of heretical groups, and radical philosophical shifts that created deep rifts in the intellectual world. To oversimplify a bit, one of the more profound features was the mechanistic nature of much of the philosophical and scientific thought of the early Enlightenment, and with it a false dichotomy between a fully independent universe without the need of God's

4. Buschart and Eilers describe this kind of posture in their exposition of retrieval: "Retrieval can be done in such a way that one responsibly looks back and faithfully moves forward. The Christian tradition is engaged in such a way that it resources the church's life and receives the deposit of faith." Buschart and Eilers, *Theology as Retrieval*, 274. Our goal is to move forward by retrieving Edwards's theological insights into our own context.

providential activity and a sovereign puppeteer who overtakes human freedom.[5] At the heart of this issue is the God-world relation, a topic that had seen much upheaval in the post-Cartesian (and, maybe more poignantly, post-Newtonian) world that Edwards lived in.[6]

Edwards was on the forefront of trying to reconsider nature, the God-world relation, space, matter, time, and so on, in an attempt to recast the world in a decisively Christian vein. What we find is Edwards brilliantly articulating what Avihu Zakai calls a "reenchantment of the world" in the face of its collapse into mechanism and materialism. In short, his account seeks to radically rethink creation in light of its Creator, articulating a classical account of creation in the face of Enlightenment reason, and doing so from within Enlightenment categories. But in doing so, Edwards became more entangled in its faults than he might have realized. As noted above, views on the God-world relation can easily assume an overly simplistic either-or paradigm: "Either God is sovereign, and therefore determines everything"; or "God is not sovereign and does not causally engage his creation"; or even, "Either God is an explanation for events or else events can be explained solely by their own causal nexus." Edwards was, of course, much more sophisticated than this, but that does not mean his system can always break free from these overly simplistic reductions. William Placher notes, "To oversimplify, as spatial language became increasingly univocal and models of space more homogeneous, there was no particular natural place for God, and the natural options were to say that God was nowhere or everywhere. Descartes and Henry More, both writing in the early seventeenth century, represent these two possibilities."[7] These kinds

---

5. This reductionism fails to see the place in classical Christian theism for God's presence that not only allows for creaturely freedom but also creates it. Avihu Zakai summarizes the issue in Edwards's day: "The classical and medieval God intimately present in creation was thus transformed in mechanical philosophy into a cosmic lawgiver who exercises his dominion over the created order from above. No longer intrinsically related to the essence of material bodies, divine activity was conceived as external to tangible, created beings. Not open to divine activity, or imbued with the redemptive presence and activity, the world of nature was separated from the affairs of salvation." Avihu Zakai, *Jonathan Edwards's Philosophy of History: The Reenchantment of the World in the Age of Enlightenment* (Princeton: Princeton University Press, 2003), 110.

6. Furthermore, and as a result of these intellectual trends, Edwards felt the weight of Hobbes's materialism, writing a note to himself to attack it with his notion of idealism. WJE 6:235.

7. William C. Placher, *The Domestication of Transcendence: How Modern Thinking about God Went Wrong* (Louisville: Westminster John Knox, 1996), 131.

of either-or scenarios, often left implicit in the assumptions of the day, helped give traction to the rise of deism, the recovery of Arianism, and radical accounts of determinism—all within the church itself. It is within this ethos that beliefs concerning human autonomy and goodness prevailed against accounts of original sin, where natural revelation was pitted against special revelation, and where the clear and accountable features of mechanism were wielded against the seemingly mythological notions of God's providential activity.[8]

### God's Fullness and Creaturely Existence

Against much of the intellectual current of his day, Edwards sought to employ what many now consider "radical" philosophical notions of idealism, occasionalism, continuous creationism, and panentheism as a response to the issues he saw in the philosophical, scientific, and theological climate he was working in.[9] Importantly, it seems clear that Edwards believed he could utilize this radical philosophy in an attempt to buttress a rather traditional Reformed view of reality. Edwards's theology was always unique, but it was also a consistent attempt to creatively articulate Reformed theology (without, in his mind, somehow subverting it). However, because of his philosophical maneuvers, Edwards ended up radicalizing certain features of the God-world relation, human freedom, and the Christian view of evil thereby pressing at the bounds of Reformed orthodoxy. Interestingly, on each of these points, Edwards does attempt to provide formulations that mirror more classical approaches to these issues. He is not attempting to radicalize his theology, but in the end, in one way or another, his attempt to make sense of his classical inclinations in his Enlightenment context pushed him in a radical direction.

---

8. Avihu Zakai's chapter "Theology and Scientific Reasoning," in *Jonathan Edwards's Philosophy of History*, 85–127, provides a helpful overview of this era and the intellectual movements that Edwards is responding to.

9. This is not to say that everyone agrees with this assessment, or that there isn't a way to take one of these views in isolation from the others and advance a less radical theory. For instance, idealism seems to be a much better view than the materialism that Edwards was writing against, and in our own day idealism is seeing something of a retrieval of its own. For one example, see *Idealism and Christian Theology*, vol. 1, *Idealism and Christianity*, ed. Joshua R. Farris, S. Mark Hamilton, and James S. Spiegel (London: T&T Clark, 2016).

In his work *The End for Which God Created the World*, Edwards articulates a view of God's relation to creation that is at once traditional and provocative. The overall claim—that God creates for his own glory—is straightforward. But Edwards went further. He wanted to give an in-depth account of the glory of God and the fullness of the divine life that would not pit God's infinite self-regard and fullness against the overflow of his life to the creature. On the one hand he had to address why a God who is infinitely happy in the pure actuality of his own delight would create, and on the other hand he had to protect against the notion that God somehow needed creation to be God. Edwards wanted a traditional account of aseity and God's creative action, but he also wanted to analyze it to a degree few had attempted.

Kathryn Tanner provides a helpful distinction to articulate the two main directions theologians often take when pressed with balancing God's aseity and self-giving. Tanner compares a contrastive and a non-contrastive account of divine transcendence, arguing that a contrastive notion of transcendence, where God is "characterized in terms of a direct contrast" with created being, leads explicitly or implicitly to the belief that "God becomes one being among others within a single order."[10] In a contrastive relation God inevitably becomes a part of a single continuum with his creation, rather than truly transcendent. Transcendence itself breaks down, to be replaced by a range of being or causality where God becomes just another object in existence. Tanner continues,

> Far from appearing to be incompatible with it, a non-contrastive transcendence of God suggests an extreme of divine involvement with the world. . . . Divine involvement with the world need be neither partial, nor mediate, nor simply formative . . . it may be the immediate source of being of every sort.[11]

Tanner maintains that when one recognizes God as truly transcendent in a "non-contrastive" sense, then God can be present fully in creation without somehow undermining creation's integrity. It is not only that God's immanence in creation is compatible with God's transcendence. Rather, it takes this kind of transcendence to allow for "the radical

10. Kathryn Tanner, *God and Creation in Christian Theology: Tyranny or Empowerment?* (Minneapolis: Fortress, 2005), 45.
11. Tanner, *God and Creation in Christian Theology*, 46.

immanence by which God is said to be nearer to us than we are to ourselves."[12]

What Tanner articulates illuminates one of Edwards's focal points in *End of Creation*. There, Edwards says,

> God's acting for himself, or making himself his last end, and his acting for their sake, are not to be set in opposition; or to be considered as the opposite parts of a disjunction: they are rather to be considered as coinciding one with the other, and implied one in the other.[13]

Notice the non-contrastive nature of Edwards's description. One of the ways Edwards develops this notion is through his account of glory, which he understands as having three "levels."[14] The first and primary "level" of glory is God's life of infinite fullness. This fullness is the procession of God's understanding and will that provides the archetype for the beatific vision, and, as we have seen, religious affection. The second level of glory is the external overflow of this fullness. God gives himself to his creation, and as such he overflows in understanding and will. The third level, therefore, is the creatures' reception and participation in this divine overflow.[15] This is a partaking of the divine nature such that creatures share, by grace, in what is God's by nature. This is always done through Christ by the Spirit, and as such it is a part of the fullness that is God's life. Creatures partake in this life in a finite way through Christ—a way that entails a mediated immediacy in Christ by the Spirit.[16] God does not offer glory in the pattern of his own self-glorification, as if his infinite fullness simply provided a model for his redemptive activity. Rather, God's fullness is such that God overflows out of his plenitude for the sake of the other, all while seeking his own glory. Therefore, Edwards avers, "God is all in all, with respect to each part of that communication of the divine fullness which is made to the creature."[17] By advancing an account of God's glory

12. Tanner, *God and Creation in Christian Theology*, 79.

13. WJE 8:440.

14. The term "levels" is mine (Strobel's) and not Edwards's.

15. WJE 8:527–36.

16. This is how Edwards can say that the saints are "in some respects *divine* in glory and happiness." WJE 18:241. Emphasis added.

17. WJE 8:442. As we have already noted, Edwards goes on to say: "Here is both an *emanation* and *remanation*. The refulgence shines upon and into the creature, and is

that includes the creature, Edwards is not contrasting the divine glory with human glory, as if one must choose between them. God being glorified does not require, necessarily, for creatures to lose glory; rather, God's glorification entails within itself the glorification of his people.

Edwards's non-contrastive inclination is the focus of our attempt to retrieve and adapt Edwards's insights. In short, if we take the broad structure of this specific inclination—that God and creatures should be addressed in a non-contrastive manner—and remove that insight from Edwards's more radical notions, can we retrieve this in a way that does justice to his thought without its negative features? Edwards had an impulse to try to create an account of God's immanence in creation that did not somehow undermine creaturely freedom and activity but served as the foundation for it. Even if he did not take this impulse to its final conclusions, we can do so. For the sake of our theology of retrieval, we seek to take this insight and rework it for our own use.

### God-World Relation

To understand Edwards's "classical" inclinations more fully—that God relates to creation out of his fullness and not in spite of it—it is important to address how this relation works. This is the overarching issue that governs the following, since accounts of freedom and evil will both be directly linked to the God-world relation. In Edwards's *End of Creation*, he presents his classical impulse well. First, he grounds the whole of God's life *ad extra* in his infinite fullness, claiming "that no notion of God's last end in the creation of the world is agreeable to reason which would truly imply or infer any indigence, insufficiency and mutability in God; or any dependence of the Creator on the creature, for any part of his perfection or happiness."[18] It is impossible, Edwards continues to argue, that God is "the subject of any sufferings or *impair* of his glory and felicity from any other being." Furthermore, "the notion of God's creating the world in order to receive anything properly from the creature is not only contrary to the nature of God, but inconsistent with the notion of creation; which

---

reflected back to the luminary. The beams of glory come from God, and are something of God, and are refunded back again to their original. So that the whole is *of* God, and *in* God, and *to* God; and God is the beginning, middle and end in this affair." WJE 8:531. Emphasis in the original.

18. WJE 8:420.

implies a being's receiving its existence, and all that belongs to its being, out of nothing."[19] Notice that, for Edwards, creation's status *qua* creation is maintained by receiving its existence from God and being created out of nothing. This coheres well with Edwards's idealism, continuous creationism, and panentheism, even though those views, along with his occasionalism, make it difficult to give the fullness of creation its due.

Importantly, Edwards shows his theological acumen by grounding God's creative act on God's fullness.[20] Intuitively, one might think that Edwards would follow his classical insights into an account of concursus and secondary causality. But that is not what we find; at least not obviously.[21] Rather than God's fullness allowing him to talk meaningfully about creation, what Edwards ends up doing is talking about God *instead of* talking about creation. For example, Edwards can talk about creaturely causality "with the vulgar," and therefore give an account of creaturely causation (including secondary causality), but it is all done within an overarching account that undermines creaturely causation and reduces it all to God's causation. Along these lines, it is relevant that Edwards says, "God is the sum of all being and there is no being without his being; all things are in him, and he in all,"[22] and "the first Being, the eternal and infinite Being, is in effect, Being in general; and comprehends universal existence."[23] Taken in isolation, one might read these passages as simply a forceful emphasis on God as the Alpha and Omega, but more is going on here. Edwards's panentheism, idealism, occasionalism, and understanding of continuous

19. WJE 8:420.

20. Webster, again with his characteristic insight, avers, "The coming-to-be of all that is not God—that there is now not one order of (divine) being but two orders of being (uncreated and created)—can be thrown into relief only against the background of the repleteness and simplicity of God. Further, the act of creation does not bring about a state of affairs in which God's fullness now includes his relation to creatures. As creator God does not cease to be perfectly alive and active without the creature; he remains supereminently himself apart from what he has made. The 'beginning' of heaven and earth is no beginning for God." John Webster, "Creation out of Nothing," in *Christian Dogmatics: Reformed Theology for the Church Catholic*, ed. Michael Allen and Scott R. Swain (Grand Rapids: Baker Academic, 2016), 137–38.

21. This, of course, was already seen in the development of Edwards's philosophical theology in chapters three and four. Edwards can give an account of secondary causality, in a sense, from within his determinism, but, with his understanding of continuous creationism and occasionalism, it does not end up doing the work it was meant to do, which was to carve out adequate space for creaturely causation.

22. WJE 20:122.

23. WJE 8:461–62.

creation point to deeper issues in his thought. The problem is not that Edwards moves too quickly away from God's aseity to an account of creation. Rather, the opposite is true.

Edwards struggles to find a way to talk about a creation affirmed by modern scientific modalities, a creation that seems to function on its own, and yet still to affirm God's transcendence and providential government. But this is where Edwards's non-contrastive inclinations could have been employed. Edwards could have sought a way to follow non-contrastive theological inclinations into a view that allowed for God's creative activity, immanence, and providence within a robust God-world relation. Kathryn Tanner writes:

> Talk of the creature's power and efficacy is compatible with talk about God's universal and immediate agency if the theologian follows a rule according to which divinity is said to exercise its power in founding rather than suppressing creating being, and created being is said to maintain and fulfill itself, not independently of such agency, but in essential dependence upon it.[24]

She continues, focusing in on Edwards's specific problem: "The theological occasionalist may suggest it is improper to say that both God and created beings bring about the effects in the created order: genuine efficacy cannot be predicated of both God and the creature." On the contrary, to "exclude genuine created efficacy as a possible direct effect of God's agency is to misunderstand, then, the nature of the transcendence implied by the supremacy, sovereignty and holiness of God. In the Christian tradition, God's greatness does not require any denial of the creature whose being is constituted in dependence upon 'him.'"[25] This is precisely the problem we find in Edwards. Recalling the image of a flip book, where flipping the pages makes the pictures appear to move, we find an adequate

---

24. Tanner, *God and Creation in Christian Theology*, 85.

25. Tanner, *God and Creation in Christian Theology*, 87. John Webster narrates the "contrastive" temptation well, along with a more fruitful way forward: "God is not to be reduced to the status of a stupendously large being over and against other, smaller beings. Precisely as the one who is uncreated, God is creative. Possessing unlimited blessedness, God does not have his being in competition, reserving being and life to himself. Beyond threat, God is also beyond envy, no other possible reality having the capacity to enhance or diminish his perfection. As the one who has life in himself he can give life to the world, he can be infinitely generous without self-depletion." Webster, "Creation out of Nothing," 138.

understanding of how Edwards sees creaturely causality (where each picture represents one "world-stage"). But certainly this kind of account does not allow for a sufficiently robust created order. Creation, for Edwards, does not have any actual causal activity; and, as we saw earlier, his panentheism, occasionalism, continuous creationism, and idealism push the creation back onto God in a way that seems to undermine necessary features of creation's being and freedom. But this seems to be a less than adequate account of God's creation and its relation to its Creator.

It is not difficult to understand why Edwards would turn to radical philosophical notions as a way to push back against the mechanism and contrastive notions of transcendence assumed in his day. But even with his non-contrastive impulse, Edwards's philosophical maneuvers take away what gains he made by employing it. By turning to panentheism and idealism, even if he does work hard to maintain the Creator-creature distinction (which he does), he has still created a contrastive account of the God-world relation. William Placher narrates this problem concerning transcendence:

> Increasingly, Christian writers in the seventeenth century, since they did not want to think of God as utterly beyond their comprehension, thought of God's otherness in terms of distance and remoteness from the world. Though they do not use the terms, they were in effect contrasting *transcendence* with *immanence*. Such a "contrastive" account of transcendence . . . makes divine transcendence and involvement in the world into a zero-sum game: the more involved or immanent, the less transcendent, and vice versa.[26]

To maintain sovereignty in a contrastive paradigm entails that God is not just the first mover but the only mover. This has disastrous consequences, and it is here, precisely, that we need to follow Edwards's non-contrastive theological impulse. This involves rejecting Edwards's route through his radical philosophy and the theological development he advances, reconceiving what it might look like to navigate similar terrain with a different conceptual vehicle, so to speak. To do so, we briefly introduce two areas implicated in his contrastive development of transcendence and immanence, showing again how Edwards's theological

26. Placher, *The Domestication of Transcendence*, 111.

inclinations could have offered him another way forward than the one he in fact took—all in the service of theological retrieval.

## Freedom

It is safe to assume that if the God-world relation is off kilter, then human freedom is an area where this will manifest similar problems. This is precisely what we find. Richard Muller introduces the discussion of freedom of the will in Reformed theology by addressing the "basic terms of the traditional debate" as "the limited and dependent freedom of the will and the problem of choice."[27] Muller argues that Edwards shifted the ground of the discussion by claiming that "the real issue was not the freedom of will but of the person, in conjunction with the intellect, to choose freely according to its nature and arguing the determination of the will itself."[28] Furthermore, Muller believes that Edwards departed from the Reformed tradition by introducing philosophical necessity into his thought.[29] In this sense, instead of being the prime example of the Reformed view on freedom, Muller sees Edwards as an aberration of the Reformed tradition, one that negates creaturely contingency in a way foreign to Reformation thought. Whereas the Reformed tradition was able to focus on God's fullness and creaturely contingency through the notion of primary and secondary causality, Edwards flattens out this schema with his notion of continuous creation and occasionalism. The purpose, as Tanner noted, was to make sure that God remained sovereign, but the assumptions behind this purpose are faulty and fail to grasp the depth of insight gained by his patient attention to God's life *in se*.

The theological structure of Edwards's understanding of God's infinite actuality, we have seen, had the available resources to carve out space for human freedom. But in *Freedom of the Will*, we discover a dif-

27. Richard A. Muller, "Jonathan Edwards and the Absence of Free Choice: A Parting of Ways in the Reformed Tradition," *Jonathan Edwards Studies* 1, no. 1 (2011): 11. This article, originally a lecture, began a debate between Muller and Paul Helm on the matter in *Jonathan Edwards Studies* 4 (2014).

28. Muller, "Jonathan Edwards and the Absence of Free Choice," 11.

29. Muller's volume *Divine Will and Human Choice* is particularly helpful in giving an overview of the arguments and the Reformed views on these issues. Muller, rightly in my opinion, points to the categories themselves (i.e., libertarianism and compatibilism) as problematic and reductionistic. See Muller, *Divine Will and Human Choice*, 310–11.

ferent sort of argumentation. Edwards's work exposits the "freedom of the will," but does so with an eye on the discussion of how his view of freedom comports with ethical issues.[30] We've already seen the philosophical notions Edwards presupposes, and it is clear that the notion of freedom cannot have any real causal import.[31] Rather, for Edwards, freedom of will is simply acting according to one's strongest desires. One wills what one finds most agreeable, what Edwards calls the "strongest motive."[32] By framing the discussion this way, Edwards can offer an account of freedom, one that, he believes, addresses the issues related to moral agency, virtue, reward, punishment, etc., and he does so within an entirely deterministic framework.

Another way to think about Edwards's view involves returning to the example of the flip book once more. Let us say that each picture in the flip book is of a person who is running. There is no actual movement going on because the flip book is comprised of still photos. But in each photo there is a person whose strongest motive is to run, and who is therefore willing to run. It is irrelevant, in how he frames the discussion, that God is re-creating the world every instant and that each new picture is not directly causally related to the one preceding (although, from a human point of view, the relation will appear causal, such that humankind can reason according to the nature of causation).[33] Edwards thinks he can, in fact, talk about a kind of secondary causality, despite the fact that there is no actual creaturely causality:

> They [human creatures] have a secondary and dependent arbitrariness. They are not limited in their operations to the laws of matter and motion, so but [sic] that they can do what they please. The members of men's bodies obey the act of their wills without being directed merely by the impulse and attraction of other bodies in all their motions.[34]

30. Edwards's work is unquestionably profound, but it is not the nature of its brilliance that we are addressing. Rather, our interest concerns how Edwards reworks the debate on freedom.

31. Edwards states, "I sometimes use the word 'effect' for the consequence of another thing, which is perhaps rather an occasion than a cause, most properly speaking." WJE 1:181.

32. WJE 1:144, 142.

33. As we have seen in the earlier chapters of this book.

34. WJE 23:203.

Edwards's view of freedom allows him to talk about the secondary operation of humankind within God's primary causality, but what he means by it is decisively different from the tradition before him. He has changed the discussion from within his philosophical framework. Because of the philosophical system Edwards employs, he can talk about creaturely freedom and causation within each world-stage, but as we have seen there is no actual creaturely causation available—nothing obtains for long enough to cause anything to happen. Edwards "talks in the vulgar," as it were, making it sound as if his view accords with how we tend to view the world; but once his philosophical positions are clarified, a much different picture appears. Edwards employs non-contrastive theological language, where God's causation does not create a zero-sum game with creaturely causation, but his philosophical material undermines the ultimate meaningfulness of this language (and a zero-sum game emerges). This is how Edwards can make a claim that sounds precisely like a classical view of concursus (even though he is talking about efficacious grace) and yet means something very different:

> We are not merely passive in it [efficacious grace], nor yet does God do some and we do the rest, but God does all and we do all. God produces all and we act all. For that is what he produces, our own acts. God is the only proper author and fountain; we only are the proper actors. We are in different respects wholly passive and wholly active.[35]

Edwards is able to make these affirmations from within his system, but the notion of freedom has been reconceived and the nature of "action" has been recalibrated such that there is no actual creaturely causation. But his goal seems to be something akin to concursus. In contrast, note the focus of Wilhemus à Brakel as he articulates concursus:

> The second act of providence is *Cooperation, (concursus)*, that is, *the concurrence of the power of God with the motions of His*

---

35. WJE 21:251. Note how similar this sounds to Tanner's discussion of Aquinas: "Thomas illustrates this rule for talk of created efficacy in statements about two orders of causality. Created causes are *secondary* causes with respect to the *primary* creative agency of God. God as a creative agent must be said to will any order among things that created causes carry out; created causes are therefore subordinate to God's own agency." Tanner, *God and Creation in Christian Theology*, 91–92.

*creatures.* All creatures have received an independent and unique existence from God so as to move in a manner unique to themselves. They set themselves in motion, as man for instance walks, speaks, and works—all of which he does of himself. Since every creature exists, however, by the energizing and preserving power of God, and would not be able to exist without this, each creature's activity comes about by the influence of God's cooperative power, without which it would not be able to move. As is its manner of existence, so likewise is its manner of motion; both existence and motion are dependent upon God.[36]

For Brakel, the creature has real causal power and the space to be a creature, without somehow undermining God's sovereignty or preserving power. Providence is still its own distinct action of God without having to become an act of creation (as with a view of continuous creation). Edwards is unable to take the insights from his tradition and maintain them in the Enlightenment context in which he worked. He has imbibed the theological impulse at the heart of Brakel's statement, but he ends up radicalizing the God-world relation and undermining its real import. Unfortunately, by failing to provide an account of the creature's "independent and unique existence," and by focusing solely on God's causal activity, he ends up undermining the fruit of his careful attention to God's transcendence and his relation to creation. In part, Edwards is responding to an ideology he fears will remove God from the world, leaving behind a system without need of God's providential upholding or his immanent activity in the created order. Edwards is not interested in a creation removed from God, and this is where his philosophical genius really lies. But, in our minds, there are better ways to advance these insights than through panentheism, occasionalism, continuous creationism, and idealism.

36. Wilhelmus à Brakel, *The Christian's Reasonable Service*, vol. 1: *God, Man, and Christ*, ed. Joel R. Beeke, trans. Bartel Elshout (Grand Rapids, MI: Reformation Heritage Books, 1992), 336. Emphasis in the original. I am not suggesting that Edwards was in conversation with Brakel, but rather, he is a near contemporary of Edwards working within the same theological tradition. Brakel articulates well the Reformed view of concursus as "the continuing divine support of the operation of all secondary causes (whether free, contingent, or necessary)." Richard A. Muller, "*concursus* or *concursus generalis*," in *Dictionary of Latin and Greek Theological Terms: Drawn Principally from Protestant Scholastic Theology* (Grand Rapids: Baker Books, 1985), 76.

## Implications

To Edwards's credit, he wielded a classical notion of Christian orthodoxy in a day when classical was seen as outmoded, and he managed to do so in a framework that was decisively modern. Edwards sought to argue for the Christian view of God as "all in all" in a new philosophical and scientific world, and, in doing so, he offered a robust account of God's life *in se* to ground creaturely reality. To retrieve Edwards's insights, we suggest that we follow his non-contrastive theological impulse against the undercurrent of much of his thought. To show why we think it is important to distance ourselves from his understanding of the God-world relation, we turn to one final issue that this creates for his theology—evil as glorifying God.

Because of his philosophical convictions, it would seem Edwards has to accept the notion that God is glorified by evil. Furthermore, although Edwards desires to affirm the basic idea of evil as privation of the good,[37] his philosophical inclinations make that affirmation difficult. In Edwards's ideal world, evil becomes a real feature of a system devoted to the glory of God. The system, as a whole, glorifies God, and therefore each gear in the grand machine is oriented to God's glory. Although not irrelevant, the issue is not so much whether God permits sin rather than decrees it, or whether God is, or is not, the positive cause of it.[38] Edwards addresses those questions with characteristic precision and caution. The

37. He seems to be assuming this, for instance, in his discussion of Taylor's work in WJE 3:251, and he seems to assume it as well when he states, "Disagreement or contrariety to being is evidently an approach to nothing, or a degree of nothing, which is nothing else but disagreement or contrariety of being, and the greatest and only evil; and entity is the greatest and only good." WJE 6:335.

38. This is not to say that these questions are not of fundamental importance. As Oliver Crisp notes elsewhere, "Edwards seeks to drive a wedge between causal and moral responsibility with respect to divine action in the world. . . . If one of the agents involved in a particular action is divine, and if a theological determinism such as Edwards' obtains, then the distinction between causal and moral responsibility cannot hold. God is the causal and moral agent responsible for that action, and therefore, for sinful actions." Oliver D. Crisp, *Jonathan Edwards and the Metaphysics of Sin* (Aldershot: Ashgate, 2005), 74. This doesn't include the element of occasionalism. Taking that into account Crisp writes, "If God alone causes all things, then he is both causally and morally responsible for all events that come to pass, since he alone has directly caused all those events to come to pass" (74), noting that this is true even though Edwards did not make the connection himself.

bigger issue concerns (1) the "substantial" nature of evil in an ideal world, and (2) evil, as an aspect of this ideal world, taking part, as it were, in glorifying God. For Edwards, the reason why evil must glorify God is not because of biblical precedent or the obvious demands of divine sovereignty, but because of his accounts of continuous creation, occasionalism, and idealism within a contrastive notion of transcendence. With the proper account of secondary causality and concursus, Edwards could have an account that speaks more meaningfully about God's sovereign activity in the world, and how his creation brought glory to himself without having to make the unfortunate claim that evil glorifies God. Yet, according to Edwards's philosophy, it seems difficult to avoid this problem.[39]

It is helpful to consider evil as a test case for the God-world relation because of its obvious pastoral import. To say that God needs evil to glorify himself seems to undermine the goodness of God. In light of evil, God can glorify himself through the creaturely condition, but that is different from saying that somehow God creates, sustains, and re-creates evil for his own glory (which, it seems, Edwards must say). In Edwards's sense, Jesus's lament over Jerusalem is odd indeed, since he should have gloried in its coming rejection: "O Jerusalem, Jerusalem, the city that kills the prophets and stones those who are sent to it! How often would I have gathered your children together as a hen gathers her brood under her wings, and you were not willing!" (Matt. 23:37). On Edwards's philosophical assumptions, and the theological buttressing he develops based on that, God should glory in destruction in a way that does not seem to mesh with much of what goes on in Scripture. This is not to say that this somehow undermines God being wrathful, but instead that this needs to be understood within an entire rejection of evil as such rather than God somehow needing evil for the display of his glory. Edwards had resources in his tradition to affirm God's rejection of evil—being able to name evil "evil" without qualification—and yet he chose another path. This is another place at which we should reject the structure Edwards employed and advance other theological insights for the sake of biblical fidelity.

---

39. There are many treatments of Edwards and the problem of evil, and the philosophical material can be dense. Crisp addresses the breadth of the issues, of which there are many, to fully understand the implications of Edwards's view. See Crisp, *Jonathan Edwards and the Metaphysics of Sin*, 54–78.

## Taking Stock

I (Strobel) have suggested that the fundamental impulse for retrieving Edwards's theology and going beyond his own conclusions is a non-contrastive view of the God-world relation. If we attend to the broad features of Edwards's non-contrastive account, we can say that his view seeks an articulation of the fullness of God's presence and action that creates the context for real creaturely power and causation (even if he cannot, in the end, say this himself). In his theological analysis, we do not have to choose one side over and against the other, as if one has to decide whether God creates for his own glory or for the glory of creation. Edwards clearly rejects this kind of reductionism. On his view, God's focus is so fully upon himself—his fullness is so infinitely actual in himself—that he is able to be for the creature.

> God, when he beholds his own glory shining forth in his image in the creature, and when he beholds the creature made happy from the exercises of his goodness, because these and all things are from eternity equally present with God this delight in God can't properly be said to be received from the creature, because it consists only in a delight in giving to the creature.[40]

We can advance these insights to say that the fullness of God's glory is the foundation for God to be for creation and to create space for the creature to have its own unique creaturely existence. This creaturely mode of existence should not somehow bracket God away from humankind, but it is within God's freedom, glory, and love that human persons come to know freedom, glory, and love according to proper creaturely causation.

While it may seem hard for some to understand how Edwards's employment of panentheism, continuous creationism, idealism, and occasionalism seeks to function according to his non-contrastive inclination, each of these can be read as an attempt to navigate the concerns just articulated. This approach may fail, ultimately, to do justice to what we've just tried to narrate, but it is, nonetheless, an attempt to address these issues by focusing on God's fullness and humanity's existence within that fullness. Edwards's panentheism seeks to articulate a God-world relation where transcendence and immanence are not set against each other, and

40. WJE 18:238.

where he can meaningfully speak to Paul's affirmation that "in him we live and move and have our being" (Acts 17:28). Edwards's idealism, similarly, sought to move beyond the all-consuming focus on the materiality of creation, to do justice to the biblical call to look "not to the things that are seen but to the things that are unseen. For the things that are seen are transient, but the things that are unseen are eternal" (2 Cor. 4:18).

Similarly, Edwards's occasionalism was meant to provide an account of creaturely freedom from within God's free activity, and, therefore, in the words of Donald Bloesch, "Edwards perceived that grace does not override the will but releases the will for creative action."[41] As we've seen, Edwards is able to affirm this only by reconceiving the nature of freedom, but, as Bloesch rightly notices, the impulse to affirm a sort of creaturely freedom is clear. Unfortunately, the direction in which Edwards advances his insights gives an account of freedom that seems anything but free, at least as freedom is normally conceived. Instead of reconceiving the nature of freedom, Edwards could have followed his non-contrastive impulse to discover space for creaturely freedom within God's own freedom and presence. Instead, his move to occasionalism and continuous creationism takes away the ultimate meaningfulness of secondary causality. But Bloesch's insights are correct. Edwards was attempting to construct a kind of God-world relation in which the creature's will was not overridden but was released in freedom. Each of Edwards's views pushes in a direction that we believe can be more adequately developed through classical constructions of the God-world relation, freedom, and evil. This retrieval, therefore, is not somehow foreign to Edwards's theology but is an extension of insights fundamental to his thought that push beyond his own conclusions.

Ultimately, Edwards was seeking a distinctively Christian metaphysic, one that refused to make creation far from God—somehow external to his presence—but sought a mode of creation as participating in God without losing its integrity. Because of this, there are aspects of Edwards's theology that overlap with the classical understanding of the "Christian-platonist synthesis," what Hans Boersma calls a "sacramental ontology," or a participationist metaphysic.[42] To do so Edwards turned

41. Donald Bloesch, *Essentials of Evangelical Theology*, vol. 1: *God, Authority, and Salvation* (San Francisco: Prince Press, 2001), 204.

42. In explaining this term, Boersma writes, "The 'sacramental tapestry' of the subtitle speaks of a carefully woven unity of nature and the supernatural, according to which created objects are sacraments that participate in the mystery of the heavenly reality of

to philosophical notions that helped his overall polemic against heretical groups but that ushered into his thought unwelcome aberrations that created tension with his theological tradition. To "become Edwardsean" implies, it would seem, that we take up his project to reconsider the whole of creation around God, and that we do so while attending to some of the more troubling fruit of his conclusions and attempting to discern a better way.

## Theology after Edwards

To advance a distinctively Edwardsean mode of theologizing, therefore, entails a patient attention to God and his infinite blessedness. Following Edwards's theological impulses, we should claim that God's fullness and presence do not somehow undermine creaturely realities but underwrite them. This should lead to a Christian vision of reality that refuses to pit God's transcendence and immanence against each other, but provides, instead, a robustly classical theology that meditates deeply on God *in se* (in himself) and God *pro nobis* (for us). Based on God's redemptive activity governed by love and wisdom, as we discovered in chapter five, an Edwardsean form of retrieval could utilize those insights to establish the creature's unique existence from within that activity and not reduce it to that activity. This is the direction that seems more fitting for us to take today.

Becoming Edwardsean, therefore, is following Edwards as he faithfully seeks to do justice to "the upward call of God in Christ" (Phil. 3:14). It means attending deeply to the blessedness of God (Ps. 16:11; 1 Tim. 1:11; 6:15) and God's infinitely transcendent being, all the while coming to understand that it is this God who is for us in Jesus Christ. Becoming Edwardsean is grounding life in the glory of God, recognizing that God's fullness does not somehow undermine his self-giving for our good, but establishes it. This holistic vision of theology is not just a rejection of oversimplification and reduction but, for Edwards, includes a distinctively churchly and pastoral theologizing. For Edwards, there was no bi-

---

Jesus Christ." Hans Boersma, *Heavenly Participation: The Weaving of a Sacramental Tapestry* (Grand Rapids: Eerdmans, 2011), 8. I think Edwards has parallel concerns. Edwards's notion of the universe being "full of images of divine things, as full as a language of words" is relevant here. WJE 11:152.

furcation between academic and churchly theology, between systematic and biblical, or between theology and spirituality.[43] (Edwards defines the task of divinity as *"the doctrine of living to God by Christ."*)[44] Edwards could wield his intellect for densely academic treatises on freedom and virtue and yet recognize that he was called to help his people discern the work of the Spirit, and so he advanced his intellectual rigor for a study of religious affection. Because Edwards was ultimately oriented by the glory of God, he was not bound by the kinds of restrictions we often put on ourselves and others, and instead he simply gave himself to the service of God. Because of this, everything he did was driven by the love and glory of God. Love was the prevailing notion that drove his theological enterprise because the God of love so fully fueled his devotion and so completely captivated his imagination. Becoming Edwardsean, therefore, implies this kind of theologizing; it is theology done before the face of God for the glory of God.

43. This is not to say that Edwards couldn't distinguish between these various genres of theology, but rather that he saw the calling of the divine to include all of them. He might have focused his written work on polemical theology more than anything else, perhaps, but that said more about his context than about his overall calling. His calling was grounded in a much more holistic notion of the theological task than we know today.

44. WJE 22:86. Edwards would, of course, be able to make distinctions between speculative and practical divinity, but that would be for the sake of clarification and not calling. See WJE 22:87.

# Further Reading

There is a growing body of literature on Jonathan Edwards, initially stimulated by the work of Harvard historian Perry Miller in the years following the Second World War. Over the last twenty years, this literature has diversified and matured to the extent that current research now focuses on the full range of Edwards's interests across cognate disciplines—from theological and philosophical studies of his work to literary and historical reflection on his intellectual merits. With this development in mind, the following annotated list intends to orient new readers to the growing body of literature on Edwards's works. Although not exhaustive, it is indicative of the most important works that a newcomer to Edwardsean studies should consider.

## I. Works by Edwards

### 1. The Yale Works

The standard critical edition of Edwards's works, published by Yale University Press, is now complete. The print edition runs to some twenty-six volumes. Although it comprises critical editions of all Edwards's major works, it does not include everything Edwards wrote. A more complete collection of his works can be found online at the fully searchable, open-access version of Edwards's work on the website of the Jonathan Edwards Center at Yale University (http://edwards.yale.edu/). This online collection includes unpublished sermon outlines, miscellaneous volumes such as Edwards's "Book of Controversies," partially printed in previous, nineteenth-century editions of Edwards's works, as well as correspondence and sundry notebooks, and runs to seventy-one volumes in total—a staggering forty-five volumes more than the print edition. This website is an outstanding resource for Edwards scholarship, containing a number of useful resources in addition to the online edition of Edwards's works (e.g., bibliographical essays). Included below is the full list of the letterpress edition of the Yale Works with the abbreviated titles:

WJE 1    *Freedom of the Will.* Vol. 1 of *The Works of Jonathan Edwards.* Edited by Paul Ramsey. New Haven: Yale University Press, 1957.

WJE 2    *Religious Affections.* Vol. 2 of *The Works of Jonathan Edwards.* Edited by John E. Smith. New Haven: Yale University Press, 1959.

WJE 3    *Original Sin.* Vol. 3 of *The Works of Jonathan Edwards.* Edited by Clyde A. Holbrook. New Haven: Yale University Press, 1970.

WJE 4    *The Great Awakening.* Vol. 4 of *The Works of Jonathan Edwards.* Edited by C. C. Goen. New Haven: Yale University Press, 1972.

WJE 5    *Apocalyptic Writings.* Vol. 5 of *The Works of Jonathan Edwards.* Edited by Stephen J. Stein. New Haven: Yale University Press, 1977.

WJE 6    *Scientific and Philosophical Writings.* Vol. 6 of *The Works of Jonathan Edwards.* Edited by Wallace E. Anderson. New Haven: Yale University Press, 1980.

WJE 7    *The Life of David Brainerd.* Vol. 7 of *The Works of Jonathan Edwards.* Edited by Norman Pettit. New Haven: Yale University Press, 1984.

WJE 8    *Ethical Writings.* Vol. 8 of *The Works of Jonathan Edwards.* Edited by Paul Ramsey. New Haven: Yale University Press, 1989.

WJE 9    *A History of the Work of Redemption.* Vol. 9 of *The Works of Jonathan Edwards.* Edited by John F. Wilson. New Haven: Yale University Press, 1989.

WJE 10   *Sermons and Discourses, 1720–1723.* Vol. 10 of *The Works of Jonathan Edwards.* Edited by Wilson H. Kimnach. New Haven: Yale University Press, 1992.

WJE 11   *Typological Writings.* Vol. 11 of *The Works of Jonathan Edwards.* Edited by Wallace E. Anderson and David Watters. New Haven: Yale University Press, 1993.

WJE 12   *Ecclesiastical Writings.* Vol. 12 of *The Works of Jonathan Edwards.* Edited by David D. Hall. New Haven: Yale University Press, 1994.

WJE 13    *The "Miscellanies": Nos. a–z, aa–zz, 1–500.* Vol. 13 of *The Works of Jonathan Edwards.* Edited by Thomas A. Schafer. New Haven: Yale University Press, 1994.

WJE 14    *Sermons and Discourses, 1723–1729.* Vol. 14 of *The Works of Jonathan Edwards.* Edited by Kenneth P. Minkema. New Haven: Yale University Press, 1997.

WJE 15    *Notes on Scripture.* Vol. 15 of *The Works of Jonathan Edwards.* Edited by Stephen J. Stein. New Haven: Yale University Press, 1998.

WJE 16    *Letters and Personal Writings.* Vol. 16 of *The Works of Jonathan Edwards.* Edited by George S. Claghorn. New Haven: Yale University Press, 1998.

WJE 17    *Sermons and Discourses, 1730–1733.* Vol. 17 of *The Works of Jonathan Edwards.* Edited by Mark Valeri. New Haven: Yale University Press, 1999.

WJE 18    *The "Miscellanies": Nos. 501–832.* Vol. 18 of *The Works of Jonathan Edwards.* Edited by Ava Chamberlain. New Haven: Yale University Press, 2000.

WJE 19    *Sermons and Discourses, 1734–1738.* Vol. 19 of *The Works of Jonathan Edwards.* Edited by M. X. Lesser. New Haven: Yale University Press, 2001.

WJE 20    *The "Miscellanies": Nos. 833–1132.* Vol. 20 of *The Works of Jonathan Edwards.* Edited by Amy Plantinga Pauw. New Haven: Yale University Press, 2002.

WJE 21    *Writings on the Trinity, Grace and Faith.* Vol. 21 of *The Works of Jonathan Edwards.* Edited by Sang Hyun Lee. New Haven: Yale University Press, 2002.

WJE 22    *Sermons and Discourses, 1739–1742.* Vol. 22 of *The Works of Jonathan Edwards.* Edited by Harry S. Stout and Nathan O. Hatch. New Haven: Yale University Press, 2003.

WJE 23    *The "Miscellanies": Nos. 1153–1360.* Vol. 23 of *The Works of Jonathan Edwards.* Edited by Douglas A. Sweeney. New Haven: Yale University Press, 2004.

WJE 24    *The Blank Bible.* Vol. 24 of *The Works of Jonathan Edwards.* Edited by Stephen J. Stein. New Haven: Yale University Press, 2006.

WJE 25    *Sermons and Discourses, 1743–1758.* Vol. 25 of *The Works of Jonathan Edwards.* Edited by Wilson H. Kimnach. New Haven: Yale University Press, 2006.

WJE 26   *Catalogue of Books.* Vol. 26 of *The Works of Jonathan Edwards.* Edited by Peter J. Theusen. New Haven: Yale University Press, 2008.

### 2. *The Hickman Edition*

There are several earlier editions of Edwards's works dating from the nineteenth century. Of these, the Hickman edition of Edwards's works is widely available and still in print. It remains useful, despite the extremely small text and the fact that it contains corrupted versions of a number of important works (e.g., "The Mind," *Charity and Its Fruits*). However, in the case of *Five Discourses on Important Subjects, Nearly Concerning the Great Affair of the Soul's Eternal Salvation,* one could argue that the arrangement of the Hickman edition is superior to that in WJE 19, since it follows the format in which Edwards himself saw the *Five Discourses* through the press. The full bibliographical entry for this version of Edwards's works is:

Edwards, Jonathan. *The Works of Jonathan Edwards.* 2 vols. Edited by Edward Hickman. 1834. Reprint, Edinburgh: Banner of Truth Trust, 1974.

## II. Works about Edwards

### 1. *Annotated Bibliographies of Works about Jonathan Edwards*

Lesser, M. X. *Reading Jonathan Edwards: An Annotated Bibliography in Three Parts, 1729–2005.* Grand Rapids: Eerdmans, 2008. This is an invaluable reference work.

Manspeaker, Nancy. *Jonathan Edwards: Bibliographical Synopses.* Lampeter: Edwin Mellen, 1981. This work has been superseded by Lesser (listed above).

Minkema, Kenneth P., and Harry S. Stout. "Jonathan Edwards Studies during the Career of Sang Hyun Lee." In *Jonathan Edwards as Contemporary: Essays in Honor of Sang Hyun Lee,* edited by Don Schweitzer, 239–60. New York: Peter Lang, 2010.

## 2. *Biographical Studies of Edwards*

Allen, Alexander V. G. *Jonathan Edwards: The First Critical Biography.* 1889. Reprint, Eugene, OR: Wipf & Stock, 2008. Contained in the Jonathan Edwards Classic Studies Series, reissued in conjunction with the Jonathan Edwards Center. This is the first critical biography of Edwards. Prior to its publication, biographical works on Edwards were largely hagiographies, although the biography by Samuel Hopkins (listed below) contains much useful anecdotal evidence concerning Edwards's habits and character.

Gura, Philip. *Jonathan Edwards: America's Evangelical.* New York: Hill and Wang, 2005. This is a short, readable account of Edwards's life, focusing on his place in early American evangelicalism. Compared with the two Marsden biographies listed below, however, it makes scant use of the results provided by Edwardsean research over the last few decades.

Hopkins, Samuel. *The Life and Character of the Late Reverend Jonathan Edwards.* 1796. Reprint, Northampton: S & E Butler, 1804. This is the earliest biography of Edwards, written by his admiring disciple. It is an interesting artifact of the period and offers much valuable information on Edwards's personal life and influence.

Marsden, George. *Jonathan Edwards: A Life.* New Haven: Yale University Press, 2003. This book is the standard critical biography of Edwards and is likely to remain the benchmark for the foreseeable future. Highly recommended.

———. *A Short Life of Jonathan Edwards.* Grand Rapids: Eerdmans, 2008. This is not an abridgement of Edwards's larger life but a retelling, including an interesting comparison with Benjamin Franklin.

Miller, Perry. *Jonathan Edwards.* New York: William Sloane, 1949. This is the book that sparked the contemporary interest in Edwards. It is still a landmark work, although not entirely trustworthy on important matters of Edwardsean interpretation.

Morris, William S. *The Young Jonathan Edwards: A Reconstruction.* 1991. Reprint, Eugene, OR: Wipf & Stock, 2005. This published version of the author's 1955 University of Chicago PhD dissertation is the most thorough treatment of Edwards's early intellectual development written to date.

Murray, Iain H. *Jonathan Edwards: A New Biography.* Edinburgh: Banner of Truth, 1988. This is a very readable work in the tradition of evangelical hagiography.

Sweeney, Douglas A. *Jonathan Edwards and the Ministry of the Word: A Model of Faith and Thought*. Downers Grove: InterVarsity, 2009. This is a fine, readable, and extremely informative work that focuses on Edwards's ministerial context.

Tracy, Patricia J. *Jonathan Edwards, Pastor: Religion and Society in Eighteenth-Century Northampton*. New York: Hill and Wang, 1980. This is an excellent critical study of Edwards's ministry that details the social history of life in Northampton. It offers fascinating insights into the lost world of eighteenth-century colonial New England.

Winslow, Ola. *Jonathan Edwards, 1703–1758*. New York: Collier Books, 1940. This Pulitzer Prize–winner is very useful as a critical biography. It is nevertheless dated in some respects—not least in its advocacy of the "tragic Edwards" view, according to which Edwards is regarded as a thinker whose creativity was stymied by his commitment to an outdated theological system.

### 3. Other Introductory Works on Edwards's Thought

Carrick, John. *The Preaching of Jonathan Edwards*. Edinburgh: Banner of Truth, 2008. This is the first monograph on Edwards's preaching.

Gerstner, John H. *Jonathan Edwards: A Mini-Theology*. Wheaton: Tyndale, 1987. This is a short but solid introduction to Edwards. However, it includes several mistaken notions about important aspects of his thought.

Lucas, Sean Michael. *God's Grand Design: The Theological Vision of Jonathan Edwards*. Wheaton: Crossway, 2011. This is a popular introduction to Edwards's thought. It focuses mainly on his practical and pastoral works and is aimed at seminary students. However, it does not deal with Edwards's philosophical works in any detail, which is a significant shortcoming. It also operates with an outdated view of Edwards's doctrine of the Trinity.

McDermott, Gerald R., ed. *Understanding Jonathan Edwards: An Introduction to America's Theologian*. New York: Oxford University Press, 2009. A helpful, readable collection of essays from a range of Edwards scholars that is accessible and fairly up-to-date.

Nichols, Stephen J. *Jonathan Edwards: A Guided Tour of His Life and Thought*. Phillipsburg: P&R, 2001. This is a descriptive rather than critical introduction that is rather superficial.

Smith, John E. *Jonathan Edwards: Puritan, Preacher, Philosopher.* London: Chapman, 1992. This book represents a broadly reliable introduction to Edwards's ideas, although it is out of print. It is also quite dated in that it does not take full account of recent discoveries about the sources of Edwards's ideas.

Smith, John E., Harry S. Stout, and Kenneth P. Minkema. *A Jonathan Edwards Reader.* New Haven: Yale University Press, 1995. This is a fine single-volume compendium of a great range of Edwardseana, with a useful introduction by some of the most senior Edwards scholars working today. Highly recommended.

### 4. Intermediate Accounts of Edwards's Theology

Caldwell, Robert, III. *Communion in the Spirit: The Holy Spirit as the Bond of Union in the Theology of Jonathan Edwards.* Eugene, OR: Wipf & Stock, 2007. This is a helpful, clearly written treatment of Edwards's pneumatology that is worth reading.

Cherry, Conrad. *The Theology of Jonathan Edwards: A Reappraisal.* Bloomington: Indiana University Press, 1966. Although this is a fine work, it primarily focuses on the concept of faith in Edwards's thought and is now dated.

Crisp, Oliver D. *Jonathan Edwards among the Theologians.* Grand Rapids: Eerdmans, 2015. A series of studies of Edwards's thought, some of which place him in dialogue with other important Christian theologians.

Gerstner, John H. *The Rational Biblical Theology of Jonathan Edwards.* 3 vols. Powhatan: Berea Publications/Ligonier Ministries, 1991–94. This is a massive, uneven work that is not always reliable on the substance of Edwards's theology; its interpretation of Edwards is rather eccentric at points.

Holbrook, Clyde A. *The Ethics of Jonathan Edwards: Morality and Aesthetics.* Ann Arbor: University of Michigan Press, 1973. A careful, workmanlike treatment of Edwards's ethical thought that still repays careful study.

Holmes, Stephen R. *God of Grace and God of Glory: An Account of the Theology of Jonathan Edwards.* Edinburgh: T&T Clark, 2000. A very thorough monograph that is clear and well written. Nonetheless, in various places Holmes reads Edwards through a "Barthian" lens.

Jenson, Robert W. *America's Theologian: A Recommendation of Jonathan Edwards*. New York: Oxford University Press, 1988. An interesting overview that often paraphrases Edwards and is helpful in several areas, particularly Edwardsean Christology.

McClymond, Michael J. *Encounters with God: An Approach to the Theology of Jonathan Edwards*. New York: Oxford University Press, 1998. A clear, well-written piece of work, but controversial; McClymond wishes to shift scholarly attention away from the major treatises that Edwards penned during his lifetime to other, less well known works.

McDermott, Gerald R., and Michael J. McClymond. *The Theology of Jonathan Edwards*. New York: Oxford University Press, 2012. This is the first single-volume treatment of the whole range of Edwards's thought. Despite the book's forbidding size, its individual chapters are very readable. It is a standard work of reference on the full panoply of Edwards's thought.

Pauw, Amy Plantinga. *The Supreme Harmony of All: The Trinitarian Theology of Jonathan Edwards*. Grand Rapids: Eerdmans, 2002. This is an important work on Edwards's trinitarian theology, although it has been superseded by more recent work in this area.

Studebaker, Steven M., and Robert W. Caldwell III. *The Trinitarian Theology of Jonathan Edwards: Text, Context, and Application*. 2012. Reprint, New York: Routledge, 2016. This work offers some of Edwards's main trinitarian writings alongside detailed exposition and discussion of his doctrine, interacting with the most recent secondary literature on the subject.

## 5. Advanced Accounts of Edwards's Theology

Bezzant, Rhys S. *Jonathan Edwards and the Church*. New York: Oxford University Press, 2014. This is the first book-length treatment of Edwards's understanding of the church, and it showcases a neglected aspect of his constructive theological vision.

Bombaro, John J. *Jonathan Edwards's Vision of Reality: The Relationship of God to the World, Redemption History, and the Reprobate*. Eugene, OR: Wipf & Stock, 2011. A revised version of the author's 2003 University of London PhD thesis, this work probes the deep structures of Edwards's philosophical theology.

Cochran, Elizabeth Agnew. *Receptive Human Virtues: A New Reading of*

*Jonathan Edwards's Ethics.* University Park: Pennsylvania State University Press, 2010. This is an accessible, stimulating rereading of Edwards's moral theology. It is based on the author's PhD dissertation at the University of Notre Dame and is the best short treatment of his ethics in print.

Crisp, Oliver D. *Jonathan Edwards and the Metaphysics of Sin.* Aldershot: Ashgate, 2005. This is a technical treatment of the metaphysical issues informing Edwards's doctrine of sin, and it is a gift to insomniacs everywhere. This work is based on the author's University of London PhD thesis.

————. *Jonathan Edwards on God and Creation.* New York: Oxford University Press, 2011. This is a substantial revisionist work on Edwards's philosophical theology, and it provides an alternative to Sang Lee's important work (see below).

Elwood, Douglas. *The Philosophical Theology of Jonathan Edwards.* New York: Columbia University Press, 1960. This is now somewhat dated, but it still offers some penetrating insights into Edwards's thought, and it is clearly written.

Fiering, Norman. *Jonathan Edwards's Moral Thought in Its British Context.* Chapel Hill: University of North Carolina Press, 1981. A careful and scholarly book in which the author reaches important conclusions about the sources and shape of Edwards's moral philosophy. Highly recommended.

Hastings, W. Ross. *Jonathan Edwards and the Life of God: Toward an Evangelical Theology of Participation.* Minneapolis: Fortress, 2015. This revision of the author's University of St. Andrews PhD thesis studies Edwards's understanding of participation in the divine life in dialogue with Karl Barth.

Lee, Sang Hyun. *The Philosophical Theology of Jonathan Edwards.* Expanded edition. Princeton: Princeton University Press, 2000. This is a standard work on Edwards's philosophical theology that is essential reading for any Edwards scholar. It is intellectually demanding.

Morimoto, Anri. *Jonathan Edwards and the Catholic Vision of Salvation.* University Park: Penn State University Press, 1995. This is a controversial work on Edwards's understanding of the order of salvation (*ordo salutis*) in which the author argues that Edwards's understanding of infused habits and dispositions places him much closer to the views of Thomas Aquinas and Roman Catholic thought than to Reformed theology.

Schweitzer, William H. *God Is a Communicative Being: Divine Communicativeness and Harmony in the Theology of Jonathan Edwards*. London: T&T Clark, 2012. An account of Edwards's understanding of the way in which the divine Trinity communicates itself in the created order with reference to Edwards's biblical-theological work. It is based on the author's University of Edinburgh PhD thesis.

Strobel, Kyle C. *Jonathan Edwards's Theology: A Reinterpretation*. London: T&T Clark, 2012. This study offers a fresh reading of Edwards's theology that emphasizes the inner-trinitarian structure of his thought. It takes issue with almost all of the recent scholarship on Edwards and is based on the author's University of Aberdeen PhD thesis.

Studebaker, Steven M. *Jonathan Edwards' Social Augustinian Trinitarianism in Historical and Contemporary Perspectives*. Piscataway: Gorgias, 2008. A detailed, revisionist account of Edwards's trinitarian theology that takes a line of thought different from Amy Plantinga Pauw and the present work. It is based on the author's Marquette University PhD thesis.

Sweeney, Douglas A. *Edwards the Exegete: Biblical Interpretation and Anglo-Protestant Culture on the Edge of the Enlightenment*. New York: Oxford University Press, 2015. An important treatment of the biblical sources of Edwards's thought in his biblical exegesis that demonstrates that he was saturated in the biblical traditions.

Tan, Seng-Kong. *Fullness Received and Returned: Trinity and Participation in Jonathan Edwards*. Emerging Scholars Series. Minneapolis: Fortress, 2014. A work that locates Edwards's thought in the history of ideas but that does not interact with some of the key, recent work on Edwards. It is a revision of the author's Princeton Theological Seminary PhD thesis.

Wilson, Stephen A. *Virtue Reformed: Rereading Jonathan Edwards's Ethics*. Leiden: E. J. Brill, 2005. This is a dense, thorough account of Edwards's ethics, and the most detailed to date.

### 6. Edited Works on Edwards

Hatch, Nathan, and Harry Stout, eds. *Jonathan Edwards and the American Experience*. New York: Oxford University Press, 1988. A very helpful collection of essays on key issues in Edwards's thought.

Helm, Paul, and Oliver D. Crisp, eds. *Jonathan Edwards: Philosophical*

*Theologian.* Aldershot: Ashgate, 2003. This is a standard reference work dealing with a number of key philosophical and theological issues in Edwards's thought.

Lee, Sang Hyun, ed. *The Princeton Companion to Jonathan Edwards.* Princeton: Princeton University Press, 2005. This work offers an excellent range of essays covering Edwards's thought.

Schweitzer, Don, ed. *Jonathan Edwards as Contemporary: Essays in Honor of Sang Lee.* New York: Peter Lang, 2010. This is a state-of-the-art contribution to Edwardsean studies, containing essays from some of the most important scholars in the field on a range of crucial issues in Edwards's theology.

Stein, Stephen J., ed. *The Cambridge Companion to Jonathan Edwards.* Cambridge: Cambridge University Press, 2008. This is another fine reference work, more historically orientated than the *Princeton Companion.*

Strobel, Kyle C., ed. *The Ecumenical Edwards: Jonathan Edwards and the Theologians.* Aldershot: Ashgate, 2015. This important theological resource brings in a number of contemporary, non-Edwardsean theologians to analyze aspects of Edwards's thought in light of the Christian tradition and particular theologians.

Wainwright, William J. "Jonathan Edwards." In *Stanford Encyclopedia of Philosophy.* This is the best short philosophical introduction to Edwards's work. It can be found online at: https://plato.stanford.edu/entries/edwards/.

# Index

CPSIA information can be obtained
at www.ICGtesting.com
Printed in the USA
LVHW031258080221
678705LV00008B/256

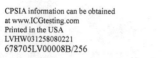

9 780802 872692